MAN BECOMING

MAN BECOMING
God in Secular Experience

Gregory Baum

Herder and Herder

1971
HERDER AND HERDER NEW YORK
232 Madison Avenue, New York, N.Y. 10016

Library of Congress Catalogue Card Number: 71–110889
© 1970 by Herder and Herder, Inc.
Manufactured in the United States

CONTENTS

PREFACE

THE ideas of this book presuppose that a development has taken place in the Catholic Church, first in the way of experiencing the Gospel and then in the manner of understanding and formulating it. The first religious philosopher clearly to understand this was Maurice Blondel, at the turn of the century. Since then, as the new cultural conditions spread in the western world, the new mode of looking at the Gospel became more widely acknowledged and eventually exerted a strong influence on the composition of Vatican II's conciliar documents.

This development takes place in individual Christians. A Christian meets his crisis when the spiritual experience of his culture is no longer reconcilable with the religious outlook he has inherited and God seems to be more powerfully present in the former than the latter. Such a crisis often results in what is called, superficially, a loss of faith. The Christian then gives up his religion. But if there are available to him theological methods by which he may reinterpret and reassimilate the inherited religion, he may discover a new unity of religious experience, where the Gospel celebrated in the Church sheds light on and intensifies the Spirit-created, redemptive values present in the culture to which he belongs. He may then, as a Christian, transform this culture along the line of its own deepest dimension.

I wish to relate the circumstances under which the crisis occurred to me. When I joined the Augustinian Order in the late forties, I had adopted a strongly Barthian emphasis in the understanding of the Gospel: salvation and wisdom are in Jesus Christ and nowhere else. This stress, needless to say, tied in well with the spiritual tradition of religious life: what counts is not life, but supernatural life. I remember how scandalized I was when, at that time, friends of mine took me to a lecture at St. Michael's College, Toronto, that dealt with the famous article of St. Thomas, then unknown to me, proposing that the supernatural life is offered to every child on the threshold of his rational life. I then readily and happily followed the more central Catholic tradition that the Church's sacramental worship elevates men to a level of life unavailable outside of it and properly called divine.

However, at the end of the fifties my convictions about life underwent a considerable change. While continuing my studies at the university, I was doing ministry in a parish in Neuchâtel, Switzerland, where, after a period of comparative separation, I again came into contact with men and women and learned to participate in the important events of their lives. Very slowly the conviction took hold of me that there is no radical difference between Christians and non-Christians. The same dynamics take place in everyone, whether inside or outside the Church: people have the same fears, receive the same challenges, come to the same possibilities of transformation and self-destruction. To say that Christians are better than others or live on a more elevated plane does not make sense. While there are indeed great Christian men and women inspired by trust and generosity, following Jesus on the road of simplicity, love, and candor, there are also great men and women without religion who have been marvelously transformed into selfless, open, and trusting persons. Holiness is as universal as sin.

I came to regard the distinction between the supernatural, elevated life of Catholics and the natural, purely human life of other people as a dangerous illusion with devastating effects on the Catholic community. The pretense to have access to a higher life not available elsewhere tended to make Catholics blind to the holiness present in others and, with more damaging effects, insensitive to their own failings and vices. It was difficult for Catholics to learn from others and come to self-knowledge. Believing itself to be alive with supernatural life, the Catholic community was often prevented from discovering how deeply involved it was in prejudices, in hidden antipathies, and in the promotion of destructive social outlooks which the culture to which it belonged had already transcended.

I was then engaged in a study of the Church's relationship to anti-semitism. This made me realize how deeply Christians, dedicated to the Church's liturgical life and seeking holiness, can be involved in self-delusions and perpetuate hostilities and injustices to outsiders. I had to ask myself what the source of cultural self-criticism was that first made anti-semitism a moral political issue and demanded greater justice for a socially oppressed people. It was certainly not the Christian Church. It was rather the ideal of the modern, liberal, democratic society, which Catholic churchmen consistently rejected. Here, too, it appeared that holiness is as universal as sin and that marvelous things happen among people wherever God chooses to act. It is from this modern society that the Church, after a period of strong resistance, has learned many social and intellectual values that have become part of the Christian conscience. I refer here to modern systematic self-criticism, to freedom of research, to honesty in scholarship, to respect for people with whom one disagrees, to equality of all before the law, etc. Catholics had to struggle before these ideals were acknowledged in the Church. While I admitted, even at that time, that modern society and the liberal values retained their ambiguity and were in need of an ongoing critique to free them from their destructive ideology, I became firmly convinced that the contemporary culture that has been created through them revealed aspects of the Gospel that had hitherto been hidden or totally unknown.

At the end of the fifties, when these convictions became strong in me, I did not know how to relate them to orthodox Catholic doctrine. I even wondered if I could remain a Catholic. It was then that I began to read the works of Karl Rahner. This original thinker and great theologian presented a theological anthropology which was in harmony with my own experience of life. It is possible, according to Rahner, to affirm the uniqueness of the Church and at the same time to hold that the mystery of new life is operative in every single human being. Jesus Christ has revealed what takes place in the heart of every person. The Church proclaims the mystery of redemption that is universal and constitutive of human history.

This new doctrinal perspective brought out that human life is the same everywhere; the dynamics of life are identical in every man. On the one hand, he is threatened by sin and self-destruction, and, on the other, he is ever sum-

moned, gratuitously and beyond expectation, to new dimensions of truth and love. No wonder, then, that holiness
is present outside the Church as well as within. No wonder
that we may meet people within the Church who crush
their vitality and disrupt their peace, while we encounter
outsiders, with or without religion, in whom new life and
joy are constantly being created. Not that Christians are
worse than other people. The new doctrinal perspective
brings out, rather, that salvation is always and everywhere
gratuitous. It happens where it happens. Holiness and creative self-possession are always gifts, the unexpected marvels created over the uncertain ground of self-deception.

The shift of perspective began to influence my theology
only slowly. Profound ideas make their way into man's
consciousness little by little; they reveal their implications
step by step. Only through a gradual process of self-cor-
rection do we eventually come to an intellectual picture
more wholly consistent with our central intuition. While I
began to have increasing hesitations in regard to the ecumenical movement, which at that time was strongly influenced by the exclusivist stress of Barthian theology, I
rejoiced in the ecclesiastical developments at the Vatican
Council, on which the universalist trend, so brilliantly
expounded and defended by Rahner, had considerable effect. The new consciousness which had come to me in the
late fifties, first as question mark and source of anguish
and then as a new way of seeing, had been generated in
some Catholic thinkers decades ago; by the sixties, it was
affecting the spiritual outlook of the widest circles in the
Church and even reached institutional expression in the
conciliar documents.

Ultimately, the shift of perspective touched the very concept of God. For if grace is secular and present in human

life everywhere, the old piety loses its power and meaning. God himself becomes a problem. Is it still possible to believe in an outsider-God? In my theological studies I found support in the work of Paul Tillich and had sympathy for the contribution of Bishop John Robinson and other exponents of secular theology, but on the whole I have always tried to work out my own method and my own language in greater continuity with Catholic life and thought. Then as now I have the desire to be radical and orthodox at the same time. I submitted my theological ideas to Catholic audiences all over North America and learned a great deal from the discussions and the questions that arose on these occasions. I often had the joy of being told that I had put into theological language what people had been convinced of all along, possibly without being able to put it into words. The task of the theologian, after all, is to interpret the faith-experience of the Church. The new perspective itself is based on the Church's spiritual experience in a new culture. The obedience to God's Word which the theologian seeks is not conformity to scripture conceived of as the record of revealed teaching but rather to scripture understood as the life-giving principle in the Church.

Over two years ago, I began to write a book in which I wanted to present this shift of perspective, analyze its beginning at the turn of the century and its influence at the Vatican Council, and then interpret Catholic teaching, including the doctrine of God, in the light of this new perspective. I was interrupted in my work when Charles Davis left the Catholic Church and asked theologians to explain why, in the face of so much inner contradiction, they continue to regard the Catholic community as the true Church. In my reply to him, *The Credibility of the Church Today,*

I adopted the new perspective and interpreted the Church and her teaching in the light of it. In another study, *Faith and Doctrine,* I worked out the implications of the new approach for Christian apologetics. When I returned to my manuscript in the spring of 1969, I found that some of its material had been used in these two publications and that some was no longer interesting, in particular the detailed examination of the conciliar documents. I decided to re-write the chapter on the new perspective and to deal, in several chapters, with the objections raised against it in the discussions with my audiences. In the second part of the book I wanted to apply the principles of re-interpretation to the doctrine of God—which I regard as the crucial issue for the Church at this time.

What is original in my approach? The systematic re-fusal to objectify the divine is not original: it has been carefully worked out by theologians who are more concerned with philosophical issues than I am. Many contemporary writers, moreover, acknowledge that by looking at life in a particular way or from a particular angle, one is able to discern the signs of divine transcendence in ordinary human situations; there is a sort of empirical basis for theological reflection. What is original in this study is the application of a psychologically-oriented phenomenology to show that ordinary human life is not ordinary at all but, in fact, highly dramatic, a field of conflict between forces of self-destruction and powers—unexpected powers—of creativity and new life. The reason why I do not give references to works on psychology throughout this book is that I have acquired my own familiarity with psychological depth analysis in my long association with Communication Therapy, a psychotherapeutic institute in Toronto. If looked at carefully, with methods sufficiently refined, it becomes apparent that the process of growing up and becoming human is a great drama, a drama which the Christian interprets as a participation in the paschal mystery. A phenomenological analysis of personal growth is able to discern transcendence in the midst of human life. It is possible, in other words, to give a description, in ordinary terms drawn from secular experience, of God's redemptive presence to human life.

If it is true that the divine mystery of redemption is operative everywhere in human life, if it is true, in other words, that the first and foremost means of grace is life itself, then the sacramental Church which is meant to serve and intensify this mystery becomes of secondary importance. If the institutional Church in fact intensifies the new life offered in the community, then there is reason for rejoicing. But if it fails to do this—and at this time the disappointment is widespread—it comes to be of minor importance for Christians, and occupies a small corner in their consciousness. But this sort of boredom with the institutional Church does not mean indifference to the divine. That God is alive means that tomorrow will be different from today.

MAN BECOMING

I. THE BLONDELIAN SHIFT

MAURICE BLONDEL was the initiator, in the Catholic Church, of a new style of thinking about that transcendent, redemptive mystery in human history which we call God.[1] He developed his views at the turn of the century, in conflict with the ideas current in the Church of his day. Blondel confronted the philosophical and theological

1. Maurice Blondel is not well known in English. In this chapter I have used his essay of 1896, usually referred to in English as the *Essay on Apologetics,* and his article of 1904 called *Histoire et dogme*. These two works have been translated and presented by A. Dru and I. Trethowan in M. Blondel, *The Letter on Apologetics, and History and Dogma,* London, 1964. These are, apart from some letters, the only works of Blondel translated into English. I have also used Blondel's doctoral dissertation, the two-volume master piece *L'Action: Essai d'une critique de la vie et d'une science de la pratique,* first published in 1893. A careful presentation and important study of this major work is James Sumerville's *Total Commitment,* Washington, 1968. Sumerville is presently working on a translation of *L'Action*. A useful introduction to Blondel translated into English is Jean Lacroix, *Maurice Blondel, An Introduction to the Man and his Philosophy,* New York, 1968. To study the influence of Blondel on Catholic theology, I refer to R. Aubert, *Le problème de l'acte de la foi,* Louvain, 3rd ed., 1958, pp. 227–294, and 317–337; H. Bouillard, *Blondel et le christianisme,* Paris, 1961; Y. Congar, *Tradition and Traditions,* New York,1967, pp. 359–368; and J. Heaney, *The Modernist Crisis: von Hügel,* Washington, 1968, pp. 83–107.

1

trends recommended by the official Church with the patterns of thought characteristic of the contemporary intellectual culture, for he insisted that creative thinking, even in the Christian Church, must take place in dialogue with the thought that preoccupies men in the present. If we use past philosophical systems, we may solve the problems of the intellectual life to the satisfaction of the specialized group to which we belong, but by so doing we isolate ourselves from the wider intellectual community and refuse to participate in the process, involving the whole of society, by which new insights are generated and men come to deal effectively with their actual problems. Access to wisdom is found only in the process by which men create their spiritual culture.

From the outset of his reflections, the Christian vision of life espoused by Blondel convinced him that God is present to human history and that his presence is the source of new life in the aspirations, conflicts, and thought-forms constituting the human reality in every generation. Thanks to this divine presence, he felt, mankind is always in a state of giving birth to the new. The Christian thinker who seeks to understand the meaning of God as revealed in Christ must open himself to dialogue with contemporary culture. Through the experience of reality proper to his own generation, he will be able to lay hold of and express the divine reality in which he believes.

Blondel is not always easy to read. His paragraphs are not always clear nor his style consistently elegant. But again and again we hit upon passages in his books that are brilliant expressions of his thought, lucid, concise, and nuanced, enabling us to participate in a truth that is both highly personal and unrestrictively universal. Blondel expresses the need to participate in the contemporary intellectual experience in a paragraph which, I think, is great literature.

> There are two ways of looking at the history of philo-
> sophical ideas. Either we remain outside the main stream
> which sweeps through the world of thought and radically
> exclude everything which is opposed to the system which
> we have adopted (for reasons which, judged from our
> chosen eminence, seem to us sound enough)—and that
> is to cut ourselves off from the only sort of life which is
> really fruitful. Or else we try to perceive that stirring of
> parturition with which humanity is always in labour, we
> set ourselves to profit by this vast effort, to enlighten it,
> to bring it to fruition, to kindle the smoking flax, to be less
> ready to suppose that there is nothing of value for our-
> selves even in those doctrines which seen most opposed
> to our own, to go to others so that they may come to us—
> and that is to find the source of intellectual fruitfulness.[2]

THE REJECTION OF EXTRINSICISM

Blondel could not avoid a conflict with the official theology of his time. He worked out a new approach to the problem of God in contrast with the apologetical theology taught in Catholic schools and recommended by the official Church. He believed that implied in the official apologetics were ideas about God and divine revelation that were irrecon-cilable with the modern experience of reality and, hence, made it impossible for intelligent and critical people to be believing Christians. According to the official apolo-getics, God is a divine being facing man from beyond history, and divine revelation is the communication of

2. *The Letter on Apologetics, and History and Dogma*, p. 147.

heavenly truths to men caught in their own limited, earthly knowledge. Blondel called this approach "extrinsicism." Against the extrinsicist trend of Catholic theology, Blondel insisted that the only message modern man can accept is a truth that has an intrinsic relationship to life, a truth that answers men's questions or corresponds in some way to their experience of reality. A message that comes to man wholly from the outside, without an inner relationship to his life, must appear to him as irrelevant, unworthy of attention, and unassimilable by the mind.

To understand the rejection of extrinsicism more clearly, let us look at the Church's official apologetics. During the nineteenth century, wrestling with the issues raised by rationalism and fideism and resisting the extremes of both, Catholic theologians had introduced a radical distinction between faith and its rational credibility. They acknowledged with the entire Christian tradition that faith is a free gift of God and hence essentially indemonstrable. Yet what can be demonstrated, they added, is the divine origin of the message believed by faith. What can be proven, ultimately by reference to miracles, is that the message preached by the Church is not of human making; it is a divine message and hence, however startling to the human intelligence, it is worthy of belief or is credible. This radical distinction between faith and its credibility enabled Catholic theologians to reject the rationalistic view that faith is demonstrable and yet to retain an element of rationality in the act of believing. It permitted them to affirm, against the fideists, the rational foundation of Christian faith and yet to agree with the fideists on the gratuitous and indemonstrable character of this faith. The price that Catholic theologians had to pay for the solution of separating faith and credibility was the exclusion of God's revelation from the spiritual process by which man comes to know what is important and true. According to the official theology of the nineteenth century, there was no inner continuity between the rational discernment of credibility and the Spirit-created acknowledgement of the divine Word. In other words, the credibility of faith remained totally extrinsic to faith itself.

What, more precisely, did the customary apologetics mean by the credibility of faith? The apologists were not content simply to show that Christian faith was a reasonable option. They did not reflect on the Christian message and examine how it is related to human life and experience, except to show that there is no intrinsic contradiction between faith and reason. The main thrust of their apologetics was to prove the divine authorship of the message. What counted was the demonstration that the Church's message has a suprahuman and hence a divine origin. The Christian message is credible when it can be rationally shown that it comes from God. However startling it may appear to human intelligence, a message coming from God is always worthy of belief. Faith, in this perspective, is understood as a grace-created act of obedience to divine authority.

The apologetics of the nineteenth century regarded the gospels as reliable historical documents recording the life and the teaching of Jesus. Jesus appears in them as a messenger sent from God. He claimed that his message is divine; he insisted that he was not communicating a human wisdom accessible to human insight, but that his teaching, his acts, his entire life have a divine meaning which is the salvation of the world. He could not have been an impostor. He was the man without guile, unable to utter an untruth; he was the man of humility, incapable of inventing a story to make a place for himself; he was a man obedient to the divine summons, unable to usurp a mission to which he was not called. But in the eyes of the nineteenth-century apologists, the ultimate proof of the divine origin of Christ's message lay in his miracles. The miracles provided proof of an empirical kind that Christ was sent by God and that his message is credible.

The apologists of the nineteenth century also reflected on the Church as the teacher of the message. Can it be demonstrated, they asked, that the Church's message is of divine origin? The Church proclaims that the Gospel is a message which she herself has divinely received. But are there any miracles associated with the Church's life that demonstrate the divine origin of her message? The apologists of the last century, supported by the teaching of Vatican I, thought that the history of the Church disclosed miraculous dimensions. While ordinary human societies are threatened by divisions, are confined to a single race or nation, are made vulnerable by the sins of their members, and are unfaithful to the ideals of their founder, the Catholic Church manifests in her historical existence a unity, a universality, a holiness, and an apostolicity that reveal miraculous proportions. In the context of human societies, the Catholic Church is a moral miracle. Her very existence indicates the divine origin of her message. While it is impossible, by its very nature, to demonstrate the Christian faith, it is possible to prove the credibility of this faith thanks to the miracles present in the life of Jesus and the history of the Church.

Blondel protested against this sort of apologetics. He objected to it, not because he did not share the confidence of the traditional apologists in the historical reliability of the biblical books or in the miraculous character of the

Church's historical existence; he objected to it, not simply because he had a different interpretation of the miraculous in human life. He rejected the traditional apologetics because of the understanding of divine revelation implicit in it.

Traditional apologetics did not attach much importance to the content of the Christian message: what counts is simply its divine authorship. What the message is about has little to do with the genesis of faith in the mind of the believer. This implies that any message at all, whatever its content, as long as its divine origin is certified by miracles, can be the object of faith and become a way of salvation. Faith, in this context, appears as the obedient acceptance of a heavenly message, independently of its meaning for man and its effect on human life. This, Blondel said, implies an extrinsicist understanding of divine revelation.

The criticism of extrinsicism has become widely accepted in Catholic theology of the twentieth century. Karl Rahner has repeatedly illustrated the extrinsicist understanding of divine revelation by sketching a telling caricature. Christians sometimes imagine, Rahner says, that God in heaven knows many marvelous truths and that he has decided, for the sake of human salvation, to reveal some of these truths to men. If men believe these truths on his authority, they will be rewarded with eternal life. To make it more difficult for men and to increase the demands on their obedience, God revealed very complicated truths to them. He told them the most unlikely propositions he knows. If men, by the sacrifice of the intellect, rely on divine authority and acknowledge these propositions as true, they shall enter the salvation promised to them.

This is obviously a parody. It certainly does not repre-

7

sent the best theology of faith to be found in the Catholic tradition. The great theologians in every age have always taught that the articles of faith are not separate truths revealed to men but that in their totality they communicate the living, self-revealing God in Jesus Christ. For St. Thomas, for instance, the object of faith (*objectum materiale*) is lastly God himself, whom we attain through the truths revealed by him.[3] In and through the divine teaching, God himself comes to the believer.

At the same time, Rahner's caricature reveals an outlook that is widespread among Christians and, at times, even encouraged by ecclesiastical preaching. We are often told that it is difficult to believe, and by this is meant that the truths revealed by God are beyond the understanding, that they demand the sacrifice of the intellect, and that the more opaque they are to human understanding, the greater the merit in believing them. When Christians have difficulties with certain doctrines, for instance with the dogmatic statements on the Trinity or the eucharist, they are sometimes told by ecclesiastical authorities that there is a special merit in not understanding, is being baffled by a teaching that sounds unlikely, and in obediently accepting a position that has no other link with the human mind than that God has revealed it to men.

It is, of course, true that it is difficult to believe; but, as we shall see, this means that it is difficult to believe the Good News that God is on the side of man, that he continually summons us, and that he is at work in us and in others.

When Maurice Blondel, in his famous *Essay on Apologetics,* rejected the extrinsicism implicit in the apologetical theology of his day, he raised the issue that has preoccupied

3. *Summa Theol.,* II-II, 1, 1.

the entire Christian community in the twentieth century. This issue may be called the quest for relevance. In all the Churches, theologians now realize that the irrelevant cannot be believed. It is no longer possible, they say, to regard divine revelation as information about heavenly realities that are added to human life from outside. The ordinary Christians in all the Churches have begun to complain that the religion they have inherited often deals with a realm that has nothing to do with life and hence distracts them from what they regard as their primary task and mission, namely *to live* responsibly. Some Christians have gone so far as to say that the ecclesiastical order and the language of worship appear to them as an exotic teritory with no relation to the landscape of their daily experience. The old time religion, they say, is like a tropical garden artificially maintained in a modern city. Religion has become an island in the midst of life, belonging to a strangely different realm. This strangely different realm, according to Blondel, does not exist. The God who is supposedly alive in a special world, separated from our own, from which he intervenes at certain times in the course of human history, does not exist at all. There is no outsider-God. Blondel's rejection of extrinsicism raised the problematic of the death-of-God theologians. The question arises whether the Gospel gives witness to an insider-God. In any case, the task of the theologian is to show how the Gospel ties in with human life, how on the one hand it offers a critique of human life and thus manifests its transcendence, and how on the other hand it transforms human life and thus demonstrates its relevance.

Blondel first rejected extrinsicism in dealing with the apologetical issue. Not long after his *Letter on Apologetics,* he denounced it a second time, this time in connection with an important controversy that took place in the early years of the twentieth century. Blondel intervened in the modernist controversy aroused by Loisy's celebrated book *L'Évangile et l'Église* in his own essay entitled *History and Dogma*. Loisy had tried to show that scientific study was capable of discerning the divine in the history of Christian origins. Against this Blondel asserted that history is always studied with certain presuppositions, even though they may be unavowed. The scholar who approaches the available documents in what he regards as an objective and scientific way inevitably makes a selection of his material, focuses on certain aspects of the documents, and—more important still—tends to identify history as recorded with history as actually lived by man. This identification is a false presupposition implicit in the work of the "objective" or "scientific" historian. This approach to the study of the past Blondel called historicism. History as recorded, he pointed out, presents us with a portrait or picture of reality. The historian who adopts the scientific method uncritically identifies the portrait with the reality without considering the possibility that the reality may be more complex and more profound than the portrait available to him by scientific history. Loisy tried to apply scientific history to the biblical and historical documents recording the story of Jesus and the early Church —this, at least, was Blondel's interpretation of Loisy—in order to demonstrate the divine origin of the Christian religion and thus to construct a new defense for the truth of the Catholic Church. Blondel tried to show that Loisy's historicism was actually undoing the foundation of the Christian faith.

In this connection Blondel also criticized the manner in which the apologetically-oriented theologians of his day approached the historical documents and used them for the defense of Christianity. These men—Blondel called them "veterists" in contrast to the "modernists"—made no serious attempt to understand history as it was lived by past generations. They simply focused on the miraculous in the story of Jesus and the early Church, and once the miracles were established, they rapidly moved away from the available records to the Church's dogmatic teaching on the person of Christ and the nature of the Christian community—to the dogmas, that is—for which the miracles supplied the rational basis. Traditional apologetics was not concerned with doing justice to the historical documents nor with gaining an historical understanding of what happened in the generation of Jesus and his followers. In this perspective, what happened then is only extrinsically related to what the Church believes today. What happened then are simply the miracles that demonstrate the credibility of the Church's dogma. Whereas Blondel was convinced that unless the life of Jesus and the experience of the early Church tie in with the dogma of the Church, this dogma has no foundation in human history and hence is not credible in the present culture.

Against historicism on the one hand and extrinsicism on the other, Blondel worked out his famous theology of divine tradition. He affirmed, contrary to the extrinsicism, that divine revelation takes place in human life and creates history. From this it follows that there is a depth dimension to human history, especially to the history of Christian beginnings, which cannot be grasped by the historicist approach to the study of the past. Historicism makes the gratuitous assumption that history as recorded in documents or embodied in ancient monuments is identical with the history that took place in people's lives, and hence closes itself in principle against acknowledging a deeper dimension of history. But in Blondel's view, the Christian historian studies the origins of the Church with a clearly acknowledged and ultimately indemonstrable presupposition, namely his faith. He believes that the deepest dimension of what happened at the beginning of Christianity continues to be present in the Church of later ages right up to the present time. This deepest dimension is the divine self-communication which constitutes the Church as the community of believers. The Christian historian does not identify the historical portrait of the early Church, derived from the documents, with the total reality of the Church at that time. Blondel recommended, of course, the application of critical historical scholarship to the available sources. He did not defend or encourage the obscurantism that is so often the result of the apologetical approach to Church history. What the Christian historian should try to do, according to Blondel, is to understand and evaluate the historical experience of the early Church, described with the help of the critical methods, in the light of the ongoing supernatural reality, namely divine tradition, which constitutes the Church—then and now.

The deeper reason for Blondel's approach to the study of history will become clearer further on. For him the study of history is never simply descriptive, it is always interpretative. The deepest dimension of what reality means to people and hence the most accurate understanding of their history are not available in what they say and think; it is their action, their involvement in life, that embodies the meaning to which they have committed themselves. To discern this meaning and hence to write their history will always be a task of interpretation and never simply a description of what has happened. The

Christian historian, therefore, even while using the most advanced methods of scholarship, will come to the understanding of the Church's history only if he interprets what happened in the light of a deeper dimension accessible to him by faith. An historian who operates out of a different set of presuppositions may agree with the Christian historian on the purely descriptive plane of what happened, but will inevitably differ from him in the understanding and evaluation of the Church's historical roots. Loisy's endeavor is grandiose but abortive, for the scientific method is radically incapable of discerning the divine in human history.

Blondel's rejection of extrinsicism, in the two contexts mentioned here, points out very clearly the uneasiness he felt in regard to the miraculous as a theological category. Blondel did not deny the possibility of miracles, but he refused to assign miracles an important place in his theological synthesis. If a miraculous interference in the order of nature took place, he reasoned, we would not be able to recognize it as such. Why? Because the so-called order of nature can never be totally known. The surprising, the unlikely, the gratuitous may well be part of what we call the natural order. We shall have occasion to return to Blondel's view of miracles in a later chapter.

THE METHOD OF IMMANENCE

After rejecting extrinsicism, what positive approach to Christian theology did Maurice Blondel recommend? He adopted the philosophical method proper to the intellectual culture to which he himself belonged. He was convinced with his own generation and the present culture that the only way to come to truth is to examine carefully man's experience of reality and hence that no truth can be acknowledged by the human mind which does not in some way proceed from it. Man cannot accept an idea as true unless it corresponds in some way to a question present in his mind. If a truth were added to man's mind totally from without, it would exist in his mental processes as a foreign body and could not be assimilated into his quest for truth. The experience of reality itself, which constitutes human life, is the one way in which the truth is accessible to men. This approach to truth Blondel called immanentism or, more properly, the method of immanence.

The word "immanentism" can be used in two distinct ways. Immanentism as a system claims that reality is proportionate to man's finite mind and thus denies the possibility of a transcendent reality. Needless to say, Blondel rejected immanentism as a system since it is in direct contradiction to the Christian Gospel. Moreover, he tried to show that immanentism as a system is philosophically untenable, demonstrating its falsity by applying immanentism as a method (or the method of immanence) to the study of reality.

The method of immanence claims that there is no truth which does not in some way arise from man's experience of reality. Truth is available in life. No affirmation can be true which does not correspond to the growth and development of the human mind. This, as we shall see, does not lock man into an inevitably finite framework: if there is a transcendent in the finite, then the experience of reality itself and man's sustained reflection on it will eventually lead to its recognition. Blondel thought that by applying the method of immanence he could demonstrate the presence of the transcendent in human life. In his basic philosophical treatise, entitled *L'Action,* he presented a phenomenology of the human spirit. He tried to prove that a systematic reflection on human life and its development leads to an acknowledgement of the divine and, in fact, to the threshold of the Christian Gospel.

For Blondel, the faculty of the real is not the intellect but man's involvement in the whole of life. His epistemology is non-Aristotelian. For Blondel, action is the organ of truth. The word "action" as used by the French philosopher refers to man's willing, choosing, and doing, understood as the profound and many-leveled self-affirmation by which he becomes himself and determines his own history. From the first moment of his life, man is summoned to action. He becomes himself, remains who he is, and enters into his destiny by involving himself in his life through action. Even man's refusal to be engaged is action: for even by electing passivity does a man create his own future.

Truth, Blondel said, is present in man's action. If we reflect on a man's action, we find implicit in it his values, his vision of life, his view of reality. Action incarnates man's grasp of reality and offers him the possibility of knowing it conceptually. The evaluation of life and the discernment of meaning take place in human action before they become concepts in the human mind. Living is prior to philosophizing. We are able to formulate the truth in concepts only as we reflect on the human action by which men constitute their history. The proper method for finding the truth, therefore, is to study human life, human experience, human history, and to discern the structure of

15

reality implicit in human action. If reality transcends man and the finite universe to which he belongs, it will manifest itself in the structure of human action.

Is there an abiding structure in human action? Can the mind discover a universal pattern in the actions of men? Blondel thought so. He tried to show by a careful analysis of man's willing and doing that there is a structure in all human action that becomes the key for the understanding of man's relationship to the whole of reality. The entry into philosophy is through the analysis of human life. Blondel tried to show that there is an inner law or "a logic" in human action which enables the philosopher to make statements of a universal nature about reality. There is a necessity in action. In the unusual terminology of Blondel, action is determined. The determinism of action does not mean for Blondel that man is not free to make his life as he chooses, but, rather, that whatever choices man makes, the inner structure of his action will be the same —has to be the same. What is this determined structure present in all action?

Reflection reveals that a man acts because he wants to be more truly himself. A man wants to be who he is. He realizes that in some way he is not yet who he is. He must constantly reach out and deal with situation after situation in order to become who he is meant to be. Between a man and himself there is an infinite distance which he constantly seeks to fill in, without ever wholly succeeding. There is in man a spring of action, an unending concern or an inexhaustible willing (*la volonté voulante*) which gives rise to an unending chain of concrete choices, of freely chosen acts (*les volontés voulues*), by which he tries to realize himself more fully. By an unshakable determinism of action, man is forever making free, individual choices (*volontés voulues*) for the sake of fulfilling the necessary will or thrust at the core of his being (*volonté voulante*) to become more truly himself. This is the logic of action.

The detailed phenomenology of the spirit which Blondel carried out in the two large volumes of his work *L'Action* sought to provide a demonstration of the necessary structure of human action and to establish, on the basis of it, the necessary orientation of human life and the nature of reality. What interests us here in this vast philosophical enterprise is Blondel's conclusion that every man is carried forward by action to an important option in his life, which determines who he will be. Every man, by the logic of his action, is led to discover the impossibility of exhausting the deep willing at the core of his being in a finite universe. Man's unending concern leads him to wider and wider action. He discovers the world in which he lives and successfully organizes it; he comes to love other men and assumes responsibility for his life and theirs; he expands his love to include his family, his nation, the whole human race: and even then he discovers that the deep willing at the core of his being is not exhausted. The distance between himself and himself is still infinite. A man is summoned to the inevitable option: either, following the drive of his limitless concern, he opens himself to the infinite; or he encloses himself in the finite order and thus violates the thrust of his own action.

This option, Blondel held, is the threshold of the supernatural. A man may open himself to the infinite either by acknowledging an infinite (the self-revealing God) to which his necessary willing can go out without reserve or, at least—if he has not heard of God—by refusing to invest the finite with infinite value, by regarding life as open-ended, by being ready to transcend it if a higher summons is available. If a man opts for openness, his life becomes, in the language of the theologian, supernatural. Here man has opened himself to, and relies on, divine grace. This supernatural may be called undetermined: it has as yet no content. As a Christian, Blondel believed that the content of the supernatural which is present as summons in every man's life, is in fact revealed in the Gospel of Christ. This supernatural, as the saving reality constitutive of redeemed humanity, enters every man's life through the fundamental option to which he is inescapably led.

If a man refuses to open himself, in this option, to the infinite, he encloses himself in his own finite house, does violence to his necessary willing, and thus condemns himself never to be who he is meant to be. He elevates an aspect of the finite order to be the infinite for him and thereby commits a sin of idolatry. To choose against openness in this crucial option is to elect death.

Blondel insisted against his theological adversaries that his method of immanence does not reduce the supernatural to a part of nature. Grace is free, totally free. While man is indeed capable of discovering, by reflecting on human action, that for the sake of becoming himself he is in need of an order beyond the finite, he is, at the same time, totally incapable of achieving this by his own resources. Blondel insisted that the supernatural does not arise from within man's nature. It is a gift. It is offered freely in the option to which every man is inevitably led by the logic of his action.

This philosophy of action enabled Blondel to replace traditional apologetics, with its extrinsicist view of revelation, with a totally new approach. There is no apologetical value, Blondel wrote, in showing that divine revelation is possible and has in fact taken place. This could never create an obligation for man to believe. Revelation here remains extrinsic to personal life. An adequate apologetics, Blondel held, must explain why it is imperative to believe. The scriptures consistently stress that the one thing necessary is to have faith, and that to refuse to believe is to initiate one's own undoing.

The apologetics of the threshold—this is what Blondel named his method—sets forth the imperative of faith. The fundamental option to which a man is brought by the inner structure of his action challenges him to believe, to be open to the infinite, and thus to enter true life, or to refuse faith, to lock himself into a finite frame, and thus to go counter to his own destiny. While this option is offered to men everywhere, it is only in the Christian message that its reality is fully and concretely spelled out—in the life, death, and resurrection of Jesus Christ. There, in Christ, we are brought face to face with the option that determines our personal history. As we open ourselves to this message in faith, we enter into new life—life caught up in God's grace, which is the only way for man to become truly himself. This is the imperative of the Gospel.

The theology of Blondel transforms the entire mood of the Church's self-understanding. Here the Christian does not see the Church as the circle of white surrounded by a world of darkness. On the contrary, here the Christian sees himself as belonging to a graced humanity. God is redemptively present to human life everywhere. In this new mood, the Christian apologist does not say to the unreligious person: "Listen, this is the message of the Gospel and here is the proof that it is of divine origin. If you accept this teaching in faith, then you will share in the gifts God promised to those who believe his Word."

According to Blondel's philosophy of the threshold, the Christian message is not added to human life from without. The Christian apologist will have to say to his unreligious friend: "Listen, this is the message of the Gospel. It tells you the wonderful things that have happened in your life. Try on the Gospel, listen to it and act in accordance with it, and then tell me if it does not correspond to and illumine your own experience of life." Men come to believe the Christian message not because they accept an abstract proof of its credibility, but rather because they discover that the message discloses to them what has been going on, and is still going on, in their lives. They discover in the Gospel the full content of the option to which they have been led by the inner logic of their action. To the man who accepts the Gospel in faith, it is not a message added to his life from without; it is, rather, the clarification and specification of the transcendent mystery of humanization that is gratuitously operative in his life.

Blondel wrote his monumental work *L'Action* shortly before the so-called modernist crisis in the Church at the beginning of the twentieth century. He was deeply concerned about those very issues that preoccupied the men referred to as modernists. Like them, he wanted to reconcile the Christian faith with the contemporary experience of reality. It was no wonder that he was often classified with the modernists, even though in his own writings he refuted the positions of modernists and veterists alike. Blondel was often understood as teaching that the Church's revealed dogma simply expressed the aspirations of man's own creative mind. He was accused, moreover, of agnosticism, of subjectivism, and of preferring action and feeling to truth, thus encouraging a kind of pragmatism. These accusations were based on a false reading of his work. There was nothing of the anti-intellectual in Blondel: he sought knowledge with passion and perseverance. But he realized that all knowledge is based on a set of indemonstrable presuppositions, presuppositions that are ultimately options that men make as they relate themselves to reality and create their history. Blondel analyzed man's willing and choosing as the organ of reality and hence as a source of truth. For this reason, he held that action is the only vessel in which man can receive the supernatural. Only if man has thus received the supernatural and then reflects on his action, is he able to know something about it and put it into words.

Moreover, he readily acknowledged that divine revelation in Christ comes to us through the preaching of the Church. What he tried to prove was that this divine teaching, this dogma, comes to us not as a truth unrelated to the human mind but, rather, as the proclamation of God's redemptive involvement in the dynamics of human life. How is this self-revealing God present to men? Since Blondel wrote on this subject as a philosopher, albeit a philosopher at the threshold, he examined man's openness to the supernatural only in terms of the fundamental option, to which he was inevitably led by his action. Although Blondel affirmed the supernatural character of human life, he did not show to the satisfaction of the theologians how God is in fact supernaturally present in man's history, because he did not subject human life to a *theological* analysis. But there was not a trace of naturalism in Blondel. The dogma of the Church may be called the expression of man's religious experience, but only because the living, self-revealing God is present to man in the action that constitutes his history, and creates an experience that is, properly speaking, supernatural.

21

Blondel's vision of human life differed considerably from the view traditional in the Christian Church. In much of Christian theology and in most of Christian preaching, it was customary to divide mankind into two groups: the Church enlivened by grace and the world dominated by sin. It was traditional to regard the Church as the community in which divine pardon was available to men and the world as the place of darkness, in which grace was exceptional. We find such a gloomy picture of humanity in many, if not in most, of the spiritual writers. Pascal and Newman regarded the world in this way. Even when Catholic theologians spoke more positively of human life in the world as "natural" and hence as non-hostile to divine grace, the world remained the place where wisdom and holiness were not at home. The world was defined by the absence of grace. This traditional view of the world, one might add, had many practical consequences. It largely determined the Church's understanding of her mission among men and the relationship of Christians to other religions and to their secular environment.

Blondel looked upon the world of men in a different light. For him the divine revelation in Jesus Christ made known the redemptive involvement of God in the whole human race. Wherever men are, God is supernaturally present to them in the process of their humanization. The Church where Christ is proclaimed and the world where he is not explicitly acknowledged may and must be clearly distinguished, but the summons of grace and the gift to enter into new life are available to the whole of mankind. The sin that pervades human life must not make Christians insensitive to the saving presence of God operative in the lives of all men. People may indeed reject the divine summons and opt for death rather than new life, but this is

22

possible in the Church as well as in the world. Despite the sin into which men are born, in Christ the whole of mankind is divinely graced.

The rejection of extrinsicism and the acknowledgment of God's redemptive presence in human history I call the Blondelian shift.

THE NEW FOCUS OF THE GOSPEL

While Maurice Blondel's view of a graced humanity was a radical departure from the customary theology, was it really untraditional? The scriptures of the Old and New Testament record many universalist themes, revealing the presence of grace in the whole of mankind.[4] The prophetic literature of Israel presents divine creation not as an event that took place in the past but, rather, as the ongoing action of God in the world, creating people and their history. The offer of redemption is part of this divine action. Israel as well as the nations of the world were being created through God's gracious presence to them. This tradition was adopted in the New Testament. Several New Testament writers tried to show that Jesus Christ, the true man, in whom the destiny of mankind is revealed, was actively involved in the creation of mankind from the very beginning. In the Pauline literature, Christ is presented as the first-born of every creature as well as the image of the

4. There exists no complete study of the universalist themes in the scriptures. One has to consult biblical commentaries and monographs on such Old Testament themes as the redemptive meaning of creation, the covenant made with Noah, and the message of the Book of Jonah, and on such New Testament themes as Christ the second Adam in Pauline thought, Abraham the father of the faithful and the type of every man, the cosmic reconciliation wrought by Christ, and the preexisting Logos in Johannine literature.

invisible God. We are told that in Christ all things are created, in him all things continue to hold together: the whole universe is created by him and for him. Christ is both creator and reconciler of men. In this perspective, Christ is acknowledged not only as the head of the Church but as the head of the entire human race (cf. Col. 1, 15–20). He upholds the universe by the power of his word (cf. Heb. 1, 3). Divine redemption is operative in the history of mankind. The same theme, in different terminology, is taken up by the fourth gospel. Here we are told that the Word, the eternal Word that became flesh in Christ, created man and his world at the very beginning, continues to create history now, and enlightens every man that comes into the world (cf. John 1, 1–9). Divine redemption is present in the creation of the world and the history of man.

While these themes are not central in the Old Testament, and in the New Testament are overshadowed by the complementary emphasis on salvation solely through Christ preached by the Church, the ecclesiastical tradition did not overlook the universalist trend altogether. Some of the ancient fathers, especially those of the East, taught that in Christ the whole of human life, including the cosmos, has been elevated to the supernatural order. Man's history on earth is not simply defined by his natural powers: it also includes God's supernatural call inviting man into divine fellowship. Human destiny is supernatural. In fact, some of the ancient writers used the term "nature" to signify the actual human situation in which man is born, including the sin which damages him and the grace which elevates him into fellowship with God.[5] Man's

5. Cf. M. Schmaus, *Katholische Dogmatik,* II, 1, Munich, 1962, p. 215.

nature, for these writers, is to be in conversation with God.

The great theologians of the Catholic Church always retained this tradition. It was generally acknowledged that between sin and grace there is no neutral middle ground. The state of pure nature was studied by theologians simply as a possibility; they thought that insisting on this possibility is the only way of defending the gratuity of divine grace. But in actual fact, they agreed, human life is supernatural. There is a single destiny of man, which is fellowship with God. And since the final cause of man is supernatural, the dynamics of human life are also supernatural. Thomas Aquinas, for instance, taught that divine grace is offered to every man born into sin, from the first moment of his conscious life.[6] If the child responds positively to the divine call by orienting his life to the proper end as it is discernible to him, his inherited sin is forgiven and he enters into the state of grace; if he rejects the offer and refuses to orient his life to the proper end, he confirms his inherited misery by his own mortal sin. In terms of a largely Aristotelean psychology, Thomas Aquinas here gives witness to the traditional theme that God is redemptively present to the whole of mankind.

While God's universal will to save and the universality of sufficient grace were acknowledged in all theological treatises, these themes never entered into the center of theological reflection, and so never modified the Christian approach to the world or became an essential part of the Church's preaching. In general, the teaching of the Church as well as her legislation and practice gave expression to the sharp division between the Church as the fellowship of grace and the world as the place of God's absence. The theological thought of Blondel, developed in dialogue

6. *Summa Theol.,* I-II, 89, 6.

with contemporary experience, moved the traditional theme of universal grace into the center of the Christian message.

The Vatican condemnation of modernism in 1907, while not specifically including the work of Blondel, prevented his thought from having an influence on the official theology taught at ecclesiastical schools. Blondel's achievement of rethinking the relationship of history and grace affected only a few scholars.

Under the influence of Blondel, the Belgian philosopher Joseph Maréchal developed a new approach to the understanding of Thomas Aquinas. While Blondel had demonstrated the profound unity between willing and knowing, and proposed that the will itself, through action, was in some way also a cognitive faculty, Maréchal, on rereading St. Thomas, found that the same sort of unity between willing and knowing was acknowledged by the medieval theologian, except that for him it was the intellect that in some way, by reaching out for its object, was also a faculty of willing. Maréchal analyzed this intentionality of knowledge and tried to show that implicit in the act of knowing are many presuppositions, as well as an orientation of life towards the absolute.

On the basis of Maréchal's research, a new school of Thomism came into being—at first under some pressure from official Thomism—a school that followed the critical realism of St. Thomas but turned its attention away from the object known to the subject who knows.[7] The Maréchalian Thomists studied the presuppositions in the knowing subject and found that implicit in the act of knowledge is a special self-experience and a definite orientation towards reality. This transcendental method—the term "transcendental" was adopted from nineteenth-cen-

7. Cf. O. Muck, *The Transcendental Method,* New York, 1968.

tury German philosophy concerned with the presuppositions of knowledge as an approach to metaphysics—was followed by such theologians as Karl Rahner and Bernard Lonergan, who each in his own way clearly distinguished between what a man knows explicitly and puts into words and the vaster truth that is co-known and co-intended in his explicit knowledge. This distinction, central to the transcendental method, enabled these Catholic theologians to reject the extrinsicist understanding of divine revelation and adopt a new approach to the Christian faith. The divine message preached by the Church is not new knowledge added to human life from without; rather, it makes explicit as thematized knowledge the divine self-communication that is gratuitously offered in human life itself and that, when accepted, is implicitly co-known and co-intended in the knowledge of the finite world. This philosophical approach made it possible for the theologians to hold that the divine message uttered by Christ brings into explicit and formal consciousness the mystery of God's self-gift, which is offered to all men and which may be acknowledged, implicitly and unreflectively, in the act of knowing the world. Here Christian faith is not new knowledge. It is, rather, the new consciousness created by the Christian message. Following the principles of transcendental Thomism, a great number of theologians came to acknowledge the Blondelian shift. They rejected the extrinsicist understanding of divine revelation, regarded the whole of human history as being under the influence of God's grace, and tried to present the Christian faith as the explicitation and specification of the redemptive mystery that takes place everywhere.

There were other influences on Catholic theology of the twentieth century that produced the wider recognition of the Blondelian perspective. Crucial issues such as the mission of the Church,[8] the salvation of non-Christians,[9] and the Christian attitude towards other religions [10] gave rise to an extensive body of literature which in increasing manner reflected the conviction that divine grace was offered to all men, and that it was, in fact, co-constitutive of human history. The traditional themes of "baptism of desire" and "implicit faith," which had always provided a doctrinal basis for salvation outside the visible Church, were no longer regarded as exceptions to the economy of salvation but, rather, as the description of that vast redemptive action by which the God who revealed himself in Christ was present to the lives of men everywhere.

The Blondelian perspective had been so widely adopted in Catholic theology that it influenced the composition of the conciliar documents of Vatican II. These documents teach the universality of divine grace. We do not suggest that the conciliar documents consistently adopt the new

8. J. Daniélou, *Salvation of the Nations,* London, 1949; *idem, Advent,* London, 1950; H. de Lubac, *Le fondement théologique de la mission,* Paris, 1946; A. Seumois, *Introduction á la missiologie,* Beckenried, Switz., 1952; C. Journet, *L'Eglise du Verbe Incarné,* vol. 2, Paris, 1951, pp. 1223–1251; A. Henry, *A Mission Theology,* Norte Dame, 1963; E. Hillman, *The Wider Ecumenism,* New York, 1968; K. Rahner (ed.), *Concilium,* vol. 13, New York, 1966.

9. L. Capéran, *Le probléme du salut des infidèles,* 2 vols., Toulouse, 1934; *idem, L'appel des non-chrétiens au salut,* Paris, 1961; Y. Congar, *The Wide World My Parish,* Baltimore, 1961; J. Beumer, *Lex. Theol. Kirch.,* vol. 1, cols. 343–345, vol. 3, cols. 1320–1321; R. Lombardi, *The Salvation of Unbelievers,* Westminster, Md., 1956; R. Röper, *The Anonymous Christian,* New York, 1966; H. Nys, *Le salut sans l'Évangile,* Paris, 1966.

10. O. Karrer, *Religions of Mankind,* New York, 1945; J. A. Cuttat, *The Encounter of Religions,* New York, 1960; H. Schlette, *Towards a Theology of Religions,* New York, 1966; K. Rahner, "Christianity and the Non-Christian Religions," *Theol. Invest.,* vol. 5, Baltimore, 1966, pp. 115–134; J. Ratzinger, "Religionen," *Handbuch Theol. Grundbegriffe,* Munich, 1963; J. Neuner (ed.), *Christian Revelation and World Religions,* London, 1967.

outlook: it is well known that these documents reflect several doctrinal tendencies and that the old is found in them along with the new. Yet, since the new elements were usually not present in the original drafts, since they were introduced only after the public discussion of these drafts, and since, moreover, the crucial debates on the Council floor and the significant votes of the Council fathers had to do with these new elements, it is not only permissible but even necessary to interpret the meaning of the definitive documents in terms of these new elements. If this historical approach is used in understanding them, it becomes quite obvious that the Blondelian perspective exerted a powerful influence at Vatican Council II.

Several conciliar documents explicitly acknowledge that the whole of sinful humanity is graced in Jesus Christ. These documents have been carefully examined in a number of publications,[11] and so I refer here only briefly to the principal passages in which the Blondelian shift appears.

In the *Dogmatic Constitution on the Church* we are told that God was redemptively present to men from the beginning.[12] The conciliar text takes up the patristic theme of *Ecclesia ab Abel,* the Church from Abel on to the last of the elect. Church, in this context, is the whole of

11. The most significant passages are: *Dogmatic Constitution on the Church,* arts. 2. 16; *Pastoral Constitution on the Church in the Modern World,* arts. 16, 22. Cf. the theological commentaries on these sections in *Commentary on the Documents of Vatican II,* H. Vorgrimler (ed.), New York, vol. I (1967), vol. V (1969), respectively. On the teaching of universally-offered salvation, see G. Thil's essay in the large commentary on the *Dogmatic Constitution on the Church,* G. Barauna (ed.), which has appeared in German and French and is being translated into English. On the teaching of universal grace in the *Pastoral Constitution on the Church in the Modern World,* see E. Schillebeeckx's essay in *The Church Today,* Group 2000 (ed.), Westminster, Md., 1968, pp. 60–96; and G. Baum's commentary in the Paulist Press Study-Club edition of this conciliar constitution, New York, 1967, pp. 1–36.

12. Art. 2.

humanity inasmuch as it is touched and transformed by divine redemption. Later in the same document, we are told that in the present, divine salvation is offered not only in the Church but wherever people are, in other religions and in secular situations.[13] We are told that even the atheist, the man who denies the existence of God, is by this fact alone not excluded from the means of salvation. What counts, ultimately, is man's engagement in life. Why? Because the man who reaches out for what is true and holy, whatever his theoretical statements about reality, is in fact under the influence of divine grace. In this context, the conciliar text acknowledges what some modern authors call "secular grace." Divine salvation is what happens to the man who finds in himself the freedom to turn away from his selfishness to a new love of neighbor and greater concern for society. This divine summons to conversion is present in every man's life.

The redemptive involvement of God in the whole of mankind is clearly expressed in the *Pastoral Constitution on the Church in the Modern World*. In fact, this entire document reflects the new approach. Here the Church tries to understand her role in a sinful but graced humanity. Here the Church acknowledges that she is united to the rest of the world not only by the common misery of sin but also by the divine presence creating new life. The document specifically acknowledges secular grace: we are told that the mystery taking place in human conscience is supernatural.[14] A man engaged in life and in dialogue with others hears a voice in his own conscience which is not simply the echo of his own thoughts and impressions but a redemptive encounter with God speaking to

13. *Ibid.,* art. 16.
14. Art. 16.

him. "In fidelity to this conscience, Christians are joined with the rest of men in the search for truth." A supernatural mystery takes place in human conscience which makes men brothers in the Holy Spirit. For this reason, the *Pastoral Constitution on the Church in the Modern World* is able to say that "a new humanism" is emerging in the world, a humanism "in which man is primarily defined by his responsibility towards his brothers and towards history."[15] Man's love of his brother and his involvement in the political order constitute the locus where divine redemption is present to him. God's call is present to men, in the Church and beyond it, initiating them into the death and resurrection of Christ and continually creating in them the perfect humanity revealed in Christ. "Since Christ died for all men and since the ultimate destiny of man is in fact one and divine, we must hold that the Holy Spirit in a manner known only to God offers to every man the possibility of being associated with this paschal mystery."[16] The mystery of Christ's death and resurrection is constitutive of the universal history of man.

Thus Vatican II gave expression to the culmination of a doctrinal development by which a Christian insight traditionally acknowledged as a marginal truth had moved to the center of theological attention and began to determine the main thrust of the Christian message. The Gospel has here become the Good News about human life: divine grace is present in sinful mankind, calling all men to new life. I have called such a development the refocusing of the Gospel.[17] By this I mean that the change that has taken place is not simply the conceptual clarification of an

15. *Ibid.*, art. 55.
16. *Ibid.*, art. 22.
17. *The Credibility of the Church Today.*

obscure doctrinal issue but, rather, a significant development in the understanding of what is crucial and central in the Gospel and hence a change in the self-awareness of the Christian.

This refocusing of the Gospel, I wish to insist, is not a purely intellectual development of the Church's dogma. What takes place is, rather, that the call and meaning of Christ is experienced by Christians in a new way. Theologians then reflect on this new *experience* and try to clarify its doctrinal basis, and eventually the hierarchy tests the development that has taken place and approves it in an authoritative statement.

The new focus of the Gospel, we repeat, records the spiritual experience of the Christian community. Faced with the challenges of a new age, Christians listen to the Gospel, seek fidelity to Christ, and slowly discern what faith and obedience mean in the new situation. In this way Christians begin to experience the power of the Gospel in a new way. It is here, in ordinary life, that the refocusing of the Gospel begins.

Let me briefly describe this new experience of the Gospel by delineating two of its characteristics. First, in recent decades Christians have discovered a new sense of universal brotherhood. They have experienced fellowship not only with members of their own Church; they have shared the deep and important things of life also with other Christians and, beyond that, with people who do not regard themselves as Christians. Jesus Christ has come to stand for human solidarity as never before in the Church's history. Christ summons his followers to a brotherhood that transcends the boundaries of the Church. As we listen to other people, bear the burden with them, and share with them in the things that really count, we begin to

realize that the mystery taking place in us, which we acknowledge in faith, also takes place in them. The orientation towards holiness which Christ imprinted on us in
baptism is also present in other people. We share in the
same mystery. If communion or fellowship ever meant
anything to us in the Church, we know that this is what
we sometimes experience with other people. We live with
them in the Spirit. Whether we are able to find a theological justification for it or not, we are quite certain that
what Church means occasionally occurs in our association with other people, be they formal believers or not. It
is to this universal reconciliation that we feel summoned
by Christ.

This experience, tested by scripture and liturgy and
confirmed by dialogue in the Church, is the supernatural
driving force behind the doctrinal development at Vatican
II, acknowledging the universality of divine grace. The
communion produced by the Spirit in the Church, according to the teaching of Vatican II, extends beyond the
boundaries of the Church to include people, wherever they
may be, who are open to the Spirit. God is redemptively
present in the lives of all men.

Secondly, in recent decades Christians have discovered
a new openness to truth. Christ summons them to be open
to the truth, even the painful truth, wherever it addresses
them. Christians realize that they have learned much in
the past, that they have often changed their minds, and
hence they expect that this will continue in the future.
As they enter into conversation with others or reflect on
personal experience and political conditions, they remain
open to the new that is being uttered to them. They no
longer feel that they possess a complete system of truths,
in the light of which they are to evaluate their experience

of reality; they are open to the new which they hear, even when it hurts, even when it shatters some of their inherited ideas, so long as it ties in with their deepest convictions about Jesus Christ. Catholics have become listeners, critical listeners. They test what they hear, they try it on, they see whether it fits in with their conscience and fosters the growth and reconciliation to which Christ summons them. If it does, they acknowledge the truth addressed to them and allow it to qualify their understanding of reality.

This experience of listening and of openness to truth has been the driving force behind the theological effort to come to a deeper understanding of divine revelation. Divine revelation can no longer be regarded as something that took place only in the past. The scriptures give witness to the abiding presence of God's Word in the Church. Contemporary theologians have begun to teach—and here again Vatican II followed them—that as the Word is proclaimed in the worshiping community, as the scriptures are read in faith, and as Christians engage in spiritual conversation, something significant takes place in the Church, namely the ongoing divine revelation.[18] While this revelation has been completed once and for all in Jesus Christ, it continues to resound in the proclamation and the life of the Christian Church. Is the divine Word only present in the Church or is it also in some way addressing people in their own history? The answer to this question given by modern Catholic theology and implicitly acknowledged by Vatican II, even if not explicitly approved, is this: God's Word, incarnate in Christ and present in the scriptural and ecclesiastical witness to him, is also

18. Cf. *Dogmatic Constitution on Divine Revelation,* arts. 2, 8, 21; *Constitution on Sacred Liturgy,* art. 7. Cf. G. Baum, "Vatican II's Constitution on Revelation," *Theological Studies,* 28 (1967), pp. 51–75.

present, albeit in a hidden and provisional manner, in man's personal life and in his universal history. Dialogue with others and personal conscience is the locus of the divine Word. Divine revelation is never extrinsic to the process by which men come to self-knowledge, gain the important insights, and lay hold of the true values.

This is why the Christian must listen to truth wherever it is uttered. To be faithful to the divine Word, once for all revealed in Christ, the Christian Church must listen to what this Word, present in man's historical experience, is saying to it now. The normative apostolic witness to Christ enables the Church to discern in the chorus of voices that surround it the divine message addressed to it. Thanks to this process, in which the whole community is involved, which is tested by scripture, exposed to dialogue and even conflict, and ultimately acknowledged by the ecclesiastical authorities, the Church is able to proclaim the Word of God, faithful to the apostolic norm, as the Good News for the present.

Thus this twofold experience of Christians—the new sense of brotherhood and the new openness to truth—has both stimulated a doctrinal development and served as a test for it, until through a process in which eventually the ecclesiastical magisterium took part, the understanding of the central thrust of the Gospel has shifted. The focus of the Gospel is the Good News about human life. The Christian message preached by the Church tells us not simply the marvelous things that happen in the Christian community—this is the perspective in which the Gospel was seen in the past—but also and especially the marvelous things that happen wherever people are. The Good News is that God is present to human life. The Good News is that God has redemptively involved himself in human history.

Wherever people are, something happens. People are not simply left to their destructive inclinations and the awful games they play; a transcendent power is operative in their lives, calling them to self-knowledge and freeing them to leave their destructive past behind and enter into new life. God is present to history in the growth and reconciliation of man.

II. REDEMPTIVE IMMANENCE

GOD is redemptively involved in the history of man. We now come to the question: How are we to conceive of the divine involvement in human life? In Chapter I we have given a brief description of how Blondel understood God's presence to man. For Blondel, we recall, man was a dynamic reality: man came to be through a history. By his action man was inevitably carried forward to an option, the response to which determined him in his very being. There are certain choices in man's life which do not remain extrinsic to his being, but which co-determine the very person he is becoming. In other words, man's freedom is co-constitutive of his being. Man comes to be through a process in which he himself must make the crucial options. This is why man is called an historical being: he comes to be through an historical process in which he himself as well as his community are involved. According to Blondel, God is also involved in the humanization of man.

Blondel's view of man as historical was a turning point in Catholic theology. A static view of man had made it difficult to theologize about man. For if man is regarded as a static reality, constituted by his definable nature and caught in his own limited finality, then sin and grace tend to be looked upon as elements extrinsic to him. If man is understood in terms of the ends proper to his nature, then he tends to be regarded as a closed reality, and it becomes extremely difficult to speak of God's presence to him: God is then simply extrinsic to man. In such a view, God may be regarded as the cause or creator of man; but God's gracious coming into human life will always appear as a miraculous intervention in the unfolding of a fixed nature, either as an occasional help or as an elevation to a higher, superhuman plane, never as man's humanization.

If, on the other hand, man's being is dynamic, if man comes to be in a process in which he, the world of men, and God's self-communication are involved—if, in other words, man's being is historical—then it becomes easy for the theologian to theologize about man, to speak of the sin that dehumanizes him and of the grace by which God is present to man's becoming himself.

How, according to Blondel, is God present to human life? It would seem that the supernatural is present to man only in the option by which he opens himself to the infinite. Every man is carried forward to the inevitable choice between saving faith and self-destructive idolatry. The inner logic of action brings a man to some sort of faith in an absolute. Either a person opens himself to the infinite and thereby becomes more truly himself, or he refuses to follow the divine invitation, attaches himself to a finite reality as if it were an absolute, and violates his nature by blocking his quest for self-realization. According to Blondel, then, God is redemptively present in the humanization of man by saving him from idolatry and offering him entry into an open-ended, ever-renewed life.

The phenomenology of the human spirit presented in the two volumes of Blondel's *L'Action* is not accepted by many philosophers today with regard to the details and the stages of human development. The contemporary reader has several difficulties with Blondel's description of human life. Blondel seems too religious. Is the quest for the infinite really a common characteristic of all men? Are not people today cautious when it comes to absolutes? The necessary choice between the finite and the infinite which, according to Blondel, is the entry into the supernatural does not seem to present itself to all men, not even to all men who take life seriously. There are many people today who do not wish to reach beyond the finite world and their responsibility for it in order to be in touch with an ultimate reality beyond history. And yet these people wish to live responsibly. It seems to them, rather, that the crucial decisions which make or unmake them have to do with what is happening in their history, personal and social. The important options are this-worldly or secular. The contemporary theologian will ask the question, therefore, whether a careful description of human life might not reveal that man is open to the supernatural not only in the ultimate option described by Blondel, but in many other options that constitute the turning-points in a man's life. Is it possible, the theologian will ask, to discern the supernatural or the divine in the finite actions of man?

One wishes to reply to Blondel that human life is much more open-ended than he thought. He saw only man's forward movement towards the infinite, which was in keeping with man's nature though realizable only through God's free gift. A more realistic view of man shows that the forward movement of man to greater maturity, to wider responsibility, to a growing capacity for truth and love, is in keeping with his nature, but not built into it. Man grows against many odds. Human life is basically threatened. The very forward movement of man is in constant need of being nourished from sources beyond his own life. If the threats to human life are taken seriously, it may be possible to say that man is open to the supernatural not only in an option by which he transcends the finite but in the many necessary and often painful choices by which he perseveres in the movement toward growth and reconciliation. To modern readers it may seem, therefore, that Blondel too narrowly confines God's presence to human life to a single dramatic moment, while a careful consideration of the precariousness of life in this world, this sinful world, reveals that man is open to divine mercy in the many choices between life and death which constitute his history.

Quite generally, one might say that the more conscious a theologian is of the sinful dimension of mankind, that is of the profound ambiguity affecting every aspect of human life, the easier it will be for him to express the divine presence to human life and to give meaning to the assertion that God is redemptively involved in man's making of man.

We agree with Blondel that man is an historical being, that he comes to be through a process that passes through his own freedom, but we wish to add that this process is so gravely threatened by human sin that without divine grace man does not enter deeply into his humanity. It is difficult for man to be human. We hope to show in this study that God is what happens to man on the way to becoming human.

The process of man's becoming can be described in

terms of the two dimensions, dialogue and communion. Man comes to be through conversation with others as well as through a deeper, less conscious sharing with others in love and fellowship. While these two dimensions are inter-related and interconnected, we shall discuss them separately.

DIALOGUE

Man comes to be through dialogue with others. This becomes evident in the possession of language. We are able to speak because others have spoken to us. We achieve a certain self-awareness and are able to put something of what we are into words because we participate in the language of mother, father, the family, and the wider community. Without the language to which we are introduced, we would not have a mental life. One may even go further and suggest that a man does not achieve consciousness at all unless there was someone who summoned him when he was a baby. Unless there is a mother, or one taking her place, who calls out to the baby and evokes a response in him, there can be no conscious life. Consciousness is not a given: it comes about through conversation—being addressed and responding.

This constitutive role of dialogue, evident in the possession of language and the emergence of consciousness, continues through the whole of a man's life. Man comes to be who he is through conversation with others. Man learns from others. This is true on the level of information, and this is true on the deeper level of self-knowledge and the values of life. Man listens to others, in the family, the school, the community, to his friends and his adversaries, and his consciousness continues to be created by his response to the reality addressing him. Man is created through ongoing communication with others.

We may add that man's emotional life is produced by a similar dialogical process. The love and the hostility, the care and the coldness to which he is exposed in his childhood, evoke in him the power to respond, and produce in him an emotional life of his own. Here the sharing is on a level deeper than consciousness. Man's emotional strength, his power to trust and to love, is born out of intimate sharing with others, offered him as a child and throughout his life.

To say that man comes to be through dialogue with others does not mean that he passively absorbs what he hears and thus becomes simply the product of his environment. On the contrary, the word "dialogue" suggests that man is never simply the creation of the community to which he belongs. Man listens and responds. He becomes himself, distinct from others, by responding. These responses are truly his own. To the extent that he makes them freely, he is responsible for who he is and comes to be as a person. His intellectual life, his religion, his entire mental world is thus created by a process in which the entire community is involved and yet in which he, consciously or unconsciously, makes the important decisions. What is given to man at the beginning is to be a listener. His life is the realization of his dialogue with others.

A careful look at the dialogue through which man comes to be reveals an element of resistance and conversion. Man is not always open to what is being said to him. The word addressed to him may be a challenge, and he may be able to give a positive reply to it only if he is willing to abandon part of the world, or the self-image, that he has made for himself. This aspect of dialogue is revealed at the very beginning of man's conscious life. At first the baby looks upon the mother simply as warmth, protection, and nourishment. But as the mother continues to summon him, the baby must abandon some of his self-centeredness and recognize that behind the warmth there is the mother who calls him. At the moment when he shatters his own little system and recognizes another person, he becomes more truly a person himself. What takes place here is a conversion away from self-centeredness to the wider reality of life and people.

From the beginning, then, there are moments when the word addressed to us makes us abandon the world of our own making and enter upon new life. Dialogue is not simply a way of giving and receiving information; it does not change man simply by expanding his knowledge. Again and again as we are in dialogue with others, we must hear the painful word which overcomes us and evokes a response in us that transforms life. The word addressed to us at those moments reveals to us the truth of which we are afraid. It pierces the screen we have erected between ourselves and reality. Then we must either flee from this word and hide more effectively behind our defenses, or open ourselves to it, go through the painful passage from superficiality to greater depth, and receive the truth that has been uttered to us. Sometimes dialogue is a happy sharing; but in the course of a man's life there are those important and yet frequent moments when dialogue means conversion. Because we have listened, because we were willing to let go the little world of our own making, because we have gained a new hold on reality, we have come to be persons in a new way. Our response to the word addressed to us has become constitutive of who we are.

The dialogical structure of the human person reveals

to us that man is in need of others to become himself.
Man's sinfulness, we add, reveals that he can only grow
through many conversions. We cannot define man simply
in terms of his orientation to truth and think of his entry
into truth as a passage from knowing little to knowing
much. While part of us desires the truth, we must make the
painful admission that part of us is also afraid of it. Part
of us does not want to see. We erect screens that prevent
us from acknowledging the truth. Knowledge itself can
be such a screen. It is possible for us to rush into knowing
many things, rush into science or research, as a way to
avoid knowing what is really true. If the reality surrounding us were mute, we might never discover it. If this reality
were passive, we might successfully hide from it. But since
we are constantly being spoken to, since the word is addressed to us, we are summoned again and again in the
dialogue of life to abandon the blindness we have chosen
and to be in touch with reality. The summons addressed
to us enables us to let go our projections and to see what
is really happening in ourselves and in others. This is conversion. Man comes to be through many conversions.

Man has a dialogical structure. We have seen that some
of man's responses determine who he will be as a person.
It makes sense to say that man is summoned to create himself. His own responses in the conversation which makes him
are the determining factors of his life. At the same time,
other people are involved in this process of becoming
man. Through dialogue they have a share in the coming
to be of a person. We have also noted that this dialogue
includes a very special word. Sometimes the call addressed
to us has a very special force. It reveals to us who we are,
it judges us, it summons us to grow, it demands a reply.
It leaves us two choices: either we choose to be deaf and

thus harden in our opposition to life or we open ourselves to the truth and lay hold of reality in a new way. This word demands conversion and summons us to new life. It comes to us through conversation with others and re-sounds in our conscience.

What is the special word by which men come to be? The Christian who has met the Word of God in scripture and who experiences life with presuppositions determined by his faith recognizes this special word available in human dialogue as God's Word present in history. In the first place, the Christian knows the biblical description of God's Word as summoning, judging, revealing, as provoking decisions, as condemning if not replied to, and as life-giving if received. In the second place, he thinks that a phenomenological analysis of this special word available in human dialogue, as he experiences it and sees its effect in others (and here his sensitivity to reality is determined by his faith), shows that this word is both transcendent and gratuitous.

The special word available in human dialogue and re-sounding in conscience does not appear as man's own cre-ation. It is uttered by men but it transcends them. It stands over against them and judges them. It makes them uncomfortable. It makes known to them what they do not want to know. This special word addressing the hu-man community is not limited to the wisdom and the values proper to the age. On the contrary, it transcends the age. Because of this word, people question their own culture and become restless in their easy self-possession. Because this word is available in history, mankind is able to move forward into new environments and find cre-ative responses to new challenges. Men can never catch up with this word. For whatever self-realization they may

45

achieve, the word is there ahead of them, offering them salvation from self-deception.

The word of truth that saves us from self-deception may be uttered by a friend or an adversary. In either case, the word does not belong to the person who pronounces it. For he, too, is in need of it. He is a faithful communicator of this word only if he acknowledges that he, too, is judged, summoned, and possibly healed by the word he addresses to us. A voice which transcends the human seems to enter into the conversation of men.

The special word in human dialogue also appears as a gratuitous reality. This is, at least, the way it appears to the Christian who has an understanding of gratuity from scriptural revelation. Man knows himself threatened in many ways. He finds in himself a passivity preventing him from living, which he cannot overcome by his will power. He is aware of his inner resistance to growing up. He is conscious of the possibility that he may isolate himself from reality and thus choose his own destruction. This is the inevitable human context in which all conversation takes place. In biblical language, sin is an omnipresent dimension of human life. When in this conversation the special word addresses man, he will experience it as a surprise, a surprise that makes him angry. But if he listens to the word and acts upon it, he will rejoice in the surprise that came to him. A man does not regard his conversion to reality, evoked by this call, as his own doing. He is not proud of it as if it were his own achievement. Whenever he is summoned to take up his own life, to endorse it, to act and to be, he realizes that the response to this call demands all the energy he has, and yet he follows the summons. He does not for a moment regard the new life available to him as the product of his own efforts. Rather, he marvels at the summons that challenged him and evoked in him the strength to reply. A man can earn truth as little as he can earn friendship. While he may exert himself to the full in being good to another and in seeking the truth that counts, when he is loved by a friend and when truth is available to him, he does not regard friendship or truth as the necessary consequence of his own efforts. Truth—just as friendship—is to him a free gift that happens and gives his life a quality of newness that he could not have achieved by himself. The special word present in human life, converting a man to reality, is both transcendent and gratuitous.

Believing that God's word is present in human history, the Christian discerns this word as the special summons available in the human dialogue by which men come to be. Men are open to God's redemptive presence not only in an ultimate option between the finite and the infinite, as Blondel proposes; men are open to God's redemptive presence in the many conversions to truth and life which constitute them in their personal being. The Word of God sounds in the dialogue by which men become men. The dialogue which constitutes human life is, ultimately, a dialogue of salvation with God.

COMMUNION

Related to dialogue is the other dimension of the process by which men come to be which we have called communion. This dimension also reveals the unfinished character of man and his dependence on others. Man is in need of the community to become himself. In the twentieth century various intellectual and political trends have made us abandon the individualism inherited from a former age. We are on the whole no longer tempted to think that a man achieves self-possession by concentrating on himself, by affirming himself over against his human environment, and by resisting the demands which the community makes on him. We have come to realize that it is precisely through his relation to others, to the community, that a man comes to be himself. Others participate in a man's self-making. We have seen one aspect of this when we looked at the dialogue which constitutes the history of man. Since a special power is needed to enter into this dialogue and since this power depends on man's communion with others, we must now look at this participatory dimension, by which man is open to the community and, we believe, to the transcendent mystery of redemption.

Other people enter creatively into a man's history because they care. This is obvious in the growth of children. Unless there is a mother who cares, and later a family, or its substitute, to surround the child with affection, it is almost impossible for the child to discover himself. The child needs strength to reply to the summons addressed to him by others. But where does this strength come from? It is produced in the child through the love and acceptance offered him. If there is no love, the child will be terrified by the word addressed to him. Without the strength created in him by love, the child will not be able to face the challenges of life. He will evade the dialogue to which he is invited, or, rather, he will take part in it simply by negation. The child finds the courage to open himself to the conversation that creates his consciousness only if the care given to him by others has provided him with the strength.

What is true for children remains true for adults. The

dialogue to which we are called may offer us new life, but it is also a threat to us. To be addressed by others creates some fears in us. Can we afford to listen to them? Is there no danger that as we listen to another, we will be taken over by him and cease to be ourselves? Could it not happen that the word of the other will destroy us— either by revealing to us how insignificant we are or by bringing us under his spell and making us dependent on him? Man is always tempted to reject the dialogue to which he is called and hence to involve himself negatively and sometimes destructively in the conversation that constitutes his life. A special strength is necessary to reply to the summons addressed to us.

Strength is needed in every truly human conversation. But it is especially necessary in the dialogue in which the special word is addressed to us, the word that makes us face who we are, that reveals to us the destructive and superficial in us, and calls us to the painful conversion to a more authentic humanity. This special word—we have described it in the preceding pages—is always a threat to us. It makes us afraid. We are tempted to draw up our defenses against it. We tend to feel that if we listen to it, we may not survive the judgment contained in it. We vaguely sense the area in us where we crumble to pieces, yet we feel that we can just make it if we do not look at it too closely. If this area were to be spelled out to us and if we were to face the emptiness, the self-hatred, or the destructiveness that is in us, we might not be able to survive. In order to listen to the special word, therefore, a special strength is required. Something marvelous has already happened within us if we are able to listen to this special word and respond to it with courage.

In general, it is the love and care offered to us by others

that create in us the strength to enter into the dialogue of life. Only as we are loved and recognized do we gain the self-confidence necessary to listen and to reply. This is obviously true of the child where the love given by mother and family creates the self-confidence that enables him to listen to the call addressed to him and thus, eventually, renders him capable of separating himself from mother and family and becoming a more independent human being. Love, in other words, gives freedom. The same law holds true for the lives of men as they grow older. The love and care they receive from others create the strength in them to listen to the summons, to come to greater self-knowledge, to assume wider responsibility for themselves and thus to become more truly human. This strength comes from a certain self-possession to which men have access only if they have shared life or enjoyed communion with others. We have grave doubts about who we are if we try to derive our self-evaluation from reflecting on ourselves. Only as we are loved by others, only as we share in community, do we come to accept ourselves. We discover our worth as persons through the love of others and our share in the life of the community. The acceptance and care given to us by others produce the freedom in us to face the challenges of life and become more truly ourselves.

Love gives freedom. Love accepts another person as he is, and discerns in the other person hidden strength. Love communicates to the other a new kind of self-possession, and enables the other to act with self-confidence.

This description may seem idealistic, for in this world every aspect of human life, including human love, is ambiguous. Human love is always marked by some destructive tendencies. It is always tempted by some self-seeking. It is possible that love may become a screen for the desire to possess another person. We use love as an extension of our power: we want other people because we need them so desperately for the building up of ourselves. This sort of love does not communicate freedom. On the contrary, it binds the other, it burdens him, it does not give him the power to listen to the summons and respond in freedom. This corruption of love is already possible in the environment that surrounds the baby; for mothers and families might love the child in this possessive way, using him for their own self-centered ends, training him to supply their own emotional needs. This sort of care does not free. Possessive love does not communicate self-confidence to the child, enabling him to engage in the conversation of life, to separate himself from his family, and to become more autonomous. Since the ambiguity of life is universal, a certain possessiveness, remains part of every human love, and the quest for holiness, to which every man is summoned by the divine word, demands the ongoing purification of love and the entry into a way of sharing that renders others free.

Man needs others to become himself. This is so because dialogue is made available to him by others and because the care that makes him free to engage in it is also given him by others. Today we have become aware that even the strength to be independent of the community is given to us by the community. The child or the adolescent finds the strength to sever the infantile ties to mother and father precisely if much love and care have been offered to him by his family. A true friend gives the freedom to the other to become more truly independent of him. Friendship allows the other to have his own convictions, to disagree, and to choose his own life. Only a friendship that is largely corrupted binds the other person, demands conformity, and does not tolerate independence. Some people may want their spouses to be with them all the time, to supply them with admiration and affection, to agree with them and promote their own self-deceptions. Their spouses must conform. And the spouses may even create this dependency in their partners. But this is not love in the true sense. Such relationships will soon enter into crisis. The love offered in marriage must also make the partner free, give him a new kind of self-confidence, enable him to express his own convictions with honesty and become in some real sense independent of the other. It is precisely because husband and wife are in a certain sense independent of one another that they are able to lead creative lives and help one another in times of stress.

Further, the fellowship offered by a larger community supplies the freedom by which men become more independent of this very community. Only when the community is very sick will it tie its members to strict conformity. A healthy community gives to its members the inner freedom to stand apart, to take a critical look, and to engage in the self-criticism without which no community can grow and develop. The prophet uttering his message is nourished by the community to which he belongs and which he criticizes. Here, too, love makes free. The reformer or the critic who has not been nourished by the community will become an angry man; he will utter truth in a destructive way. If a man who has not been supported by the community listens to the special word that gives him insight, he may lack the freedom to respond positively to this call; he may make the insight an instrument for his own anger. Only if a man is freed by the fellowship to which he belongs to be independent, will he be able to stand on his own feet and become part of the community in a creative way. The fellowship available in the Church, for instance, frees or should free us to become more independent of it, to break the infantile ties to conformity, and to gain a more critical and yet more creative and faithful adherence to the community.

Man needs others to become himself. He needs the few, his friends, his intimates; and he needs the many, the wider community to which he belongs. The power to respond to the summons, supplied by the care of other people, will enable a man to grow, to become more himself, and to make his own contribution to the building-up of the community. The love we receive prepares us to give love to others. The man who is nourished by the care of others and thus enabled to respond in the dialogue of life, is carried forward by his own vitality to love others and to extend his concern to the whole human community. We may say, therefore, in a slightly different sense that a man is in need of others to become himself. A man needs others because by extending his friendship and service to them and by bearing the burden with them in love, he is in fact becoming more truly himself. The man who is free to leave himself and abandon his preoccupations with his own little problems, to be present to others and to share with them, enters more fully into his own humanity. It is confirmed by the ordinary experience of life that the man who is able to loose himself finds himself. The man who is drawn to love others and assume responsibility for the community gains a more peaceful and powerful self-confidence.

Obviously, this moving away from oneself cannot be done through will power. For if we move away from ourselves simply on the strength of our will, we carry our fantasies and preoccupations with us, and involve other people and the community which we intend to serve in our own problems. The power to move away from oneself is always a gift, a gift that is created in us through the care we have received and the word addressed to us. Something new is being generated in us as we are able to leave our own small world to be concerned about the greater community in which we participate in so many ways. We may say, therefore, that while the community supplies the care which goes into a man's growing up, the man who grows in turn will embrace others in love and create the community by his own action.

We note that in this description of human life, we have used the word "freedom" in a special sense. We have said that freedom is a gift granted to men, which enables them to respond to the summons addressed to them. Freedom here is not simply the ability to choose between inconsequential alternatives. This sort of free choice is built into the human equipment. It belongs to man and is not a special gift to him. But whenever man is challenged, whenever man is threatened by his own passive and destructive tendencies, whenever man is called to love other people or open himself to the truth, then the power to respond is not something that can be taken for granted, something that belongs to his human equipment, something over which he has power. On the contrary, a man finds present in himself a hundred hesitations to respond, to act, and to be in a new way. The freedom to enter into this dialogue or to accept the love extended to him is a power a man finds in himself at certain moments, a power over which he has no control, a power he experiences as a gift. We have suggested that this freedom is created in many by the love he has received. A man thus marvels at the freedom he finds in himself and he trembles in the hope that it will remain with him tomorrow. The freedom to enter into dialogue is a gift.

Man is constituted not only by dialogue (in which, as we have seen, he remains open to the transcendent), but also by the gifts he receives from others. Just as the summons addressed to man in his life is not totally reducible to the human, so, the Christian holds, the gifts which empower a man to grow are not totally reducible to the human. As the Christian is able to discern the word of God in the dialogue available to him, so he is able to detect a gift-dimension in human life, which is redemptive and transcends the human. The freedom to become human is God's gift to man.

Again, we do not suppose that it can be demonstrated, in a strict sense, that in the gift-dimension of life man is in touch with a transcendent mystery called God. What we propose, rather, is that the Christian who accepts the Gospel in faith is able to discern in the freedom by which man creates himself a gift that surpasses him. A phenomenological analysis of the gift-dimension in human life—to which he is sensitive precisely because he is a believer—will show him that this dimension is not only gratuitous by definition but also radically transcends the powers of man.

We notice that people give us more than they really have. The child receives care from his family which enables him to grow, even though mother and father are involved in their own problems and much of the care they offer him is wounded by the ambiguity inevitably present in their lives. The child may be hurt in many ways, but in and through the care given him, though offered in ambiguity, is provided the kind of strength that creates freedom and enables the child to grow in his humanity. And as the child grows up to become a man, he notices that his friends also give him more than they have. The gift that friends and the community provide exceeds what they themselves possess.

In and through the care offered by others caught in the ambiguity of life is presented to us the food of life which enables us to listen, to respond, and to be in a new way. Our friends realize that they do not own what they give. For when we express our gratitude to them, they are embarrassed. They know that they have not really given us what we have received from them: the gift transcended their power.

When people are in communion and help one another, there is always more involved than just these people. The freedom created in them to grow and to be reconciled is a gift which is mediated through their interaction but of which none of them is the author. Each man is caught in his own ambiguity. He is wounded and in need of others, of love, and of dialogue, to become more truly himself. Unless there were a gift available in the human community, transcending the members that make it up, the community would soon destroy itself. Sickness would come up against sickness and each man would infect the other. Fears, angers, and hostilities would begin to take over and eventually destroy the conditions of life. Yet this is not what happens, at least not all the time. When people come together to share and be friends, each mediates to the other what he does not totally possess, and their mutual enrichment exceeds by far what each member was able to put into it. The multiplication of power towards the building up of life available in communion reveals the transcendent character of the gift by which men enter into their humanity. There is a gift-dimension in human life that is not reducible to the human.

If I reflect only on myself, I might possibly persuade myself that I receive the gift which creates my freedom from the people who have come close to me; but when I reflect on the community of men, made up by people like me, involved in ambiguity and wounded by self-centeredness, then it becomes extremely difficult to suppose that the gift creating their freedom is a purely human reality, under the control of the people involved. This gift is offered from beyond man's sinfulness. The Christian believing that God has involved himself in human history discerns in this gift the saving presence of God to his people. The gift that creates our freedom is the love that God extends to every man and that engenders new power in him to grow in his humanity. This creativity in man, which we have called his freedom, is due to God's redemptive presence in human life and is offered to every person through his relation to the community. This gift, according to Christian theology, is ultimately God himself, the Holy Spirit.

This description of human life, then, enables us to give concrete and definite meaning to the claim that God is redemptively present in human life. As Word and as Spirit, God is present in man's making of man. God is present in the dialogue and the communion by which men enter into their humanity. God's presence to man as Word and Spirit establishes an orientation in human life which radically transcends man's natural powers. In Christian theology this supernatural destiny of man is called God, the Father. As destiny, God the Father is the ultimate source of man's being. But the process by which man enters life and becomes human is not a single creative moment, before which man was not and after which he is, but rather a development, a history, with many stages and pivotal

57

points, in which God is creatively present as Word and Spirit.

God is present to man in the secular process of his self-creation. The divine presence is not confined to the ultimate religious moments when man must choose between the finite and the infinite—one may wonder how many people today have these religious experiences—; we have shown, rather, that God's presence is discernible in the ordinary situations of human life, in the dialogue that constitutes man's history and in the gifts that reconcile him with himself and with others. Human life is not only open at the top, as it were, where man may opt for the infinite; it is open to the transcendent mystery in the entire process of man's humanization. The locus of the divine is the interpersonal. God is present in that area of human life where man, in fact, invests most of his intellectual and emotional energies, namely his ordinary, secular existence. We may summarize these remarks by saying that God is the mystery of man's humanization.

While God is present to man in his secular existence, we do not suggest that human life is one-dimensional. On the contrary, we have shown that there are special moments in life when man is addressed by the new and when responding to it he becomes himself in a new way. Not all the moments of life have the same power and meaning. There are pivotal points in a man's history when he is healed of some of his self-doubt and has access to a creativity not his own. There are times when man is in touch with the transcendent ground of his being. In the preceding pages we have tried to express the depth-dimension of human life, which is God, in terms of Father, Word, and Spirit. God's presence to man as Word and Spirit orientates him towards the Father. According to the Church's doctrine, the eternal Father revealed the true manhood in his Son or Word, Jesus Christ, and with him sends the Spirit into the community of men to conform them more and more to Christ's perfect manhood. God's gift of himself orientates man towards growth and reconciliation. Since the Word and the Spirit are present in man's life, it should be possible to describe in greater detail some of the experiences by which people advance in growth and achieve some reconciliation. In another study I have tried to analyze some of these depth-experiences by which men are open to the transcendent.[1]

We have come to conclusions about God's presence to human life in line with Blondel's theological anthropology, yet less removed from the contemporary experience of life. Blondel was a religious person in a traditional sense, and he took it for granted that discerning people, sensitive to the "inner light," would be religious in the conventional way. He thought that all men have a hunger for the infinite. Today this can no longer be taken for granted. For vast numbers of people, responsible people, the specifically religious decisions have become marginal issues. Central are the decisions that affect their personal and social history. We recall in this context a sentence from Vatican II, already quoted in the previous chapter: "We are witnesses of the birth of a new humanism, one in which man is defined first of all by his responsibility towards his brother and towards history." [2]

What has enabled us to come to conclusions different from Blondel's? There are two factors. First, we have acknowledged the dialogical structure of the human person. We have consistently interpreted human life as the realiza-

1. *Faith and Doctrine,* ch. 2.
2. *Pastoral Constitution on the Church in the Modern World,* art. 55.

tion of a dialogue involving all men and thus have pointed out that man is more open-ended, even in regard to the transcendent mystery, than would be suspected in a more static view of him. Secondly, we have stressed the sinful dimension in which man is born and which remains an aspect of his life. This has enabled us to affirm man's need of redemption in an unqualified manner: without divine grace man cannot become fully human. Every aspect of his life is marked by ambiguity. Theologians who stress divine immanence may possibly be tempted to neglect the otherness of God and thus become unfaithful to biblical revelation. But if they have a radical view of man's ambiguity, they are able to discern the otherness of God in the midst of life itself. If humanity is essentially threatened, if men are not at all certain whether it is possible to be human, then the affirmation of humanity implies divine transcendence. Because of God's presence to man, as Word and Spirit, humanity is possible.

The following chapters will further elucidate the presence of God to human life. This elucidation is especially necessary since the Blondelian shift raises many questions in regard to the Church's traditional teaching. If it is true that God is redemptively present in all of human life, what then is the role of the Church? What is meant by the judgment on the world? What is the meaning of the cross? We shall examine these and many other issues in the following three chapters. We hope to show that the Blondelian shift is in harmony with the Church's teaching and that, understood in the light of the new focus, the traditional doctrines assume a special relevance for the present age. In the last three chapters of this book, I wish to reinterpret the doctrine of God in the light of this new focus.

III. THE CHURCH IN THE NEW PERSPECTIVE

THE teaching that the Gospel happens everywhere raises many questions with which the theologian will have to deal. To say that God's grace is present to human life and hence constitutive of human history, both personal and social, seems to question some of the Church's traditional positions.

A first set of questions deals with the reality of the Church. If divine grace is present in all of human life, what then is the role of the Church? Does this not make the Church superfluous? Or if not superfluous, does it not abolish the difference between Church and world? The teaching that God is redemptively involved in human history raises the question whether Jesus Christ has added anything new to human life, and hence whether the traditional teaching on the redemption worked by him is still meaningful.

A second set of questions deals with Christian eschatology. How is the teaching that God is redemptively present in the humanization of men related to the traditional teaching on eternal life? Will not the emphasis on the earthly consequences of the Gospel make men forget the judgment that is to come and the resurrection of the flesh in the new age? Does not such a secular emphasis remove the eschatological tension from Christian life? This world, we have learned, is just the provisional tent in which we live during our pilgrimage; the new and everlasting world is promised us for a future age, already pressing in upon us. These are some of the difficulties we will have to deal with.

A third set of questions has to do with the meaning of Christ's teaching. The position that the Gospel happens everywhere might be understood as a kind of naturalism. Does it mean that man can save himself? Does it mean that man is ultimately responsible for his salvation and that he creates his future by relying on his own resources? The position advocated in these pages, some readers may feel, seems to promote a simple humanism. What about the supernatural which manifests itself in contradiction to man's earthly existence? What about the traditional teaching of the Church on shunning the world, on prayer and the ascetical life, on the violence which Christians must do to their own nature? Does the teaching that God is present to human life take the edge off the Gospel? Does it remove the cross from Christian life?

In this and the following two chapters, I wish to show that these three sets of difficulties do not constitute dogmatic obstacles to the Blondelian shift. This is not the occasion to deal with these sets of questions in an exhaustive manner. What I wish to do is to outline the meaning of the traditional teaching in the light of the new central insight. We follow here the general principle, clearly expressed above, that the refocusing of the Gospel demands the reinterpretation of the Church's teaching in the light of the new shift. This is demanded to preserve the self-identity of the Gospel.

THE CHURCH

If divine grace is present to human history, what then is the meaning of the Church? This question, we note, has been amply dealt with by many contemporary theologians.[1] In the Church is proclaimed and celebrated the mystery of redemption that summons man everywhere. The hidden involvement of God in the humanization of man has become fully, definitively, and unconditionally manifest in Jesus Christ, the Word made flesh, and it is this Christ that is proclaimed and celebrated in the Church. This Christ is available to men in the Church. In the Church, therefore, we have not only the source of salvation for those who belong to it, we also see in the Church God's redemptive plan for the entire world of men. The Church signifies that God has involved himself in the lives of all men to form them into a single family of brothers. The Church reveals that despite the sinfulness that pervades human life, the whole of the human race has been oriented towards growth and reconciliation. The

1. We want to refer above all to E. Schillebeeckx's article "The Church and Mankind,'" *Concilium,* vol. 1 (E. Schillebeeckx ed.), New York, 1965 pp. 69–102; and to his essay "Christian Faith and the Future of the World," *The Church Today,* pp. 60–96. From this essay we quote (p. 82): "What the Church has to offer us explicitly is already implicitly present in human life as a whole: it is the mystery of salvation. The Church reveals, proclaims, and celebrates in thankfulness the deepest dimension of that which is being fulfilled in the world. . . . The Church is in fact the world where the world has come fully to itself, where the world confesses and acknowledges the deepest mystery of its own life, the mystery of salvation fulfilled through Christ."

Church proclaims and embodies the Good News for all mankind.

What then is the difference between the Church and the rest of mankind? This difference is certainly not defined by the decision between belief and unbelief. We cannot claim that the Church is the community where people say Yes to God's Word, and the world the collectivity of men who say No to him. We realize that faith, saving faith, is granted outside the Church and that unbelief is not excluded from the Christian community.[2] What, then, is the difference between Church and world?

The Church alone is conscious of the redemptive mystery that goes on everywhere. The Christian is aware of what goes on in him and in others: he believes that in Christ the universal mystery of redemption has been made known to him. While the Word and the Spirit are present to people everywhere and, in fact, constitute their history, the Christian alone explicitly acknowledges this mystery which is omnipresent in the lives of men. We may say with Karl Rahner that the Christian is *"der ganz zusichgekommene Mensch,"* the man who has become totally conscious of who he is.

Christians alone are conscious of the redemptive mystery present in all men. They know about it from and in Jesus Christ. But is this giving enough meaning to the special position of Christians as members of Christ's body? Some readers might feel that to gain greater consciousness does not include a profound change in a man's life. Our interpretation, they may feel, tends to empty out the meaning of being Christian. Entry into the Church, we have always been taught, produces a radical transformation in

2. Cf. J. B. Metz, "Unbelief as a Theological Problem," *Concilium,* vol. 6 (J. B. Metz, ed.), New York, 1965, pp. 59–78.

people. Does our teaching render an account of this transformation? A moment of reflection will convince us that the entry into a new consciousness indeed creates a radical change in the lives of men. When men come to know the mystery that occurs in them and their community, they are able to reorientate their lives in accordance with this mystery and make it a principle of their own self-making. This is a radical reorientation of life.

Even as we reflect on the ordinary forces of good and evil that influence us, we realize that our consciousness of them produces a significant change in our lives. These influences may be operative in us all the time. They may help us or they may weaken us. But as soon as we know them for what they are, we are able to relate ourselves to them in a conscious way and orientate ourselves in the light of this knowledge. I may be exposed to the destructive influence of another person who has a certain power over me. But as soon as I become conscious of this, as soon as I recognize the influence this person has on me, I am called to a decision: either I reject the evil influence and become free, or I acknowledge the evil influence and submit to the destruction of my life. While the influence has been there all the time, the consciousness of it has provoked a significant turn in my personal history. The same holds for the good influence people have on me. I am supported in many ways by the goodness and wisdom other people offer me. There may be a person who has a specially beneficial influence on me, even though I do not fully realize this. Then I find out. I become conscious of what goes on. As soon as this happens, I must make a decision. If I am willing to receive the gifts that are being shared with me, I must respond to this person in a new way and make this friendship a factor in the determination of my future. The new consciousness enables me to reorientate my life so that this person has a special place in it.

To say, therefore, that the Christian is conscious of the redemptive mystery, incarnate in Christ and operative in the lives of all men, indicates the profound transformation occurring in people who come to believe in Christ. Even if these people have been open to God's saving presence in their lives, even if these people, prior to their contact with the Church, have been alive by faith, hope, and love, the acknowledgment of Christ makes the hidden grace conscious to them and demands a decision in regard to Christ, the author of grace. God's Word in Christ becomes a factor in the determination of their lives. Becoming Christian, even for men in grace, implies a reorientation of their lives. Now that they acknowledge the redemptive mystery present in Christ, they can open themselves to it, proclaim it in their faith, celebrate it in the community, intensify their involvement in it, and make it the central factor in the important decisions of their lives. We conclude, therefore, that to express the difference between Christians and other people in terms of greater consciousness is not belittling the difference between Church and world. Greater consciousness of the hidden mystery means personal transformation. It is possible, we conclude, to affirm the universality of grace and at the same time to speak of Church in a meaningful way. The Church is the community where God's universal redemptive presence is proclaimed, celebrated and possessed in Jesus Christ.

Yet this statement must be followed immediately by a certain corrective. Already the New Testament spoke about the kingdom of God in a dialectical way. On the one hand, salvation is available in the name of Christ alone, and on the other, not those who say Lord, Lord enter the kingdom, but those who do the will of the Father (cf. Mt. 7, 21). On the one hand, the believer has access to Christ as the only way to the Father, and on the other, it is not those who profess the name of Christ who enter salvation, but those who love and serve the least of his brethren (cf. Mt. 25, 31–46). Christ is present in the proclamation of the Church and the community gathered at worship; and yet this affirmation must be qualified by the equally fundamental teaching that Christ is encountered in all men who suffer and are in need of help— that is, in the whole of humanity (cf. Mt. 25, 31–46). We are told in the New Testament that unless we love, we do not know God (cf. 1 John 4, 8). The profession of faith or the recitation of the creed is no guarantee that we are in touch with the saving reality the creed proclaims; unless there is a special, loving inner disposition divinely created in us, the divinity we acknowledge is not the God and Father of Jesus Christ at all. And if this special Spirit-created love exists in a man, then God is in fact redemptively at work in him, even if he has never heard of the name of Jesus and the Church's creed. This is the irony of the Gospel.

It is necessary, therefore, to speak of the Church and humanity in dialectical terms. On the one hand, we affirm that the Church is the community in which Christ is proclaimed and celebrated. The Church is the community where humanity has become fully conscious of its divine destiny, and hence the community which has the mission to serve this destiny in the world. At the same time, divine redemption goes on everywhere. The marvelous things that happen in the Church are also available outside. For this reason it is very difficult to define the difference between a Christian and a man who does not acknowledge the Christian creed. While the Christian is constituted as such by his faith in the divine truth, it may happen that he is less transformed by it than his neighbor who has no explicit knowledge of it. The distinction between Church and world, though clearly revealed in the scriptures, does not draw a clearly visible boundary line through the human race, creating two kinds of communities, Christian and non-Christian, that face one another. What is true, rather, is that the fellowship produced by the Spirit in the Church extends beyond its visible boundaries to include other men in whom the Spirit creates new life.

Church, understood in this perspective, is the divine message about man's life in community. Ecclesiology, we suggest, is not simply the theological study of the Christian Church; it is, rather, the critical study, based on divine revelation, of what happens in human society.[3] How is society threatened by the sinful forces in life? What are the structures of redemption available in the community? Ecclesiology is the study of the Spirit's presence to the sick society. What happens in the Christian Church is the specification and clarification of that mystery of communion which, thanks to God's mercy, is present in all the societies of men. The Christian Church, in other words, is not something altogether new that Christ has created. Through Christ's action, rather, the Church specifies and clarifies (and thus raises to consciousness) the divine involvement in the redemption of the human community. Scriptural revelation sheds light not only on man's personal existence; it also and especially illumines man's social existence. The marvelous things that happened in

3. Cf. G. Baum, "Where is Theology Going?" *The Ecumenist,* no. 3 (1969), pp. 33–36.

Israel and finally in Jesus Christ enable us to detect the patterns which, thanks to God's mercy, are available in all human communities. Ecclesiology, we repeat, may be regarded as the theological study of human society. Admittedly, this approach has not often been developed.

THE SACRAMENTS

If we reject the extrinsicist understanding of divine revelation and regard the Church created by Christ as the specification and clarification of God's redemptive presence to human society, then it should be possible to find secular equivalents of all the gracious elements that constitute the Church. Because the ever self-identical divine Word is present in human history, it should be possible to show that what God is doing in the Church in an explicit manner, through the faith-consciousness of those who acknowledge Christ, he is doing in the rest of humanity, with varying degrees of intensity, in a more hidden and implicit manner. We may speak, for instance, of the secular equivalent of faith, hope, and love. The self-same gifts which create the new man in the Church are also given, as dispositions of mind and heart, to people touched by the Spirit beyond the Church's boundaries. The Word present in human conversation may summon a person and evoke faith in him, and the Spirit at work in human fellowship may create love in the hearts of men. There are moments in a man's life when the word addressed to him by another person, a work of literature or a human incident, discloses to him how unreal he has become, and by offering him a convincing image of what he could become, initiates his conversion to new life. These moments are the secular equivalents of

69

preaching. There are works of art, there are secular plays and novels, there are incidents of personal history that celebrate the Word of God and make his power available to men.

We may also look for the secular equivalents of the sacraments. For what God is doing through the sacraments in an explicit fashion, he is doing in a more implicit manner through the words and gestures that are part of life itself. There is a good dogmatic basis for the shocking statement that there may be more communion taking place in the tavern on Saturday night than in the church on Sunday morning. The sacraments appointed by Christ reveal to us how God offers transformation to men through the ordinary events of their lives.

Eucharist

It is possible, for instance, to speak of the secular meaning of the eucharist. The eucharist tells us not simply how Christ is present to the Church as it gathers for worship; it tells us what God offers to men who eat at the same table, engage in human conversation, and enjoy the same gifts together. Eating together can be a redemptive happening.

Let us reflect for a moment on the role of eating in human life. Like any human activity, eating is ambiguous: it is also in need of redemption. It is never totally free of excessive self-seeking. It could even be a self-destructive thing. A man may devour his food to feed his isolation. He may make eating a substitute for more important things from which he shies away. Or the longing for food may be a man's desire to remain a baby and have an ever-present mother to look after all his troubles. There may be redemption in eating together with others, even though men are also more vulnerable to the destructive while they sit around the same table. Eating together could be an enforced coming together of people who try to avoid one another all day, accompanied by a carefully screened conversation by which each tries to keep the other out of his life, a nervous juggling with words, interrupted occasionally by jokes that hurt and remarks by which some triumph over others, until the longed-for moment arrives when everyone rises from the table, each to his own isolated life. Such meals are devastating. They feed the sickness in us: they nourish what is skeptical and untrusting in us; they encourage our fears and our angers; they heighten our alienation from human life.

The Good News implicit in the eucharist is that God offers men redemption through common meals. The marvelous may happen when people eat together. Eating itself is redemptive in the sense that here a man acknowledges his need of food and, hence, of other people. Even the person who delights in his independence, even the individualist, even the man who is ashamed of his body gets hungry several times a day. Unless he is willing to recognize his need and let other people help him fulfill it, he cannot survive as a human being. Eating means opening oneself to others. Meals may even link many countries and several continents on the same table. The food and drink may come from all over the world: the table cloth, the china, and the silverware may unite the industries of many nations. How many people are involved in producing the food, in harvesting it, in packing and shipping it, in selling and buying it, in the whole organization through which these transactions become possible! In eating we

71

depend on the cooperation of the millions. A meal may celebrate the unity offered to the human race and, at the same time, accuse us of complicity in the awful fact that vast numbers of men are hungry. If we consider how a meal shared with others offers men redemption from their pride and individualism and opens them to the human community, to the few who eat with them as well as to the wide world, we see that eating may indeed be sacramental.

Eating, moreover, is accompanied by words. If a common meal is to be truly human, it must be the occasion of conversation. Eating together places us in a context which invites the trusting exchange of words. Sharing the same food, acknowledging our common need, and helping one another to fulfill it, opens us to fellowship and creates a special kind of friendship among us. The Word is present at the table. To those who eat together in a human way is offered reconciliation and the inner rebuilding of life. The wounds inflicted by our self-centeredness are in part healed by the love that is being shared. As friends eat together, the eucharistic mystery is offered to them—not in its explicit and specified form as Christ personally present, but in the implicit and more general form as the Spirit present, by whom all men may share in Christ's death and resurrection.

Baptism

How does the Blondelian shift affect the understanding of baptism? The man who acknowledges Jesus Christ as God's Word made flesh enters the community of the faithful, the body of Christ, through the sacramental rite of baptism. But if not only sin but also divine grace is universal in human history, what, then, is the meaning of infant baptism? Why should it be necessary to baptize small children? Our first response to this question is that however important infant baptism may be, we must not think for a moment that without it little children who die will go to hell or limbo. It is true that the theologians of the past have often affirmed this; yet they did this not because they had a special message regarding the lot of little children but, rather, because the revealed teaching on original sin and the gratuity of grace seemed to demand that babies who die without baptism be assigned to a place that was not heaven. Thanks to a doctrinal development, however, it has become possible today to affirm man's inherited sin and the unmerited character of God's grace, and at the same time to hold that a man born into this sinful world and becoming a sinner, is, nonetheless—this is the Good News!—oriented towards divine salvation in Jesus Christ. Man is born into sin, but present in his life are not only the divisive powers that create his self-alienation, but also through dialogue and communion with others the redemption offered by Word and Spirit. Despite the sinfulness into which a child is born, God is redemptively present in the process by which he comes to be man. Even without baptism, the future of a child is Jesus Christ.

Nonetheless, infant baptism is meaningful. It may happen, of course, that in certain traditional environments the common practice of infant baptism makes people look upon the Church as part and parcel of their cultural inheritance. Parents may come to regard baptism as a ritual which implies no personal commitment. Infant baptism by general custom may promote a non-critical, conformist, purely cultural kind of Christianity or, worse, constitute the legal link between the Church and civic society. In such circumstances it may be pastorally useful or even imperative to limit infant baptism.[4] But in other circumstances, infant baptism may be a meaningful celebration of the sacrament, even if the child is not yet capable of believing. Even in the baby, I contend, the baptismal insertion into the Christian community produces a radical change.

Since man comes to be through a process in which his community is actively involved, it is obvious that to transfer a child from one community to another causes changes in him of the most profound character. If a child born in New York of American middle-class parents is, after a few days, taken to South America to be raised by Brazilian peasants, his life undergoes a radical change. He will come to be through a very different process of dialogue and communion. Not only will he grow up in a different language, he will come to be by responding to different people, different values, different customs. He will come to be quite different from what he would have been had he stayed in New York. To suggest that the translation from New York to Brazil is something that remains external to the child, or that no real change takes place in the child because he is not conscious, would be quite superficial. Because man comes to be through a process in which the whole community is involved, the insertion of the child into a new community creates a change intrinsic to his life. Similarly—*mutatis mutandis*—the insertion of a child into the Christian community creates a profound

4. In 1952 the French hierarchy imposed restrictions on the baptism of infants belonging to non-practicing Catholic families. Cf. *La Maison-Dieu,* no. 32 (1952), pp. 90–117.

change in him. Infant baptism orientates the child towards Christian faith, towards participating in the Christian community, towards the celebration of the sacraments and a share in the Christian imagination. The child's consciousness will be created by a dialogue in which the Word, preached by the Church, will have a part and a communion in which the sacraments play their role. If we regard man as a finished reality, then we might think that nothing changes at infant baptism; but if we understand man as an historical being coming to be through dialogue, then we see that infant baptism produces a radical change in the child who receives it. Something changes in the process which constitutes him as a man. The Christian who regards a sacrament as a special way of Christ's presence has no difficulty in acknowledging the meaningfulness of infant baptism.

Liturgy

It is possible to believe in the universality of divine grace in this sinful universe and at the same time to acknowledge the uniqueness of the Church as the community of salvation. What does this mean for the understanding of the Church's liturgy? Liturgy is the sacramental celebration of the marvelous things that happen in human life. Liturgy, I insist, is not a sacred action which separates men from the ordinary situations of life and brings them into touch with the otherness of God. In liturgy men do not turn their backs on secular life to be in more direct contact with the heavenly realities. We wish to avoid such an extrinsicist understanding of sacramental worship. The radical distinction between the sacred and the profane has been overcome in the person of Christ. In Christ it is revealed that the locus of the divine is the human. In him it is made manifest that God speaks in and through the words and gestures of men. The Christian way of worship, therefore, can no longer consist in sacred rites by which men are severed from the ordinary circumstances of their lives. Christian liturgy is, rather, the celebration of the deepest dimension of human life, which is God's self-communication to men.[5] Liturgy unites men more closely to their daily lives. Worship remembers and celebrates the marvelous things God works in the lives of men, purifies and intensifies these gifts, makes men more sensitive to the Word and Spirit present in their secular lives.

Liturgy is important in the Church, but it is never a substitute for life. The primary means of grace is always and everywhere human life. It is here that men are first encountered by the Word, and here that they are first graced with the Spirit. The message of Christ enables men to discern God's presence in their lives and to turn whole-heartedly to the divine Word personally present in Christ. The sacraments of Christ enable men to celebrate the deepest dimension of their lives, namely God's gift of himself, in a way that renders this dimension more powerful. Liturgy, then, brings men in touch with the self-revealing God as he is present in the life of the community, creating fellowship and new life. The otherness of God, as we shall see further on, is not accessible at the edge of human life, at the threshold of another world, but at the very center of life where men are summoned and graced to create their future.

5. Cf. E. Schillebeeckx, in his article "Theology of Renewal Talks about God," *Theology of Renewal,* L. K. Shook, ed., vol. 1, New York, 1968, pp. 102–103.

This leads us to the secular equivalent of prayer. If we reject the extrinsicist understanding of the Christian Church, then the prayer which is God's gift to the Church must also be available in secular life. We shall deal with this subject at greater length in a later chapter. At this point we simply recall that prayer is primarily listening and responding to the divine Word. Christians pray when they listen to the Word which God has spoken and is still speaking in the history of salvation, and when they reply to this Word with faith and gratitude. The divine conversation called prayer always begins with God. His Word uttered first evokes the response of man. Since this Word is not only present in Jesus Christ proclaimed by the Church but also in human life and history generally, prayer understood as listening and responding takes place among the non-religious as well. The man who reflects on human life, on his own and on that of the community, who seeks to detect in it a message sent to him, who listens to what his experience means for his growth as a human being, and who responds to the summons available in his life with confidence and courage is, in fact, in the strict theological sense, praying. There is a contemplative dimension in the life of every man who wants to become truly himself. Christian prayer is the specification and clarification in Jesus Christ of the contemplative dimension by which God enters into dialogue with every man.

THE CHURCH'S MISSION

We now come to the more difficult subject of the Church's mission. Does the teaching that God is redemptively present to human history invalidate the Christian mission?

Why should the Church address itself to the people of the world if divine salvation is offered to them where they are? This is the question that is being asked in the Christian Churches today. In the process of rethinking the Church's mission at this time, diverse and sometimes conflicting views are being proposed and defended.

A diversity of view in regard to the mission appeared even at Vatican Council II. Three documents dealt with the Church's mission in distinct and slightly divergent ways. One of them, the *Decree on the Church's Missionary Activity,* developed the traditional understanding of the mission as the evangelization of unbelievers. *The Declaration on the Church's Relation to Non-Christian Religions,* on the other hand, regarded mission as creative dialogue between Christians and members of other religions. The *Pastoral Constitution on the Church in the Modern World* looked upon the Church's mission principally as her effort to enter into solidarity with the whole human race and to serve others so that life may become more human on this earth. These three views of the Church's mission are similar inasmuch as they all consider it as belonging to the essence of the Church, as the divinely-appointed ministry in the recreation of man in the image of Jesus, and as the commission to serve the mystery of redemption so that God's will be done on earth as it is in heaven. These three views agree that the Church's mission is to serve the kingdom of God coming upon us. At the same time, these concepts of the mission differ greatly from other points of view, and Vatican II did not succeed in reconciling them in a single doctrinal synthesis.

The New Testament itself does not seem to contain a perfectly consistent teaching on the salvation of the nations.[6] These are the great missionary passages in which Jesus sends the apostles into the world to announce the Gospel and to baptize men in the name of Father, Son, and Spirit (cf. Mt. 28, 18–20). There is, furthermore, the shining example of the apostolic Church wholly involved in the evangelization of Jews and Gentiles. At the same time, there are New Testament passages insisting that in Jesus Christ God has reconciled all of humanity with himself in an irrevocable fashion and that the effect of God's work in Christ is as extensive and more profound than the consequences of Adam's fault (cf. Col. 1, 20; Eph. 1, 10; Rom. 5, 15–19). The nations are now part of the covenant which God first made with Israel. We are told that what counts for salvation is to listen to God's voice and do his holy will (cf. Lk. 11, 28). Thus, in a story told by Jesus, it is not the Samaritan, the outsider, but the true believer who is in need of conversion. Jesus foretells that the last judgment of mercy will come upon man not according to his profession of faith, but according to the love he extended to the least of the brethren (cf. Mt. 25, 31–46).

The New Testament gives witness to the Church as the unique instrument of salvation and at the same time acknowledges the universality of God's salvific care for his people. It may well be that several concepts of the mission are in harmony with New Testament teaching and that it depends on the historical situation and the guidance of the Spirit what particular understanding of the mission the Church acquires in a given age.

Today we witness a strong tendency to understand the

6. Cf. J. Jeremias, *Jesus' Promises to the Nations,* London, 1958; Ferdinand Hahn, *Mission in the New Testament,* London, 1965.

mission of Church primarily as service to mankind. As Christ came as God's servant, so the Church is sent into the world to serve others in order that the whole human community become more conformed to God's plan for it. Today the Church's mission is often understood as the unification and socialization of the human race. The Church declares herself in solidarity with mankind, especially with the underprivileged and exploited, and by bearing the burden with others, it labors with them to make life in society more human. In particular, the Church is sent to create fellowship among men. The Church's task is not to separate men from their environment and group them in a walled community of their own. Today we have passed from a closed to an open understanding of Church. The fellowship created in the Church extends beyond its boundaries to include other men in whom the Spirit is at work. The Church is, therefore, creator of community in a special sense. Since she initiates her members into the mystery of communion, they in turn have the mission to create fellowship in the environment in which they live, a fellowship uniting as friends not only Christians but all men open to friendship, truth, and the sharing of new life. It is by becoming an open-ended movement in society that the Church exercises her mission to collaborate in the reconciliation of mankind.

I wish to add, however, that we cannot leave the Gospel out of the definition of the Church's mission. The Church is indeed sent to cooperate with all men in the transformation of human society, but what is specific about her mission is the proclamation of Christ. Now, how is the Church's witness to Christ offered to men? At a time when we thought that divine grace was largely confined to the

Church, and hence regarded the rest of the world as afflicted with spiritual ignorance, this witness was given by preaching Christ to the nations. The Church was the white circle in the field of darkness, and her mission was to carry the light given to her to men caught in the darkness of their environment. But if God is redemptively at work in the whole of mankind, the Church must listen to others before she may speak to them. The white circle in the dark field no longer describes the Church's situation in the world. The Church must discern Christ's presence in the religions, the cultures, and the value systems that she encounters. Only after she has become aware of the wonderful things which, despite man's universal sinfulness, God has worked in other communities can the Church offer her own witness to Jesus Christ. Therefore, the Church's proper evangelical mission today is dialogue with other people, whether they be members of other religions or have no religion at all.[7]

To understand what this dialogue means, we must for a moment consider the development that has taken place in the Catholic evaluation of other religions and other value systems in general. The traditional Christian attitude towards other religions has been almost totally negative. The teaching that Jesus Christ is the one mediator between God and men seemed to exclude other religions from any access to divine salvation. At best, some Christian teachers were willing to concede the possibility of a good "natural" religion, that is the acknowledgment and worship of God based on man's own powers. The Blondelian shift in the understanding of human history, characteristic

7. Cf. Juan Segundo, "Fundamental Theology and Dialogue," *Concilium,* vol. 46 (J. B. Metz, ed.), New York, 1969, pp. 69–79.

of the twentieth century, has opened new possibilities for the appreciation of other religions.[8] The teaching that Jesus Christ is the one mediator between God and man no longer implies to us the limitation of divine grace to the Christian Church. The Gospel happens everywhere.

Now the question arises as to whether other religions contribute to the salvation of mankind. Do they have any part in the universal history of salvation? A growing number of Catholic theologians have affirmed that God is redemptively at work in and through other religions. This trend was greatly encouraged by Vatican II. The conciliar documents acknowledge that salvation is available in the world religions and recommend that the Church enter into dialogue with them.[9] This does not mean that Vatican II acknowledged the divine origin of the other religions or that it approved the teachings mediated by them. The Christian who believes that God has revealed himself in the man Jesus will disagree with some positions held by other religions, but he may affirm that through some elements of these religions, the divine summons becomes available to men. Through what takes place in these religions men may be converted from the superficial in life to the profound, from self-centeredness to openness and communion. Without denying the ambiguity of the world religions and hence their need of redemption—this ambiguity exists in some sense also of the Church—contemporary

8. Cf. K. Rahner, "Christianity and the Non-Christian Religions."

9. The principal passages are *Dogmatic Constitution on the Church*, art. 16; and *Declaration on the Church's Relation to Non-Christian Religions*. We quote from the latter document, art. 2 "The Church has this exhortation for her sons: prudently and lovingly, through dialogue and collaboration with the followers of other religions, and in witness of Christian faith and life, acknowledge, preserve, and promote the spiritual values and moral goods found among these men, as well as the values in their society and culture."

Christians joyfully acknowledge that men are summoned and graced by what is best in their religious traditions to become trusting, generous, loving, patient, and cheerful people, devoted to a meaning of life that transcends them.

These brief remarks enable us to understand better the nature of the Church's dialogue with other men. This dialogue, I insist, is not a purely humanitarian endeavor leading to better public relations, nor is it a hidden attempt to convert others to the Christian Church. The Church's dialogue with others is a redemptive process in which both parties are being transformed and enter more deeply into what is God's will for them. While God is redemptively present to men in every truly human conversation, we here consider a dialogue in which Christ is specifically mentioned. In the Church's dialogue with other religious traditions, the Gospel is openly sounded. Christian witness is present in dialogue!

What happens in such a conversation? Neither partner becomes teacher to the other. The Word of God present in the Church's witness is teacher to both. Through this conversation the members of other religions become more sensitive to the destructive elements in their religious tradition and learn, through a change of heart, to attach themselves more to those elements which mediate the new life. Through this dialogue they come to see the implications of their religious views, the effects these views have on their own lives and on society as a whole; they learn to detect the ambiguity of their tradition and to discern those aspects in it that promote greater openness to the transcendent mystery. The Church's dialogue with other religions effects a transformation in them. Through this dialogue people come to possess their religion in a new way and enter more deeply into God's will for them, *where they are.* (The Church, as we shall see, is also transformed by this dialogue.)

A similar kind of analysis applies to the Church's dialogue with secular philosophies or systems of values. Since these systems are created by men in particular historical situations as responses to real problems and difficulties, they are not simply "natural": they too are, in part, the crystallization of man's dialogue of salvation with God. Despite their ambiguity, despite the errors they contain, they may reflect aspects which embody authentic responses to God's Word in history and hence continue to summon men from hostility to love, from indifference to concern, from individualism to a sense of community. The Church's dialogue with these systems includes her witness to Christ and hence renders the divine critique available to others. Again, what takes place is not the creation of better public relations nor the hidden attempt to convert others; what is made available to both partners in the conversation is the divine Word offering them new life. Through such a dialogue the followers of other systems may become more aware of the personal and social implications of their convictions, may come to see some of the destructive tendencies implicit in their thought and the way of life they advocate, and may learn to discern more clearly the life-giving and humanizing elements in the systems to which they adhere. Through dialogue men come to hold their view of reality in a new way. In particular, if these systems are atheist or agnostic, their advocates may well become aware of the hidden presuppositions in their views and acknowledge in their systems the universal danger, from which no one is immune, of falling into idolatry. They may discover whether they have elevated a finite and limited principle to an absolute and thus closed themselves off from the newness which life continues to offer to them. Dialogue with the Church may make secular systems of thought more open-ended.

In particular I wish to distinguish between a closed and an open humanism. A closed humanism is based on the presupposition that reality is proportionate to human understanding. We can know what man is like. We can see through him. Whatever happens in the future is explicable through causes and forces operative among men now, and hence there will never be any real reason to marvel at life. Reality is a closed and finite system—and hence God does not exist. This sort of dogmatic humanism is quite different from the open-ended humanism that is adopted by vast numbers of people today. Such people refuse to commit themselves to the strict proportion between reality and the human mind. They do not claim that they know who man is. They are concerned with the humanization of life, with the growth and the reconciliation of people, yet they differ from the dogmatic humanists inasmuch as they do not exclude the possibility of the new happening in human life. The future is open. Man is not yet totally defined. There is, for these humanists, no sufficient evidence for affirming that reality is finite. They are open to the truth that may be uttered to them tomorrow, even if this should mean that they have to question some of their positions. Between these two kinds of humanists, the dogmatic and the open, there is a radical difference. The dogmatists tend to set up structures that enslave man in the self-understanding of a particular period in history. They tend to repress new life and the possibility of faith. The open-ended humanists, on the

85

other hand, are willing to listen to the new and modify their understanding of man. They do not defend their present insights like a fortress but are open to a future that promotes the growth and reconciliation of men in unexpected ways. (The Christian would claim that the discernment of human growth and reconciliation is ultimately a theological judgment.)

The Church's dialogue with others is a redemptive process. We note in passing that there are situations where this dialogue is impossible. There are value systems which are so destructive that to engage in dialogue with them would make Christians accomplices in the dehumanization of man. The Church's mission in regard to these systems is to be in conflict with them. In the early Church the political world of the Roman Empire was regarded as such a system. There was no dialogue with the world. Becoming a Christian meant to oppose this world. In regard to some systems the Church remains in the situation of either/or. The Church cannot enter into dialogue with antihumanistic ideologies, with racism, with any system committed against the universal well-being of man.

In showing that today the Church's mission to the world, religious and secular, is the dialogue in which she proclaims the Gospel as divine critique, we have only considered the effect of this dialogue on others. This must be complemented by the consideration of the effect this dialogue has on the Church herself. Here we categorically assert that the Church needs the conversation with her own generation to be faithful to the mystery alive in her. The Church enters redemptive transformation through dialogue with others. Since the Church becomes herself through obedience to God's Word, and since this Word is present to her not only in scripture and her past tradition but also in present history and the experience of mankind, she is bound to listen to what God is doing in other people, in other religions and in secular cultures. This does not mean, of course, that Christians open themselves uncritically to the views and values of their contemporaries. What happens is that Christians listen to what others have to say, test their message with the Gospel, and if the new insights tie in with the Church's experience of Christ, then she must receive guidance from them and reinterpret her own position. The Church needs the world to become Church! The Church must listen to the Spirit speaking in humanity to lay hold of the Gospel in a new way and to formulate the Christian message for its age. Since there is no other way for the Church to obey God's Word except through this sort of dialogue, mission understood in this sense belongs to the Church's essence. It is thanks to her mission that the Church becomes Church.

The most obvious example of this process is the Church's encounter with the values of the modern world. After the first indiscriminate rejection of these values, the Catholic Church eventually came to discern in the democratic, humanistic, and liberal ideals of modern society much that was in harmony with the Gospel and that demanded a modification of her own position. Even though the Catholic Church had not encouraged these values and, during the nineteenth century, had actually fought them, the Catholic community was humble enough in the twentieth century to listen to them and seek a new obedience to God's Word present in the experience of mankind. The inalienable rights of persons in society, including the right to religious liberty, were acknowledged at Vatican II. The participation of the many in the decisions made by the few was recognized as a Christian ideal. The Catholic Church was even willing to learn, at a great price, from the critical trends characteristic of the modern age, that self-interest in the political and personal order influences every aspect of man's life, and that the task of the wise man is to submit his own views as well as those of his society to a careful critique. In dialogue with the modern world, the Church learned to become self-critical and thus more faithful to God's Word.

These reflections on dialogue show that the Church's mission is to enter into a dialectical process of conversation and interaction with mankind, where the Word of God revealed in Christ stirs up the cultures of the world and, conversely, where the Word of God present in these cultures brings the Church to a more profound grasp of her own message. The Church is not a closed community seeking to keep herself aloof from humanity and to attract a few chosen souls to her; she is, rather, a movement in human society with open boundaries not always clearly visible, appointed as divine catalyst of a spiritual and social transformation, a movement drawing men into dialogue and even conflict so that the whole human family may become more open to God's self-communication and proceed on the way to growth and reconciliation. The acknowledgment of a graced humanity, therefore, does not invalidate the Church's mission. The mission of the Church sets up an inexhaustible dialectic in humanity by which all men are summoned to greater consciousness of the divine mystery operative in their lives. The Church is the visible instrument, the extension of Christ, by which the divine Word elevates humanity to the ever-to-be-renewed awareness of God's presence in its own self-creation.

CHRIST AS SAVIOUR

This leads us to the last point we want to examine in this section. Is it possible to reject an extrinsicist understanding of divine revelation and retain the Church's traditional teaching on Jesus Christ? If God is redemptively operative in history, what then is the place of Jesus? Why is he called redeemer and saviour? Will the Blondelian shift not inevitably lead to a depreciation of Christ's work of redemption? The reflections made in the preceding pages enable us to reply to these questions.

We admit, of course, that the acknowledgment of God's redemptive presence in history forbids that we look upon Jesus Christ as the beginning of salvation history. Jesus Christ was not God's entry into human life. We can hardly entertain the idea that prior to Christ's coming mankind was in an unmitigated state of sin or in some sort of "natural" state and that only through Christ were men offered forgiveness of sins and a share in the new life. It is commonly taught that grace was already available in Israel, and even prior to the ancient covenant, in Abraham, the father of the faithful. In fact, from the very beginning of human history, God did not leave sinful man without the help of salvation. It was this divine involvement in human history, hidden from the beginning and variously signified in Israel, that was made manifest in Jesus Christ. The divine Word which in a hidden way was present in the lives of men from the beginning, which addressed the people of Israel in the covenant, was revealed in an unconditional and definitive way in the person, in the life, death, and resurrection, of Jesus Christ. In Jesus the Word became flesh.

This revelation in Christ produced a profound change in the condition of mankind. In Christ the hidden presence of God has become known to men and, as we have shown above, has created a new consciousness in them and thus has produced a reorientation of their lives. Because in Jesus God's Word has become flesh, men have access to God in him. They can submit their life to this Word, turn to him, and be rebuilt by him; they are able to base their personal history on the knowledge of what God through the man Jesus is doing in their lives, and what he said and keeps on saying to them. In Jesus God has revealed that he is not far away, living in separation from men, and only occasionally, at sacred moments and in sacred places, intervening in history to save men. In Christ is revealed that the way of God's presence is incarnation. God acts through the human. It is in ordinary words and gestures, in interpersonal relations, that God communicates himself to men. Before Christ's coming, men may have sought the invisible God in temples and shrines; after his coming, they seek him in human life. What is revealed in Christ is that human life is the locus of the divine. Jesus is not the beginning of salvation; he is a turning point in man's universal history of grace, the beginning of a new human consciousness and a new orientation towards greater humanization. By creating the Church as the community of believers, Jesus established a dialectical movement in the history of men by which the whole of mankind was to be transformed and elevated. We saw in connection with the Church's mission that this does not mean that all men are destined to become Christian! The Church's entry into dialogue with other religions and secular cultures makes the Gospel operative in the transformation of these communities, and of the Church herself, and thus makes Christ effective in the creation of the human future.

In this brief reflection on Christ, we have looked upon divine revelation as a way of redemption. Some readers may be surprised at this. They may feel that God's revelation in Christ is one thing and Christ's redemptive work is another. If we entertain a highly conceptual understanding of divine revelation, then revelation in Christ refers mainly to his teaching, and the effect of this revelation in man is largely the faithful acceptance of this divine message. In such a theological context, it would be necessary to describe Christ's redemptive work as distinct from and transcending his revelatory work. But if divine revelation is understood in a wider and more realistic fashion, as we have done in these pages, then revelation in Christ is not simply his message but his entire being, his life, his passion, his death, and his resurrection. The whole person of Christ, as historically constituted through his personal life, including his death and resurrection, reveals to men the invisible Word of God as creator and saviour of human life. As this divine self-revelation cannot be reduced to the conceptual order but includes the whole history of Jesus, so can the effect of this revelation in men not be confined to the conceptual order but includes the transformation of their personal histories. Even in ordinary human situations, we note that if a man reveals himself to us and becomes a friend, the effect in us goes far beyond the intellectual order: what is changed in us through his self-revelation is our relationship to this man, and possibly even our relationship to others and the world around us. The encounter with God in the man Jesus Christ—and this includes his entire life, especially his death and resurrection—transforms man in a powerful manner. God's self-revelation in Christ affects not only man's understanding; it produces in him a new relationship to Christ, and hence with Christ to the invisible God and to the whole human race. It should be possible, therefore, to consider Christ's redemptive work as an aspect of God's self-revelation in him.

God's self-revelation in the whole of Christ's life, including his death and resurrection, transforms the men who encounter him in faith. Christ redeems them. Even his sacrifice is an element or aspect of the divine self-disclosure. While the divine Word summons every man to do the will of the Father and to enter into his destiny, it is only Jesus Christ who ever obeyed this call fully and completely. Because he was without sin, because the Word was in Christ and constituted his history, Jesus surrendered himself to the Father as no other man did or could. He said Yes to the Father, even when this meant entering into suffering, into failure, and eventually into death. Jesus also said Yes to the Father when this meant entering into new life after death. This obedience to the divine will as expressed in his entire life and culminating in his death and resurrection is what is sometimes called Christ's sacrifice and more often the paschel mystery. It is in this sacrifice that Jesus reveals who he is—and hence who man is and who God is.

Christ's sacrifice is revelation not simply in the sense that God manifests himself in it; it is revelation in the deeper sense that God communicates himself through it to other men who receive it in faith. In other words, the obedience of Christ to the Father is proclaimed, giving men the power to share in it. By faith men are able to participate in Christ's Yes to the Father. While by himself no man is able to do the Father's will—as sinner every man resists the divine summons on some level of his being—it is possible for man to join Jesus Christ in faith and be obedient to the Father with him. Since Christ's sacrifice is divine revelation, it is offered to men as the entry into their own reconciliation with the Father. The Yes of Christ becomes available to the believing community—in faith and in the eucharist. It is possible, therefore, to understand Christ's redemptive work in terms of divine self-revelation in him.

The doctrine that the Gospel happens everywhere, therefore, does not reduce the central role of Jesus Christ in history. The divine self-communication offered to all men in a hidden way as conditional and provisional gift entering into their self-making is visibly present in Jesus Christ as the unconditional and definitive gift by which he comes to be and forever is the Word of God in human history. In his life Christ has redeemed mankind. For in him is made known and made available the way to the Father, that is the forgiveness of sin and the entry into new life. The doctrine that God is redemptively involved in human history, we conclude, does not weaken the understanding of Church or remove the urgency of her mission, nor does it minimize the role of Jesus as universal redeemer. The Blondelian shift is in harmony with traditional Christian teaching.

IV. ESCHATOLOGY IN THE NEW PERSPECTIVE

A SECOND set of questions raised by the Blondelian shift has to do with the Christian teaching on the age to come. If we reject the extrinsicist understanding of divine revelation, what effect will this have on the doctrine of eternal life and the Church's eschatological message? If the Gospel has to do with the humanization of life on this earth, will men become so secular in their concern that the traditional hope for future life will lose its power and meaning. Is not the eschatological judgment revealed by Christ a perpetual warning against becoming too attached to life on this earth and of transmuting Christian hope into an expectation of earthly happiness?

To deal with the question of eternal life, we must examine more closely the meaning of divine revelation. We have already referred to the significant development in understanding divine revelation that has taken place in Catholic theology over the last decades and that was endorsed at Vatican II.[1] While neo-Scholastic theology

1. Consult the great commentaries on the *Dogmatic Constitution on Divine Revelation,* especially H. de Lubac in *La Révélation Divine,* vol. 1, Paris, 1968; and J. Ratzinger in *Commentary on the Documents of Vatican II,* H. Vorgrimler (ed.), vol. III, New York, 1969.

tended to regard divine revelation as truth about God and his plan of salvation, contemporary Catholic theology, influenced by biblical research, ecumenical dialogue, and the personalist trends of modern philosophy, has come to look upon divine revelation as self-revelation. God does not reveal truths about himself: he reveals himself. God communicates himself in his Word. In divine revelation God makes himself known, and the so-called truths of faith give witness to this self-revelation. The articles of faith recited in the creed do not describe an object, called God, of which man is an observer: these articles proclaim and mediate God's communication of himself. Since God comes to man in his Word, his truth is always salvational. Divine revelation is not new knowledge, it does not make men learned or well-informed about the divine; rather, it affects man's consciousness, it transforms his relationship to himself and his world, it initiates him into a new way of being. God's Word recreates man.

Truth is always salvational. What does this mean in regard to eternal life? The message of eternal life, revealed by Christ, is not additional information about a divine world, it is not information about a realm to which men have no access, it is not conceptual knowledge about an objective reality existing apart from human history. As we shall see, the message of eternal life is, like all of divine revelation, a way of God's coming to man. It mediates divine redemption and initiates men into the new life promised by Christ.

At the same time, we are subject to the temptation to regard divine revelation as a source of information about a world we have not traveled. Man is always tempted to give in to a rationalistic understanding of divine revelation. In this way man defends himself against God's Word. We resist the conversion God offers us in his truth, by regarding this truth as a piece of information about an objective order apart from human life. In this way we take the power out of the Gospel. This approach enables us to make revelation the starting point of learned speculations about God and his divine world and to escape the confrontation and transformation to which the divine Word summons us. We must reject this temptation.

Christian truth is salvational. We admit, of course, that the Christian message contains some facts. We are told, for instance, that Jesus was born, that he suffered, died, and rose for us. But these facts by themselves are not divine revelation. They become revelation only if through them God communicates himself to us. What counts in regard to the facts, therefore, is their salvational meaning. The birth of Christ as biographical information is not salvationally significant. But to believe that in this birth God reveals his solidarity with the human race and becomes brother among brothers, affects a man's relationship to this God and the world in which he lives. In this case the fact communicates the salvational message. While Christians are deeply attached to the facts associated with the Christian message, they always want to remember that it is possible for a man to accept the facts and yet be less transformed by the divine self-communication available in them than another man who has no knowledge whatever of these facts. This is the irony of the Gospel. The facts associated with the Christian message do not alter the nature of divine revelation as self-revelation. If these facts are understood through the Word that is uttered, they mediate God's self-communication. But these facts are never so closely related to God's gift of himself that he may not offer himself independently of them. To Abraham, the father of the faithful, God communicated himself prior to any of the facts that constitute the special history of salvation in Israel and in Jesus Christ.

ETERNAL LIFE

The Christian message regarding eternal life, we conclude from the above, is divine self-revelation. God reveals himself as the One who creates life out of death. God manifests himself as the faithful friend. He who has summoned and graced us reveals in the message of eternal life that he is ever faithful to his promises. The divine summons is always before us; even if we die, the divine Word shall address us offering us new life. The message of eternal life is not information about another world, but in it the invisible God makes himself known to us and transforms our self-understanding. To believe the message of eternal life means to believe that God ever creates life out of death, and to open oneself to this newness on the levels of life where we are frightened by death. The Good News is that the divine Word is always present to life. Even though we are threatened by death in many ways, even though we experience failures, breakdowns, impasses, and insoluble problems, we learn in Christ that God is present summoning us to new life. The Good News is that tomorrow will be different from today. God is creatively involved in human life.

We may not look upon the death of the body as the most frightening aspect of death. The death which threatens man is not primarily the death he shares with the animals but the specifically human death which presses upon him in situations without hope. The Old Testament was able to describe the dialectic between life and death, in which God was redemptively present to men, long before it expressed a clear teaching about life after the death of the body.

Death surrounds man on many sides. Human life, as we have seen, is built up in a gradual process of dialogue and communion, but it remains breakable at every stage. Life can be shattered. We are surrounded by traps into which we can fall. Failures, sickness, disappointments, accidents remain part of life on this earth. It is possible to fall into situations where life is destroyed. It is possible to have one's life shattered like a precious vase and despair over ever being able to rebuild it. We meet people in mental hospitals and in ordinary situations whose life has become a living death and we realize with fear and trembling that we too are vulnerable, we too could destroy our lives or have our lives destroyed by forces beyond our control. These deaths in the midst of life are what we are most afraid of. Yet the Good News, so hard to believe, is that even in these prisons we are not left without the divine Word summoning us to human life. To believe in life everlasting is to trust that out of the fragments left to us after the storm, God will create the conditions for becoming more human. Death, bodily death, is just an instance of the many deaths which threaten us in life. Believing in eternal life, then, means to believe that God is creatively present to human life even after the many moments of death. The life beyond the tomb is just a special application of this.

According to the irony of the Gospel it is possible that a man who recites the creed and affirms his belief in eternal life may, in fact, have little or no faith that God offers life in the situations of death, while another man who repudiates immortality and thinks that bodily death is the end, may in fact be borne by a faith, a divinely-created faith, that beyond the failures he endures and the traps he falls into, the summons to new life will be available to him. Our real convictions about reality may not coincide at all with the system of beliefs that we honestly profess.

Christ's message about heaven and hell, we continue, is not information about another world. Since we are always tempted to misunderstand revelation as a set of truths about a world we have not traveled and to start speculating about the life of the future, we are in need of being reminded that divine revelation is self-revelation. God reveals himself, and by doing so changes man's self-understanding and thus transforms human life. Revelation initiates man into the knowledge of who he is, of what his human possibilities are, of what he is being saved from, and towards what his life is oriented. Heaven and hell as divine revelation, then, disclose to us who we are. We are introduced to the two ultimate possibilities of human life. On the one hand, we are summoned to be open to God's Word, to become listeners, to remain learners, to continue growing, and as we do this we shall become fully human through God's gift of himself. This is heaven. On the other hand, we may close ourselves from the divine Word, we may resist the summons that surrounds us, we may make up our minds never to listen, we may choose to be deaf, and if this process is allowed to continue, we may close all the doors and windows of our house and eventually die in isolation from the dialogue with others, which is the source of life. If we create ourselves or, more correctly, destroy ourselves by this process of negation, we would be unable to hear the God who approaches us as saviour. We would have excluded ourselves from life.

This is hell. Hell, in this view, is not inflicted by God on men; rather, hell describes a state of existence which men are able to choose.

People sometimes ask the question: "Does hell really exist?" One may wonder whether this question does not want to make divine revelation into a source of information about another world. Divine revelation, we have said, is not supplementary knowledge granted to the inquisitive; it is the saving self-communication of God to men and hence the entry of the man of faith into a new self-understanding. The hell of which Jesus speaks, therefore, is real indeed. It is before us as a real possibility of human existence. It discloses to us the sin and self-destruction present within us, which could make us prefer deafness to hearing and death to life. At the same time, we may not separate the message of hell from that of heaven. Heaven and hell together constitute Christ's message, declaring the new life to which men are summoned and revealing the crucial importance of some of the decisions that men must make in their history. Some decisions in life are turning points: either we choose openness and fidelity, and live; or we prefer obtuseness and self-contradiction, and elect death. The message of heaven and hell, then, communicates God to the believing community. Through it men enter into the faith that God is good, that he creates life out of death, that he saves men from their own self-destruction, that men grow in their humanity with fear and trembling, that self-destruction is a real possibility, and that the human life in which God is present will never end. The message of heaven and hell, then, is not information about another world but saving truth producing a new consciousness in man and affecting his personal history.

We note in passing that the Catholic doctrine of purgatory, though often misunderstood as information about another world, is also a saving truth. It reveals to man the multiplicity of layers in his personal life and makes him realize that the gift of faith in God's Word, occurring in the part of his personality where he is free, does not automatically reconcile and integrate him on all levels of his being. Total reconciliation, the doctrine of purgatory implies, is a process that begins in faith and leads to conversions and often painful transformations on the more hidden levels of the human personality. If this total reconciliation does not take place in this life, the doctrine says, then God's Word present to the believer after death offers him the painful entry into a fully redeemed humanity.

Divine revelation is salvational truth. This is the basic principle we have applied in the interpretation of the Church's teaching on eternal life. Divine revelation has to do with the transformation of man now. Since salvational truth cannot be possessed once and for all like an idea or a concept but demands repeated confrontation and conversion, a special effort is required to avoid a rationalistic misunderstanding of doctrine. This is why God's Word must always be preached in the Church. When the religious imagination is allowed to use doctrine as information and construct the outlines of another world, then Christ's words on eternal life have less and less to do with the transformation of life now and become weaker media of divine revelation. If the doctrine on eternal life should ever be totally objectivized, it would cease to be divine revelation altogether. While little harm is done when the religious imagination entertains certain anticipations of eternal life on the margin of its activity, the attempt to focus on these, elaborate on them, and erect them into a speculative structure would be greatly misleading. Many questions asked about the Church's teaching on eternal life presuppose a desire for total objectivization, and to reply to them might satisfy people's curiosity for a time but would ultimately weaken the salvational power of Christ's message. The Christian must constantly submit the Church's teachings to the test of God's Word that he may be delivered from understanding them as information and be initiated again and again into their salvational meaning.

The message of eternal life tells us about God's presence to man's personal history. The wider eschatological teaching of the New Testament tells us about God's presence to history, personal and—above all—social. In the following we want to examine Christian eschatology as a way of divine self-revelation.[2]

According to the preaching of Jesus, the end of the present age is at hand. The pressure of the future events is upon us now. It is imperative for man to realize how close the kingdom is and how this closeness is to influence the decisions he makes and the life he builds. The preaching of the early Church insisted that without the acknowledgment of Christ's imminent return men are unable to do the will of God in their lives. Why? Because men are too identified with the elements of this world. Men participate in destruction not only by committing acts that are openly sinful but also by belonging to institutions that on the surface serve many useful purposes. Even the good life, even the constructive efforts of men, even the culture which they create and which creates them are caught in a sickness that give them reason to tremble as they hear the message of the end. This end is not simply personal death. This

2. For a modern re-evaluation of eschatology see *The Problem of Eschatology, Concilium,* vol. 41 (E. Schillebeeckx, ed.), New York, 1969.

end spells out judgment on the whole of human life, especially on the works of the powerful and on the behavior of nations and institutions. The eschatological message pronounces judgment on the entire history of mankind. Jesus Christ is to come on the day of days to be judge and saviour of all men. All is to be destroyed and made new. The early Church announced and celebrated the coming of the end, the eschaton, in a multitude of images with varying emphases on its destructive and renewing consequences. The eschatological message does not simply concern future happenings; it also and especially reveals the pressure of these future events on the present. The whole of life is illumined through the eschatological message.

The coming of Christ on the day of days means judgment and renewal. It is possible to interpret this message as information. It is possible to regard this doctrine as a new truth added by Christ to human knowledge. But if we do this, we remove the sense of urgency that is associated with this message in the New Testament. The end is near, and only as we acknowledge the nearness and live under the tension will we be able to live in fidelity to the divine Word. Eschatology affects life in the present. Eschatology is divine revelation and hence is a mode of divine self-communication to men, initiating them into new life, personal and social.

The impending coming of Christ has the twofold dimension of judgment and renewal. God in Jesus Christ, the Church proclaims, presses upon us as judge and saviour. Unless we open ourselves to the judgment and the newness offered to us, we cannot enter into our destiny. In the eschatological message, God reveals himself as the one who transcends and transforms history, personal and especially social.

103

THE END AS JUDGMENT

Let us first examine God's coming as judgment. All of human life, we insist, is under judgment. Even the good things we do, even the useful societies we have built up, even the holy institutions which God has summoned forth among men, are under judgment. Since sin is a dimension of the whole of human existence, we must be willing to look closely at the social reality to which we belong, to distinguish in it what is sinful and destructive from what is for life and the building of true community. We have to submit man's institutional life to a critique; while it may be conformed, on one level, to the moral law spelled out by society, it may, on the other, embody destructive trends which, because of their hidden character, are all the more devastating. The judgment of God, proclaimed in the eschatological message, challenges not simply the wicked but more especially the good people and the good things they have created, their institutions, their nations, their religions.

The Gospel is a critique. Yet we must not suppose that the Gospel offers us a set of laws according to which we are able to evaluate life. The conflict of Jesus was not with public sinners and men involved in unlawful actions; his conflict was rather with the respectable and influential section of society, with the leaders, and ultimately with the institution to which he belonged and for which they were responsible. Christ revealed the sickness of society, and because he uttered publicly what was wrong with the institution and revealed the hidden power plays and secret intentions of the leaders, he was hated by them and eventually killed. Jesus accused the institution of setting itself up as an untouchable norm by which all personal life was to be judged. According to Christ's startling teaching, the sabbath is for men, not men for the sabbath (cf. Mk. 2, 27). In his conflict with the authorities he revealed that the absolutizing trend of an institution is due in part to the leaders' desire to elevate themselves over other men and in part to the inclination of the whole institution, including the people, to elevate itself over other communities. The leaders caught in this process become increasingly alienated from themselves: they eagerly try to live up to the image demanded by their office, while they lose the capacity to listen to others and to understand the critical remarks uttered by them. Unless they be converted, Jesus told them, they will lose access to life altogether. By using their authority as a means to promote their power and status, the leaders create conditions in which the people become alienated from the institution, and thus initiate their own eventual undoing. The Gospel reveals to us that personal and social self-seeking qualifies all of human behavior. The divine critique summons men to acknowledge the sinful dimension of their personal and political lives, to be open to conversion and sweeping social change, to trust in divine mercy and hope for the unmerited possibilities of future growth.

As the eschatological message of the New Testament faded into the background of the Church's consciousness, the critical function of the Gospel came to be neglected. The message of Christ was often translated into a set of moral norms, without attending to the ongoing divine critique of human life available in this message. In particular, Christ's conflict with the leaders of the institution was hardly ever understood as divine revelation making known the truth about human society and social change. Even though the entire biblical message has to do with transition—in the Old Testament with the passover from the land of bondage to the fellowship in the desert and in the New with the passover through death to ressurrection—the Church has usually understood the Gospel in a static way. The social institutions, both religious and secular, were regarded as ordained by God, they became the measure of human behavior, they were permitted to formulate the demands of the true and the good; and hence man's moral struggle was often conceived as his attempt to conform to the ideals taught by the institutions to which he belonged. Sin was the violation of this divine order. Christians always admitted, of course, that all men would again and again fall into sin and that even institutions, even holy institutions, occasionally commit acts that go against God's law, but they tended to restrict the critique of the Gospel to what was patently unlawful and suppose that human behavior in conformity with the standards of society was not in need of the divine critique. Against this tendency, the eschatological message proclaims that all of life is under judgment. There is no aspect of human life, be it personal or social, that is exempt from this critique. The Christian must always seek to discern in history, even in the behavior approved by the institutions, what is for death and what for life. There are no islands in human life untouched by sin. All of history is in need of redemption.

One of the positive aspects of modern culture is the wide acknowledgment that human life is in need of critique. Life is not what it appears on the surface. It is, in particular, the critiques made by Karl Marx and Sigmund Freud that reveal in a profound manner the self-centeredness of human life and the effect which this self-interest has on all manifestations of human behavior. According to Marx, every society tends to create for itself a view of life, a set of values, or a doctrinal system that will protect the interests of the society against others and make it easier for the government to rule. This is often called ideology. The material needs of men are so pressing upon them, Marx believed, that their culture, their philosophy, and their religion are so many ways of dealing with these basic needs, either by protecting inherited privileges or by reaching out for more power to obtain what is needed. Marx wanted to reduce all of thought, culture, and religion to ideology. Such a reduction is obviously wrong. But thanks to Marx's insight few people today would deny that in all thought, culture, and religion there are ideological trends. Much of what passes as philosophy, as cultural values, or as religious ideals are subtly disguised ways of protecting a privileged institution against others and of making it easier for the ruling class to retain its power. It is inevitable that the self-seeking and self-elevation of man, which is the consequence of the original sin, influence every expression of his social behavior. Even the good things which society achieves are in need of redemption: they must be carefully examined to discern the ideological trend in them. Similarly, the view and values of individuals are never, in this world, totally redeemed from their economic fears. The source of one's daily bread-and-butter inevitably exerts a certain, even if unconscious, influence on one's way of looking at reality. The Marxian critique maintains that no man in his decisions and ideas ever fully overcomes his self-interest and hence is never totally free from the desire to protect his worldly advantage, and in particular that no society in the creation of its values and ideals is ever totally able to escape the tendency to promote its political superiority and protect the authority of the ruling class.

While Christians have been quite willing to apply this critique to secular society and often denounced the tendency of politicians to use beautiful language and profess high ideals as a hidden way of achieving their selfish purposes, it is only in this century that the Church has been willing to apply this critique to her own life. We have come to recognize ideological trends in our manner of proclaiming the Gospel. The Church's doctrinal system presents the Gospel with an emphasis that tends to separate the Church from other communities, elevate her above other people, defend her inherited privileges, and—above all—make it easier for the ecclesiastical government to rule. Christians have learned to recognize that the stress given by the ecclesiastical government to authority, obedience, and the institutional aspects of religion and worship is not derived from the Christian message but corresponds to the unavowed and usually unconscious ideological trend present in the governing body. The traditional catechisms, the forms of public worship, the customary theology of the ministry, and the symbols and ceremonies surrounding church dignitaries carry strong ideological overtones, to which the present generation has become sensitive. Doctrine and liturgy are often used to tighten the rule over the Christian people. And to interpret the apostolic office of papal primacy as a position exempt from criticism in the Church is pure ideology, without any foundation in dogma.

The eschatological message preached by the Church summons men to acknowledge the ideological trends in their view of life and the world. We note, however, that this critique cannot be communicated to others *directly*. It will not do to tell other people and other institutions that many of their views and values are patently ideological and hence destructive of the human community. The critique can be communicated by the Church to others only *indirectly,* if she applies it to herself. Ultimately, this divine critique can only be applied through self-knowledge. People and communities do not enter into this process by being told what is wrong; they may enter it as they see another community submit itself to the Word of God and struggle to abandon the ideological deformation of its goal and values. For this reason, we are lastly capable of applying the critique only to the communities to which we belong. Jesus himself restricted his preaching to Israel.

The self-criticism that is taking place in the Catholic Church today has a prophetic mission, for it awakens in other societies the same redemptive dynamics. We have learned that it is useless to tell other groups, other religions, other political institutions what they ought to do. Pointing to the insincerity of religious or political parties does not make the divine critique available to them. But if, in dialogue with others, we are able to apply this critique to ourselves, we make them witnesses of a redemptive process. This may stir up in them the desire for a similar transformation. In the context of what we said of the Church's mission in the last chapter, we propose that the Church's mission today lies principally in her own self-criticism.

While Marx brought out the political aspect of the ongoing critique of human life, Freud clarified the emotional aspect. According to Marx, the unjust economic order of society produces the self-alienation of man. Freud also regarded man as alienated from himself, but he gave a different account of it. Every man in society is afraid of his own hidden desires. Society makes many demands on man that remove him so much from his own wishes that he becomes mortally afraid of acknowledging what really goes on in him. To survive in his situation, he must build defenses against self-knowledge. The creativity of man in the philosophical, cultural, and religious realms is, according to Freud, largely an elaborate defense produced by unconscious compulsions, enabling him to look away from the unresolved tensions and hidden powers in himself. The entire spiritual culture of which men are proud is, according to Freud, just the manifestation of a universal illness. This Freudian reduction of all values to defenses against man's spontaneous and instinctual desires is as unacceptable as the Marxian reduction. But what is being acknowledged very widely today is that in all expression of thought, of values, of religion, there is an element of defense against self-confrontation. Knowledge itself, that is man's rational life, may be in part a defense. Because we are afraid of life, and cannot deal with our own problems, we may seek refuge in intelligence and move into the realm of abstract thought and scientific research where problems can be solved. That a concealed flight from reality may affect man's spiritual culture is the critique which, in addition to the Marxian, makes explicit the need of redemption even for the highest manifestations of the human spirit. Even rationality, according to this critique, is not an island untouched by the human misery.

The Freudian critique offends a venerable tradition of Western culture. The mainstream of philosophical thought and the political and cultural institutions have regarded rationality as the island of truth in human life. Confusion and error enter the minds of men, it has been supposed, through their emotions and the intrusion of their personal problems. The more men are able to exclude these personal factors from their quest of truth, the closer they come to rational objectivity. If men are able to detach themselves from their personal goals and the interests of society, the intellect becomes the sure organ of truth. A proposition demonstrable with arguments of universal validity is true. This intellectualist tradition of the West overlooks the fact that there are inevitable presuppositions in the process of knowing, not only logical and methaphysical ones, but even political and emotional ones. The political presuppositions were brought out by the Marxian critique. It was Freud who put his finger on the emotional presuppositions that enter into the process of knowing. Since a man can never totally escape from his emotions and his personal life, it is inevitable that these will in some way influence his quest of knowledge. If he refuses to recognize this, if he insists that the intellect is the sole organ of truth, then he is unable to discover the hidden emotional factors in his knowledge and incapable of submitting his knowledge to a critique. The man who excludes self-knowledge from the process of rational inquiry will never achieve objectivity. But if a man is conscious of the emotional involvement in the issues he studies, then he is able to examine these personal factors, test whether they are in harmony with his whole life experience, and try out whether they stand up in honest conversation with other people. Men must try to acknowledge their emotional investment in the process of knowledge. As men must be willing to discern more and more the ideological trends in their world views and remain open to a social and political transformation, so they must be ready to discover through dialogue with others and the search for self-knowledge their own emotions, fears, and ambitions operative in the process of knowledge and be ready to be converted again and again to a more total contact with reality. Objectivity in knowledge is an aim to be achieved by greater conversion to reality.

The rationalistic understanding of truth so common in the West is a good example of knowledge as a defense against the truth. Man's fear and uncertainty in regard to his feelings, including his sexuality, has made him focus on rationality as the secure position where he can stand without being threatened. From this position he defines himself as a rational being, regards the other human faculties as lower than reason, and thus assigns to the intellect the task of controlling and censoring his feelings and his intuitive contact with reality. Because man is afraid of the apparently uncontrollable powers in himself, he makes rationality the supreme element by which he defines himself, and this self-definition helps to avoid self-knowledge.

In the biblical perspective it is obvious that man's knowing and loving is closely related. We are always reminded that a certain disposition of the heart is necessary for the entry into truth. Without love truth is not available. And, conversely, truth transforms man's being and hence renders him capable of love. Truth, in the biblical perspective, is salvational.

The outer and inner situation of man determines the slice of reality with which he is in contact. This becomes sadly apparent in many discussions. Many debates on philosophical and theological issues have little to do with the subject under consideration; they are just arguments on a respectable level, about hidden conflicts and clashes of interests that are only faintly acknowledged by the participants. One may wonder whether a debate where one side wants to win over another is ever an occasion when truth becomes accessible. Such a discussion all too easily becomes a thinly disguised power-play or a defense of positions that seem emotionally necessary to one's world view. Only in dialogue is it possible to wrestle with issues in a creative way, for here the participants acknowledge from the outset that their truth is still in need of redemption and thus become open to a greater conversion to reality.

The world is under judgment. This judgment, according to the biblical message, is not simply in a distant future; it is upon us now. The eschatological pressure demands that we discern in the present where the need of further redemption lies. To believe this message, therefore, is to commit oneself to the ongoing critique of life. The Christian need not turn to Marx and Freud to become critical of human culture and discover that even its best manifestations are still marred by man's hidden self-seeking. In the Gospel he has his own source of critique. Christ's struggle with the institution reveals a critique of society and his teaching on the role of faith discloses a critique of personal life. But the Christian may turn to Marx and Freud who, when critically read, clarify each in his own way, how the great fears of man or his self-aggrandizement (which is the other side of fear) affect the creation of his human culture. The openness of man to this painful judgment, unsettling him in his presumed security, is God's gift to him. It is faith.

It is the irony of the Gospel that a man who has not acknowledged Christ's teaching regarding the impending nearness of judgment may in fact, in virtue of God's presence to him, be committed to the ongoing critique of life, however painful and unsettling it may be, while a Chris-

tian who professes the return of Christ and the establishment of the kingdom in glory may in fact refuse to submit
his life to the divine critique and may elevate certain
aspects of life, possibly even ecclesiastical aspects, to a
height where they no longer seem in need of redemption.
Which of these two men, we ask, believes in the eschaton?

THE END AS RENEWAL

We have been examining the eschatological message as
judgment. We now turn to the renewal promised for the
last day, which is now pressing upon us. According to
the biblical message, Christ is coming to make all things
new. This coming is imminent. The biblical message is
not information about what will happen in the distant
future when those listening to it will no longer be on this
earth. The message is divine self-revelation: it initiates
man into a new awareness of himself and reorientates him
in regard to the world in which he lives. The end is near.
The coming of Christ affects the meaning of human life
today. Newness is constantly upon us.

God is a coming God. He summons us to new life and
graces us to create it. He saves man from the destruction
threatening him, to which he has contributed by his own
evil choices, and he is creatively present in the process of
man's self-making. God offers the new. This means that
man's future is not totally determined by factors present in
his life today. Man is not caught in the traps and barriers
he has made for himself. Man is not defined by the categories which seemed useful to him at one time. The new is
available to him. The divine Word, present in his dialogue
with others, calls and empowers him to become more truly

himself. The Christian believes that tomorrow will be different from today. There is hope for tomorrow because the new creation is upon us.

Eschatology discloses a view of man: human life is open-ended; man cannot be considered simply in universal terms without thought to his particularity; man's future is not confined to possibilities determined by present causes. Contrary to Christian faith is the positivist or behaviorist approach to psychology and sociology which reduces man to what is knowable of him by the scientific method, which encloses men into universal categories and presumes that the human future is wholly determined by factors present in history now. This approach to man denies the possibility of the new. There is never any reason to be surprised and to marvel. The new that happens, according to this approach, must be reducible to what preceded. This deterministic approach has devastating consequences on human life. It confines man's imagination concerning his future, it constrains his creativity, it gives man a self-image that makes him a prisoner of the past. This approach induces him to put other people into fixed categories, to hear of their utterances only what fits these categories, and to persuade these people by his responses to them that these categories are their total reality. In this way men close themselves to the newness of life. As we shall see in a later chapter, this rejection of newness in human life is, in practical and concrete terms, the denial of God.

Does the eschatological message of the New Testament announce an ongoing Spirit-created evolution of the human race? Some contemporary Catholic theologians seem to understand Christian eschatology as the proclamation of man's new future in history. Teilhard de Chardin is inter-

115

preted in this way. What is revealed to us in Jesus Christ, these theologians seem to say, is that God has involved himself redemptively in human history in such a way that his victory within history itself is quite certain. According to this view, Christ's victory in death and resurrection gives us the assurance that his presence to human society in the Spirit will eventually reconcile men on this earth, initiate them into a higher form of unity, and through the creation of a new consciousness in them, elevate mankind on this earth to a more divine level of existence. Thanks to Jesus Christ, these theologians say, we know how history will end, namely well. The evolution of mankind is assured.

I have objections to this viewpoint. I do not think that Christian eschatology, revealing both judgment and renewal, tells us how history will end. The promise of renewal is qualified by judgment. It is not impossible at all that mankind may destroy itself within the next few years by an atomic holocaust. It is not impossible at all that human culture may decline in other ways by the sin and corruption at work among us. It is quite conceivable that mankind could regress from the present state of consciousness to a more primitive form. There is nothing in divine revelation that proclaims the continuing evolution of man. What the Gospel promises is that wherever men find themselves, the divine summons empowering them to become more human will be available to them.

The powers of evil in history are so enormous, even after Christ's victory, that we cannot be certain of man's evolutionary future. What we can be certain of, according to the Christian message, is that greater humanization is offered to men in every historical situation. The distinction between evolution and humanization is important. Evolution signifies mankind's entry into higher consciousness and the transformation of the human environment through God's presence in history. Humanization, on the other hand, need not involve the whole of mankind nor the transformation of the environment. Humanization signifies man's entry into greater faith, hope, and love through God's presence in his personal history. Man may grow in his humanity even if he is exposed to a dehumanizing community and the breakdown of his cultural environment. Jesus' entry into his passion and his death was for him humanization.

Divine revelation is Good News. But what is the salvational meaning of divine revelation in situations where evil is fully established or the social framework of life breaks down? What is the meaning of the Gospel to a person with a terminal illness or a man on his way to an extermination camp? The Gospel would have little meaning if it simply assured these men that one day the illness from which they suffer will be curable by the science of medicine or that concentration camps will no longer exist in a society determined by greater justice. Divine revelation is Good News for the present. Even the message of eternal life, we have seen, cannot be understood as information about the distant future. What is promised in Jesus Christ is that in all situations, even when misery invades men's lives, greater humanization will be offered to men. For how do men react in a situation of suffering? It is possible that they collapse into hatred and bitterness. It is possible that they become numb and unfeeling. It is possible that they lose the sense of personal dignity. But it is also possible in the situation of senseless suffering to become more human, to bear injustice with courage and peace, to possess oneself with confidence. The Good News is that the divine summons to humanization will address men and empower them, wherever they are. As God's Word frees men to become more truly human, even under these crucifying circumstances, they become more conformed to him who rose from the dead.

Renewal is present among us now. Wherever people are, something happens. The divine summons to humanization is available in the entire community of men: it is spelled out and celebrated in the Church. Through conversation men become open to the Spirit who recreates their lives. This is how wisdom is engendered. This is how friendship is created. At the same time, we must not underestimate the powers of evil in human history.

The contemporary theologians who interpret Christian eschatology in an evolutionary sense tend to attribute evil in human life simply to the evil choices of men. Evil, to them, is reducible to human malice. Since to men the overcoming of bad will and the freedom to choose the good is promised in Christ, the Christian may look forward to the elimination of evil in history and the evolution of mankind to a more perfect state.

THE DEMONIC

Whenever the scriptures deal with the evil in human life and reveal God's judgment on history at the end of time, they refer to the demonic. Biblical eschatology, speaking of the powers of darkness at work among men, frequently refers to the demonic. Modern theologians who no longer regard demons as separated spirits living in a world apart and occasionally influencing men on this earth often tend to forget that the disclosure of the demonic is part of God's message of salvation. Revealing himself, God has also disclosed the demonic aspect in history. Hence even if we reject an extrinsicist understanding of divine revelation regarding demons, we must still ask what is the salvational meaning of the biblical message.

According to the scriptures, God is in no way responsible for evil. The evil in human life is due to man. At the same time, the repeated references to the demonic remind us that the evil at work among us cannot be reduced to human malice. There are processes among us multiplying evil and spreading destruction that vastly exceed the harm that can be done by men's evil choices. The evil among us transcends human proportions. A theologian who neglects this transpersonal proportion of evil may suppose that Spirit-created good will is able to overcome the destructiveness in human life and hence may entertain unrealistic expectations in regard to the future of man. Yet evil has established itself much more profoundly in human history and is being perpetuated by forces which, in part at least, escape immediate personal control. Even through heroic effort and great sanctity men are not always able to stop the destructive forces in history nor to avoid all complicity with these forces. The evil present in human life is stronger than the person.

What are these forces of evil among us? What are the structures in human history that multiply evil and destruction? They seem to be operative in two distinct orders, the political and the psychic.

Let us first look at the political order. The behavior of an institution is not wholly determined by the will of those who belong to it nor even by those who exercise authority in it. Institutions seem to have a life of their own. Healthy institutions multiply good. They enable people to be helped by the wisdom and the resources of the whole community. Good laws protect people, and good organization permits the expansion of their lives in many ways. Institutions multiply good, I have said, because their beneficial effects are comparatively independent of the generosity, or the lack of it, of the men involved in it. At the same time, institutions have their illnesses: they also multiply evil among men. While all communities in this sinful world embody some group egotism and group aggression, institutions may translate these tendencies into organizational processes affecting the lives of many people. Moreover, institutions are threatened by the pathological trend to forget the purpose for which they were created and to make themselves their own end, and when they become fully dedicated to self-perpetuation, they begin to treat the people whom they were meant to serve as objects, as numbers, as items in their programming. Another pathological trend observable in institutions is the elevation of the government to a superior caste concerned with its own power and privileges. Institutions, I have said, multiply evil because the harm they do and the suffering they produce by far exceed the malice of the men involved in it. The pathological trends are operative even among good people and often against their will and intention. While these pathologies may be overcome by certain social processes, the individual, even when in a high position, seems to be unable to resist them. The system, the apparatus, the machine does harm and inflicts suffering even against the good will of the men who serve it.

There is no need to turn to the vast institutions, political or ecclesiastical, to find examples of this power to multiply evil. Every organization, even the good ones, are vulnerable to this pathology. In a company, for instance, a decision has to be made by the board of directors that will affect the lives of thousands of people. It is only after lunch that the meeting is able to discuss the proposed plan. Tired from the morning's work and the martinis before lunch, the directors sit around the table listening to the proposal made by the committee. The proposed plan seems advantageous to the organization, and even though it will disrupt the lives of many and unsettle the conditions of life for men in a vast area, the directors give it their approval, without facing these issues and assuming full responsibility for the results. They vaguely rely on the committee that proposed the plan: they may not have been delighted with it but neither were they alert enough to resist it. A half-hearted approval from each of the board members sufficed, the vote was cast, the decision was adopted, and from then on the machinery executes it with precision. After the vote, a member of the board may discover that the new policy has more destructive consequences than he thought, but now there is nothing he can do. The institution moves ahead with automatic and unrelenting regularity. Repentance, good will, holiness will not help him. Only a highly complex social process—calling an emergency meeting, convincing the other directors, finding an alternative plan, etc.—a process which is not always within reach, could possibly put a stop to the execution of the orders. While the malice involved in the decision-making was minimal, the institution moves ahead like a monster more powerful than man, repetitive, compulsive, inhumanly precise, devouring people in obedience to its inner programming.

Every institution, the best of them, is affected by pathological trends that multiply evil. The person caught in these processes faces an inhuman power, impersonal, relentless, devouring, similar to some of the biblical descriptions of the demonic.

The presence of the demonic in institutional life casts a shadow of injustice on all human activities, even the best. No one can altogether escape from the destructive processes built into the institution, unless he is ready, as was Jesus, to be executed by them. Since as citizens we profit from the institutional life of our country and as members of the Church from its organization, since we derive many advantages from the institutions on which we depend, we all participate to some degree in these social pathologies. Even withdrawal does not enable us to escape the sin of the world. The monasteries that withdraw from public life are nonetheless tied into the social and economic system by the alms they receive, possibly from the rich, by the selling of their products, by the buying they must do, and above all by the spirituality of withdrawal affecting people's political views. Social injustice is so profoundly established on this earth that all men have some share in it, all men except the martyrs, except Jesus.

These remarks are not directed against institutions as such. What I have denounced are the pathological deformations of institutional life. Since institutions are perhaps too much slandered today, it is important to stress the possibility of healthy institutional life. There are social processes by which the pathological trends may be healed. Dialogue, participation, feedback, reassessment of aims, etc. introduce profound transformation into the life of the institution enabling it to serve the people for the sake of which it was created. We must add, however, that an ambiguity remains even as institutions are improved. For every advance in social organization also offers new possibilities for power plays and group egotism. The Christian is summoned to remain critical in regard to institutions, to wrestle with the powers of darkness present in them, and to involve himself politically in the various societies to which he belongs.

How is the victory of Christ related to these demonic forces? This is the question that interests us here. In Christ, we have said, is revealed to us God's redemptive presence to man's making of man. Salvation, we hold, is visibly established among us in the Church. But the demonic powers are conquered only in the sense that they cannot interfere with the humanization Christ offers to those who believe. However terrible an institution becomes, however unjust and destructive its influence is, even if it turns into a concentration camp, the Good News is that the divine summons to humanization continues to be available to men. The Gospel claims that God will save men from despair and from bitterness, and creating a new freedom in them, will make them more human through suffering and death. But does the Gospel promise that the institutions themselves will be transformed?

Since Christ is the pivotal point of history and since he has made available forces of reconciliation able to overcome, in time, the destructive processes of society, it may well be that human history now moves in a direction of greater institutional sanity and hence of an evolution to a superior kind of humanity. But it may also happen that the social pathologies will destroy mankind on this earth and that the total victory of Christ will only take place in the new life which God then creates out of death. We do not know. The scripture does not give us any hints. While the Christian believes that even in destructive situations the divine summons will address man and make possible his ongoing humanization, he has no reason to believe that there is a divine logic in human history, overcoming all destructive situations and moving mankind towards a more perfect unity on this earth. The Church's eschatological message does not imply an optimistic view of history.

We shall only say a few words about the second area of the demonic in human life, namely the psychic. Here, too, man is exposed to repetitive, compulsive, and relentless forces that threaten to devour him and make him do awful things which he does not freely choose. The pathology of life is not only political but also personal. While I do not suggest that these psychic forces are totally independent of man's free choices, they are certainly not directly dependent on his good will. For this reason men often find themselves constrained to do—even without knowing the compulsive nature of their action—what their good will in no way intends. Psychic forces can multiply evil. We admit, of course, that psychic forces also multiply the good: some psychic patterns in us make us creative and respond to reality in an imaginative way. But illness multiplies evil. It makes us compulsively relive unresolved conflicts of the past. The pathological makes us unconsciously inflict hatred and anger on people whom we consciously respect or clamor for massive revenge against people whose disagreement with us is only slight.

The angers of a baby, overwhelmed by his impotence, are well known. There is nothing wrong with them. But when baby tantrums are compulsively relived in adulthood, possibly disguised and carefully rationalized, they can become the source of death-dealing actions. A man may get angry and resentful with a force transcending the occasion that provoked it and his action against the supposed offender may be unconsciously aimed at his mother, his father, or some other person who harmed him in the past. Or a man may disguise his hostility so successfully to himself and to others that he is able to release his anger in a hidden way, or even by setting up situations in which these others will come to harm. The possibility of causing others to suffer are infinite. The point I wish to make is that the evil which people inflict on others, in their immediate environment and the wider social contact, by far exceeds their personal malice.

If we get to know persons who have been engaged in destructive action, criminals for instance, possibly men who worked in concentration camps or organized the extermination of a race, if we have access to their fears, their anxieties, their inner pressures, and the force of irrationality in them, we may find that they are little people, highly confused, that their freedom in choosing the awful things was minimal, that they were possessed by psychic powers automatically and relentlessly demanding vicious destruction and totally senseless never-ending repetitions of inexplicable rages. These psychic forces are not totally beyond human influence, they can be modified by processes in which man's freedom is involved, but they are not under man's direct power. They are a manifestation of the demonic in life.

We have here a parallel to the multiplication of evil by the institution. As no one can totally withdraw from the illness of society but must in some way participate in it, even against his will, so can no man totally escape personal pathology. The illness is universal. What is, in this situation, the Good News? Does Christ promise to heal us of all our pathological trends? The answer is No: as little as he promised to remove all the pathological deformations from society. But what the Gospel promises is

125

the divine summons, uttered in the power of the Spirit, that enables men to become more truly human. The Good News is that the divine grace for man's growth and reconciliation will be available, even to him who is badly caught in pathological trends. On a deep level that escapes the judgment of the observer, men make decisions about the newness that is being offered them; and it may well be that a person who is gravely ill may say Yes to the divine call and be saved by God every day from collapsing into total despair and the destruction of life, and that another man who shares in the universal illness only slightly may say No to the divine offer of new life and live out some dreadful idolatry and unspeakable hatred in situations where release from these would have been available to him. But the relationship of the pathological forces to man's free choice and the responsibility of society has hardly ever been examined from a theological viewpoint. We are in need of a theology of the therapeutic.

These remarks suffice to show that the powers of darkness are firmly established in human history, in the political and in the psychic order. While we affirm that the eschatological message promises the divine offer of humanization in all historical circumstances, we are unable to conclude that it also promises the evolution of human life on earth to a superior consciousness and a new form of human unity. This may happen, but history remains open-ended. The scriptures reveal nothing in regard to it. It seems to me that the silence about the demonic makes Christians suppose that eschatological victory must mean evolution. What the eschatological message does demand is that man subject the whole of human life to the divine critique and engage himself in the political and the therapeutic orders to wrestle with the powers of evil.

V. HOLINESS IN THE NEW PERSPECTIVE

A THIRD set of objections raised against the Blondelian shift expresses the fear that it may promote a hidden naturalism and a man-centered and hence God-forgetting religion. Is the acknowledgment of God's presence in human life equivalent to a denial of the supernatural? Do we suggest that people are able to save themselves by their own efforts and the spiritual desires of their hearts? Do we wish to reduce religion to ethics? Finally, there is the suspicion that the thesis we have adopted removes sacrifice from the Christian life and instead of recommending the following of Christ crucified, it promotes an ethic of self-realization in contradiction to the Sermon on the Mount.

MORALITY IS REDEMPTIVE

We must examine these objections carefully. If they are valid, then the thesis we have adopted would certainly not be an authentic understanding of the Christian Gospel. Let us begin with the objection that the thesis supports the

Pelagian error that man can save himself. I insist that the tone and content of this theological study is opposed to any theory of self-salvation. Pelagianism is contrary to divine revelation. Pelagianism is contrary, moreover, to a profound understanding of human growth. Some things precious to man can be produced by will power or merited by personal effort, but the important things just happen to man.

This is obvious in the case of love and friendship. Love is always a gift. If a man thought that he could merit friendship, if he submitted a list of his achievements to the person whose friendship he sought and demanded love as a reward for his efforts, he would not only fail to receive the love but also render himself incapable of receiving it if it were freely offered to him. Friendship can ultimately be received only as a free gift. It is true that we make an effort to build friendship with other people, we try to do what gives them joy and supports them in their lives, but as soon as we suppose that this effort makes us earn their friendship, we put up a barrier from ever receiving it. Even if we do much for other people, even if we have made many sacrifices, the friendship we share with them, however well-founded in the good things we have exchanged, is free and unmerited. Affection cannot be demanded or earned. While we are able to reach out for it with a great effort, it can only be received freely. If, as the other turns to us and offers us affection, we suspected that this takes place as a kind of payment for what we have done for him, we grow cold in our heart and on our part become unable to enter into friendship. Gratuity is the heart of human love. How absurd it is to think that divine love can be merited.

The profound things in human life are always gifts.

Artists readily acknowledge this in regard to their work. They speak of their inspiration. They describe that in the act of creation they are overwhelmed by a way of seeing, hearing, or feeling that profoundly moves them and demands concrete expression. While the finished work is truly theirs, the artists acknowledge that the gift preceded it. If we look closely enough at life, we see that this is true of everything that is achieved by hard work. To have ideas and energy available in our life and to be free to give ourselves to a great task are powers over which we do not have control. If we do not find them in ourselves, we cannot produce them at will. Will power is useful in life, but it is powerless to make us free and creative. If, for instance, my mind is preoccupied with anxious reflections or overwhelmed by passivity or fear, will power alone cannot deliver me from this burden. To work hard, to give ourselves completely to a task, we need an inner freedom which is not wholly of our making. That is why we marvel when we have achieved something or have been able to work very hard for a period of time. "Isn't that marvelous," a man says to his friend with some excitement. "Imagine, I have been able to do this thing so well and so whole-heartedly." Unless a man is compulsive in his work, he acknowledges the gift dimension even in his greatest efforts. To say that the good things happen to people, therefore, in no way encourages a hidden quietism or a dangerous passivity. On the contrary, great effort is necessary for human growth and personal achievement. Man must again and again lay hold of his life, affirm it with his own power, and assume responsibility for it, but this effort, this spending of oneself, is possible only because of an inner freedom which is not made but given. A man knows in his heart that if he cannot spend himself, his will power, however strong, will not help him to do it, and if he has the inner power to give himself away, then his own will power is ultimately not responsible for it.

The Christian Gospel, the antithesis of any theory of self-salvation, is the key for the understanding of all human life. Man's dialogue of salvation always begins with God. The growth and development of human life through man's own efforts is always dependent on and carried by gifts which are received in the community and ultimately come from God himself. The gift-dimension of human life is God's gift of himself as Holy Spirit.

To believe in the gift-dimension of human life is to reject any kind of will-power dominated ideal of holiness. The Gospel denounces the willful man, the man who uses will power to bring himself into conformity with a set of rules or the self-image he has chosen for himself. The compulsive man who trusts in his own power and concentrates on himself in the process of growing will tend to look down on other people who have achieved less than he. He may even come to think that he can justify himself by his own efforts. It was with willful men of this type that Jesus had to wrestle in his public ministry. When the Lord told them that no man can base his self-acceptance on his own achievements, they were profoundly threatened by his message and began to hate him. Secure self-acceptance does not come about by achievements but by faith. Since all men are sinners, there is in all a certain compulsive trend fostering the illusory effort to create self-assurance by doing great things. According to the Gospel, this effort is based on the fear that God is a strict judge and that we cannot stand in his sight as we are. The compulsive trend in us persuades us that if we do many works today, tomorrow, and the day after, then we shall have peace. Peace, we are being persuaded, is conditioned in us by our achievements. But the peace that is available to the arrogant who are pleased by their own achievements is illusory. Christ's message reveals to us the divine ground of man's justification. Justification is by faith. Faith is a conversion away from the illusion of self-justification. Faith heals and goes on healing the compulsion in us which drives us to gain self-acceptance by action. Faith opens a man to the gift-dimension of his life. It locates the ground of a man's self-assurance not in his will power, but in a mystery that keeps on revealing itself in his own life. The man who acknowledges this mystery and submits to the divine Word is strengthened to do many things and to engage in action with all his power. If he believes that the source of this power is not simply his own doing but a free gift offered to him, he will not be tempted to despise others who do not move as far as he. A man of faith will marvel at his own life, he will be surprised again and again at his own achievements, he will discern in his own past the working out of a mystery of grace. Faith makes a man see in his own life a history of salvation.

These few remarks bring out the superficiality of the objection which is sometimes heard that contemporary Catholic theologians try to reduce the revealed Gospel to morality. This objection supposes that morality is the conformity of man's actions and attitudes to a set of norms and that, consequently, man's moral life is a purely human or even humanistic endeavor. Morality, in the terms of this objection, is one-dimensional. It is man's knowledge of the moral law and his willingness to put this knowledge into practice. But once we look more closely at what happens in human life, in particular in the moral decisions and the formation of a man's attitudes towards other people and the world in general, we discover a complex process of summons and response, of growth and creativity, of leaving behind patterns of childhood and entering upon new spheres of personal responsibility. Morality is not a one-dimensional process fully determined by human intelligence and human effort. Morality implies human transformation, entering into death to self-centeredness and receiving the freedom to rise to a new dimension of love. Morality is a redemptive process. In the light of God's revelation in Jesus Christ, human life is not a purely natural reality. Human life is always supernatural. God is redemptively present in the process by which man becomes more truly human. Contemporary Catholic theology is not tempted to reduce the Gospel to morality: what has happened, rather, is that theology has, for the first time, consistently applied the revealed teaching that human morality is more than natural and that God is present to man in the faith, hope, and love which are the basis of all moral life.

This leads us to the objection accusing contemporary spirituality of promoting a harmful naturalism. Catholics who follow the new theological approach, we are sometimes told, have lost the sense of the supernatural. They are exclusively concerned with human things and neglect the religious dimension of life. They suppose that God manifests his mercy in the humanization of man and hence forget God's encounter with man in prayer and worship. What are we to think of this objection?

In the first place, we insist that human life is always

supernatural. This has always been taught by the great Catholic theologians, even if they have not always applied this teaching in their evaluation of human life.[1] There is a single end of man, which is revealed to us in Jesus Christ. There is a single destiny of the human race, which is supernatural. All of human life, in the Church and outside of it, is—despite sin—orientated towards salvation in God. And since the ultimate end of human life is supernatural, so is the dynamics of human life. Sin and grace are constitutive elements of human history, personal and social. To suppose, therefore, that supernatural life is offered to Christians and another sort of life, a purely natural one, offered to people who are not Christian, goes counter to the central tradition of Catholic teaching. We cannot divide humanity into two groups of people, one called to a supernatural existence and the other confined to the possibilities of their own resources.

Similarly, it is impossible to divide the actions of man into two distinct sets, one comprising the supernatural and the other his natural acts. Popular Catholic spirituality has often used the words "supernatural" and "natural" in this way. It has often regarded the specifically religious acts of man, the acts by which man consciously refers himself to God, as supernatural, and considered the ordinary human acts in which a man encounters other people and together with them builds the human world as simply natural. According to this terminology, prayer, worship, sacraments, and the ecclesiastical life are supernatural, while man's growth as a human being and his involve-

1. See the monumental work of H. de Lubac, *Surnaturel: Études historique,* Paris, 1946; and *The Mystery of the Supernatural,* New York, 1967.

ment in the secular world are natural. Man's secular involvement may be important and must be moral: but it is not there that man encounters God. According to this popular spirituality, the secular must be subordinated to the religious and supernatural. The stress on the secular, according to this viewpoint, always implies a waning sense of the supernatural and a growing naturalism that could undermine the life of the Church. This popular spirituality, however, is not based on a sound doctrinal foundation. According to Catholic teaching, we cannot neatly divide the actions of men into natural and supernatural. Sin and grace are omnipresent to human life. Divine grace is present not only in the specifically religious aspect of human life; it is offered in the entire process by which men grow, become themselves, and by doing so create the human world. To suggest that man's secular life is not supernatural would be a Pelagian error. To suggest that the interpersonal relationships through which men come to be and keep on creating the human community are purely this-worldly, humanistic, or natural events would go counter to the entire teaching of the Gospel. Human existence is so deeply wounded and threatened by sin that the passage from fear to trust, from hostility to love, from ignorance to self-knowledge, from passivity to creativity, from self-centeredness to concern for others are never purely natural events, determined by the human resources available to men; they are always co-determined by divine grace, they are always supernatural.

Some people are not convinced by this doctrinal argument. They insist that there are natural actions that are good: for instance, teaching. A man can be a good teacher, they say, even if his relationship to God is destroyed, even if he has elected a sinful way of life; conversely, a man's conversion to God does not make him a better teacher. Surely, then, teaching is a purely natural human action, which may be considered quite apart from the supernatural order. This objection, I reply, does not take seriously enough the ambiguity of human life. Sin perpetually threatens all of man's action. This is true also of teaching. While there is an aspect of teaching that has to do with information, research, systematic presentation, techniques of communication, etc., and hence can be considered apart from the supernatural order, there is another aspect of teaching, namely the historical, that cannot be separated from the supernatural. Teaching always takes place in a concrete, historical situation in which it is threatened by sin and hence in need of redemption. The teacher is tempted, for instance, to use his superior knowledge to rule his class, possibly to manipulate it. Or he may be so preoccupied with his knowledge, his ideas, his system, that he does not hear what the students say to him. He may try to put over a system of knowledge without hearing the truth that is uttered by his class or without being willing to modify his own insights. There are an infinite variety of ways in which self-centeredness can affect the teaching in the classroom. Hence, if a teacher is able to be truly present to his class, if he can communicate his wisdom to his students without making them feel that it is his own, if he can refrain from using his superior knowledge as a means of dominating them, if he can listen to them without fear and be open to the truth that they utter, even if this demands the modification of his own conclusions, then divine grace is present in his teaching. Of course, some ambiguity always remains in man's action; even with the help of grace the need for redemption continues. We conclude that to deny that divine grace is needed for good teaching is to suppose that a man can turn away from his self-centeredness to be truly present to others by his own skill and determination.

Since, according to divine revelation, the mystery of redemption is operative in the whole of man's life, and not only in its religious dimension, the present-day emphasis on the secular need not necessarily imply a turning away from the supernatural. For some people, the stress on the secular may indeed be an escape from the supernatural, but this happens only if they regard human nature, their own human nature, as a closed reality or substance and thus make themselves insensitive to the interactions with the human community, which is the locus of God's presence. But if men turn to the secular and open themselves to the personal and social relations by which the human world is being created, then they are also open to the true God who is redemptively present in man's making of man. The conversion to the world may be an opening to the divine.

Since the whole of history is supernatural and since man comes to be in a process in which God is redemptively involved, one may wonder if it is useful to retain the term "supernatural," misleading as it is to modern ears. The term seems to designate a reality beyond ordinary human life, while in fact the divine self-communications takes place within human life and is constitutive of man's history. The term "supernatural" is useful if it reminds us that the newness which God's mercy makes available in human life transcends anything that a man can produce, relying on his own resources. This newness is always a gift making man marvel and, if he has heard of the giver, be grateful. But since God's presence in human life can be expressed in many other ways, there seems to be no special need to preserve the term "supernatural." In this book I have often replaced it by the expression "Spirit-created" indicating that human life is never simply built on man's own initiative but on a creativity ultimately due to the Holy Spirit. The thesis that God is redemptively present in history does not neglect but strongly emphasizes the Spirit-createdness of human life.

Contemporary theologians are sometimes accused of being humanists. This usually means that they advocate a man-centered understanding of religion or, at least, that they regard religion as part of the humanizing process of society. But is this an accusation at all? The divine incarnation in Jesus Christ reveals to us that God's encounter with men always humanizes them and that God's grace comes to men not only in moments of piety but more especially in their relationship to the community, the Church. It is revealed to us in Jesus that the human is the locus of the divine. God's self-revelation effects the growth and reconciliation of man. Even the acknowledgment of divine transcendence, even man's encounter with the otherness of God is not—as we shall see—a moment extrinsic to human sanctification. Even worship understood as the celebration of the (uncreated) depth dimension of human life is an important factor in the humanization of man.

Christianity may be called a humanism, to be precise a christological humanism. For in Christ it is revealed to us who man shall be or, more carefully, who the transcendent dynamism is by which, gratuitously, all men are summoned and freed to become more fully human. Divine grace recreates in men the perfect humanity revealed in

Christ. Christianity is humanistic in the sense that it reveals, celebrates, and promotes the entry of all men into greater likeness to Jesus Christ. Is this different from other humanisms? Some forms of humanism are certainly based on concepts of man not in harmony with Christ's teaching. But there is an open-ended humanism entertained by men who refuse to define human nature, who wish to remain open to the newness that emerges in the community, and who evaluate new developments in terms of the growth and reconciliation they produce on people. This sort of humanism, based on openness to, or faith in, the transcendent dynamism in the human community, is very close to the Christian Church—which alone proclaims and celebrates this dynamism as God's gratuitous gift of himself in Jesus Christ.

Is Christianity a man-centered religion? If the term "man-centered" means that a religion glorifies man, underestimates the evil in human life, and makes a divinity of human progress, then the Gospel advocates the very contrary of man-centered religion. But if the term "man-centered" means that a religion celebrates the humanization of man and regards God as the transcendent source of this humanization, then there is nothing wrong in calling the Gospel man-centered—or better, Christ-centered. Conversion to God and entry into human fellowship is one and the same orientation. Unless we deny the doctrine of the incarnation, conversion to God does not imply a turning away from man. Since God is redemptively present in the interpersonal and communal relations through which men come to be and create their common world, it is precisely by centering on man with faith that we turn to the living God.

HOLINESS AS SELF-REALIZATION

Another objection claims that the new approach proposes an ethic of self-realization and thus abandons the Christian way of sacrifice and self-denial. The great Christian tradition of self-discipline, of patience, of suffering, of the ascetical life seems to be negated by the modern emphasis on God's presence to man's self-making. Jesus himself lived a life of sacrifice. So did the apostles. The entire Church is summoned to follow the Lord on his way of the cross. The modern cult of self-realization and the quest for fulfilling all one's human possibilities seem to go counter to the spirit of the Gospel.

This criticism of modern theological trends has recently received support from quarters where one might least expect it. In his interesting book *The Triumph of the Therapeutic,*[2] Philip Rieff proposed, among many more significant points, that the therapeutic approach to man which has become popular in the wake of Freud's magnificent achievement, though contrary to his intentions, has created among men a psychologically-oriented self-understanding that contains great dangers for the survival of culture. The psychological man of the present, Rieff says, has adopted an ethic of self-realization. He is permissive in regard to his instincts and inclinations. He attempts to create conditions under which he is able to express himself with the greatest possible freedom according to the feelings experienced within himself. Rieff believes that this search for self-realization pervades our entire culture: he calls this the triumph of the therapeutic. At the same time, Rieff

2. New York, 1968.

139

holds—and in this he follows Freud's own speculations—that culture is created through the constraint men impose on their inclinations. Restriction, discipline, unfulfilment, sacrifice—these supply the energy by which men have created culture and the works of the spirit. The defenses against the instincts produce culture and make society possible. These defenses may indeed rob men of their health—Freud, in fact, regarded the creation of culture as an expression of human illness—but for the sake of the total human community and the creation of values required for the survival and spiritualization of man, health may have to be sacrificed. Health is not the highest value. The triumph of the therapeutic, Rieff thinks, has raised mental health to be the highest value and thus undermines the very forces that humanize life. The therapeutic approach to life, Rieff holds, will ultimately destroy the present civilization.

In this context, Philip Rieff refers to the theological developments taking place in the Christian Churches today.[3] He realizes that here, too, the therapeutic approach has been acknowledged. Even Christian authors, he says, speak of an ethic of self-realization which they seem to prefer to the traditional ethic of self-denial. Rieff regrets this development. He laments that today even Christians have abandoned the struggle against the instincts, which struggle, even though it be the source of human illness, is the only force that creates culture and makes society humane. This is not the only point, not even a main point, of Rieff's study. It is, however, of special interest to us because it confirms from a standpoint outside of Christianity the views of the conservative voices in the Church, often highly placed in the

3. *Ibid.,* p. 16.

ecclesiastical government, who claim that the modern emphasis on the human undermines the traditional Christian teaching on sacrifice and self-denial.

Rieff's position, we note by way of reply, is based on an anthropology that is hardly reconcilable with Christian faith. Christians cannot accept that the creation of culture and the building of a spiritual community is due, purely and simply, to the forces by which men contain their instinctual energies. With Freud, Philip Rieff has no appreciation of man's consciousness or his ego as the seat of freedom and creativity. Human creativity, however, is not simply a neurotic manifestation of instinctual powers that are prevented from achieving their natural fulfillment. Man's growth is not wholly determined by unconscious forces: his conscious ego is the seat of freedom and hence enables him to respond to the summons addressed to him, to enter into friendship and truth, and to express his spiritual awareness in the works of culture, art, literature, and religion. While human consciousness may never be totally free from the influence of the unconscious, it is free enough, or at least it may be freed, to open itself to God's living Word and to express itself in religious language and worship, which are not simply a compulsive defense against the instincts—as Freud thought—but man's free and authentic response to the divine reality present in his life.

Christians do not believe that the struggle against the instincts is the creative force of the spiritual life. The wrestling of Jesus was not against human instincts. His fight was against the law and those who upheld a system of laws as the entry into new life and the expression of the divine will. True humanity is not found, according to the New Testament, by seeking conformity to fixed moral and

141

cultural categories: true humanity is found precisely by breaking through these categories when they limit man on his way to growth and reconciliation. Jesus' opponents were gravely upset by his teaching and his style of life because, as guardians of the establishment, they felt that he undermined the morality and the cultural values they had inherited. Christ put too much trust, they felt, in the creativity that the Holy Spirit produces in the human spirit. The way of the cross which Christ took upon himself was certainly not a fight against the instincts. The cross that was laid on his shoulders was above all the persecution inflicted by the powerful in Israel and the pressure of society on the man who wanted to be free and speak the truth. By insisting that the sabbath was there for man and not man for the sabbath, Christ put a question mark behind all the absolutes regulating human behavior, to which the religious institution was deeply attached. He challenged all institutions; for in this sinful world all are tempted to regard themselves as an end in themselves and to impose their norms as absolutes for human conduct. Since the religious institution imposes its rule in the name of God, it is able to confuse man's conscience more than any other. Because Christ spoke the truth and disclosed the hidden illness in the society to which he belonged and which he loved, the leaders hated him, persecuted him, and eventually decided to do away with him.

Jesus revealed the sin of the world. He brought to light not only the powers of darkness in Israel but the crimes against human life committed by societies all over the world and in which, in some way, all men are involved as accomplices. The Christian is summoned to take up the cross of Christ, to speak the truth, to wrestle with the powers that destroy human life. In this conflict with the powers of darkness, men may have to discipline their instincts and purify their desires, but this struggle hardly constitutes the essence of the Christian life.

To suppose that the triumph of the therapeutic—which, contrary to Rieff's supposition, is far from being with us— implies the breakdown of human culture does not make sense in the Christian perspective. With Freud, Philip Rieff thinks that the source of morality and religion is simply the "superego," the censor of man's instinctive wishes, the inner judge stopping him from doing what he wants to do. Many humanists, Christian and otherwise, do not accept this. The creative source of morality and religion is the mystery of freedom that takes place in man's spirit. The Christian Gospel, I wish to add, does not reinforce man's superego, but saves him from its domination.

But Philip Rieff is correct in his observation that in Christian theology today there has been a shift from an ethic of constraint to an ethic of self-realization. This raises the important question: how can an ethic of self-realization be reconciled with the Christian teaching on sacrifice and the cross and the entire ascetical tradition? I wish to show in the following pages that man's self-realization, or the self-making which is God's redemptive work in man, is a process demanding sacrifice, discipline, and ascetical effort, even if the place assigned to these is different from that in traditional spirituality. Contrary to some Christian teachers and contrary to some Freudians, I insist that health, the health of the human mind, is not brought about easily and spontaneously as if all a man has to do is follow his instincts and impulses. Health does not come naturally. Human health is a process of growth and expansion demanding self-knowledge, a process, therefore, in which God is redemptively present to man.

The discovery of the unconscious has shown that human growth is a complex process. Depth psychology has clearly established that hidden in man are angers, hostilities, and other destructive trends that may not reveal themselves in his conscious mind and yet have a profound influence on his behavior. Even what on the surface looks like the search for happiness or fulfillment may, understood in terms of the unconscious, be the playing of a hidden game aiming at destruction or the perpetuation of suffering. For many years Freud had thought that man's instinctual life was inevitably orientated towards pleasure. On this supposition, it may not have been unreasonable to suppose that the curtailment of the instincts inflicted on man by society is the main source of sickness and misery. Philip Rieff, at least in some of his views, seems to follow Freud in this early stage. But Freud discovered at a later stage of his career that the pleasure principle, as he called it, could not account for all the manifestations of man's instinctual behavior.[4] Freud's clinical experience convinced him that there were also human impulses towards death or self-destruction. From this followed the conclusion that an uncritical permissiveness in regard to human instincts was not at all a certain road to health and well-being. By letting himself go, a man may possibly get caught in his death impulse and destroy himself. Growth and well-being, in other words, is a complex process in which discernment, self-knowledge, and conversion are indispensable.

The Christian does not wish to reduce human life to instinctual responses. The Christian acknowledges the

4. *Beyond the Pleasure Principle,* 1920.

spirituality of man. Man comes to be through a dialogue in which the human community and ultimately God himself are involved. Man is orientated—through the wholly gratuitous divine presence—towards growth and reconciliation. At the same time, the Christian also wants to take depth psychology seriously. The understanding of human growth and the description of the way that leads to holiness must take into account the crucial modern discovery of the unconscious.

According to the ascetical teaching of the past, man does foolish and destructive things because of his exaggerated self-centeredness. Man sins because he places himself in the center of his universe. Man loves himself too much and makes himself the supreme value. Giving in to this selfish tendency, he damages the lives of other men, is at odds with his own inner reality, and closes himself off from God's saving grace. Self-elevation was regarded as the root of all evil. The ascetical effort of the moral and perceptive man is to fight against the self-elevation to which, in virtue of the inherited sin, he feels a natural inclination. To grow in humanity meant, according to this teaching, a constant warfare against self-love. Man in quest of holiness commits himself to wrestle with the powerful drives towards self-aggrandizement. Traditional ascetical teaching gave a detailed description of how the Christian, trusting in God's mercy and following the cross of Christ, is to fight his connatural self-centeredness on every level of his life. Self-discipline, sacrifice, self-abnegation, self-effacement—these are the practices that would enable the Christian with God's help to oppose the trend towards self-centeredness which is deeply rooted in his personality.

The insights of depth psychology and in particular the discovery of the unconscious, including the death impulse, have considerably modified the traditional understanding of how men enter into growth and holiness. There is overwhelming evidence drawn from clinical observation and personal experience for claiming that the reason why people do foolish and destructive things is not simply their exaggerated self-love but also their hidden self-hatred. The sins and crimes of men are due not simply to the trend towards self-elevation but also to an unconscious trend towards self-destruction. What is wrong with man is not only that he loves himself too much but also, and simultaneously, that he dislikes himself, that he puts himself down, that he destroys the good things coming about in him and chooses to inflict misery upon himself—though he may not be conscious of this. Exaggerated self-love is accompanied by a hidden self-hatred. The other side of narcissism is a disgust with oneself. Megalomania is a powerful defense against the fear of being nothing. The man who loves himself excessively does not, on a deeper level, love himself enough. The man who pushes himself into the center of every conversation and every human situation has, on the unconscious level, the greatest doubts about who he is. The power drive that makes a man seek the highest place and prompts him to triumph constantly over others is a strong defense, embraced compulsively, against the hardly acknowledged feeling that he does not really exist. What is present at the root of self-elevation is a hidden self-hatred. What is wrong with us and what causes the awful things we do, is not simply that we love ourselves too much but also that, on a deeper level, we do not love ourselves at all.

Depth psychology has helped us to discover that much of the trouble we have in our lives—though not all of it—is in some sense self-chosen. The misery that afflicts us is often secretly provoked by our hidden self-hatred. We may destroy the good things that happen to us by skepticism and mistrust, we may attach ourselves to certain people because we are impelled by an unconscious desire to be betrayed or badly treated, we may set the authorities against us and be subject to unjust treatment because unbeknown to ourselves, we feel the need of punishment —the list of self-inflicted miseries that people choose is unending. The unconscious wish to be unhappy or to be punished is as universal as the more conscious wish to be unhappy or rewarded. Man does not simply love life: he also desires death. Thus is the ambiguity of human life, in which all men are born.

Though there are hints in the New Testament, as we shall see, that man is to be redeemed also from his self-hatred, the traditional ascetical teaching has recognized only man's exaggerated self-love and made man's desire to elevate himself the source of his sinful or destructive action. Traditional ascetical teaching recommended that men, trusting in the divine help, fight against this self-conteredness on every level of their lives, without warning them that by fighting the exaggeration, they might fall into the devouring trap of their hidden self-hatred. Resisting self-aggrandizement, men could back into an equally destructive trend, all the more dangerous because it is largely unconscious, which makes them seek pain and unhappiness. The ascetical tradition has often enkindled in people the hidden love of death. While it has successfully warned men of the destruction present in their self-centeredness, it has not revealed to them their hidden desire to be miserable, and hence many Christians who eagerly embraced

147

the ascetical life and resisted happiness and human fulfillment on many levels were in fact caught in the iron grip
of their destructive, though hidden, self-hatred.

Today we have discovered the danger of this one-sided
ascetical teaching. We have come to realize that even the
love of death is at work in us, and that for this reason we
must again and again lay hold of ourselves, affirm life, and
open ourselves to the newness that is being created in us.

According to Freud, the cause and instrument of the
punishment man inflicts on himself is the unconscious
faculty which he called the "superego," by which man
assimilates and makes part of himself the rules and the
orders that his mother and father and later the whole society impose on him. The superego has interiorized the
voice of family and culture. The superego is man's inner
legislator, judge, punisher, and tormentor, giving him
orders, disapproving of his actions, inflicting punishment
on him, and often making him prefer unhappiness. Man
can be well only if he is able to discern the irrational
character of the superego, escape from its messages and
its guilt feelings, and enter an area of liberation where he
can decide his course of action according to his conscious
mind.

Sigmund Freud and many of the Freudian school regarded the superego as the source of human morality. The
positivistic view of man which they had inherited from the
nineteenth century and which is still acknowledged in
wide circles, denied man's spirituality and hence the possibility of a morality intelligently discerned and freely embraced by man's conscious mind. Morality, according to
the Freudian theory, is simply due to unconscious pressures. Conscience equals superego. No wonder, therefore,
that many opponents of Freud, including Christian think-

ers, resisted the concept of the superego. They thought that the Freudian view of man undermines the spiritual basis of human civilization, and that the Freudian therapy, by releasing man from the power of superego, freeing him from guilt feelings, and allowing him to follow his instincts, put an end to morality altogether.

The Freudian discovery of superego, however, is not necessarily linked to the positivistic view of man. Today many Freudians, including Christian thinkers, are willing to acknowledge the superego as man's unconscious conscience, the set of compulsions acquired, from childhood on, under the pressure of family and society, and distinct from this, man's conscious conscience, the spiritual core of his personality, where he faces himself, where he listens to the community, and encounters the divine Word, and where he is freed to decide upon his own future. These humanistically-orientated Freudians agree with Freud that to be well and to become more human, man must escape from the irrational demands of the superego and abandon his neurotic guilt feelings, but they add that this liberation enables him to choose his actions according to conscious considerations. The aim of therapy, according to these men, is to free man from the superego, to initiate him into self-knowledge, and thus to usher him into the area of liberation where he can make his own responsible decisions.

Christians may agree with Freud, therefore, that to become more fully human man must be freed from his superego. This view does not endanger morality but rather establishes it. It would be a mistake to think that a person strongly dominated by the superego is necessarily characterized by holiness and generosity. The contrary may well be true. While the superego-dominated person religiously lives up to the commands received in childhood and the conduct recommended by society, his morality will be lacking in resourcefulness and imagination. He will tend to adopt a legalistic outlook on the moral life, he will lack a sense of humour, he will be insensitive to new areas of moral concern. The superego and the life it generates differ greatly from the conscious conscience. As an unconscious faculty, the superego is automatic, repetitive, and compulsive. As soon as the signal is given in the familiar situation, the superego commands. But it cannot adapt itself to a new situation, it cannot learn from experience, it is not open to the needs of others and the meaning of the life situation. It simply repeats, it follows the rules. At the same time, the superego can never be satisfied. Since it seeks obedience to a voice it no longer recognizes, it can never stop, it will always create guilt feelings, and unless a man can turn away from these pressures, it will generate compulsive trends in his behavior. The superego will always become an irrational accuser and incompetent judge.

The conscious conscience, on the other hand, enables man to be in touch with reality. There he listens to reason, there he listens to other people; if he is a Christian, there he listens to Christ celebrated in the Church. In this conscience a man discerns the call addressed to him and finds the freedom to respond. This conscience is the source of a morality that grows in sensitivity and concern. Since the mystery that takes place in man's conscience will make a man discover the important values, create in him a fidelity to these values, and give him a growing share in the death and resurrection of Jesus Christ.

While it is possible and indeed necessary to distinguish between the superego and the conscience, the ambiguity of human existence is such that the two calls are never totally separable in real life. Since the illness is universal, since there is an echo of superego in every spiritual moral experience of man, he must remain on guard and ready for the next conversion away from destruction to the new life offered him. Man always remains in need of being redeemed from his unconscious accuser and judge.

The scriptures, we note, do not regard man's self-centeredness as the sole cause of his sinful and destructive life. In the biblical polemics against the law, especially in the New Testament, it is revealed that in addition to this self-centeredness, there is another enemy of salvation. In his arguments with the scribes and Pharisees of his day, Jesus presented a devastating picture of the effects that law, even divine law, could have on the lives of men, and a generation later, arguing with his opponents, the apostle Paul presented the same picture in a more elaborate form. The radical doctrine of the New Testament is that a law imposed upon man from without as the condition of his salvation has a harmful effect on his life and keeps him away from salvation.[5] In the first place, such a law tempts man to identify holiness with the observance of the law; and if holiness equals observance, then a man is able to make himself holy by his own will power. The law, therefore, tends to encourage a compulsive view of human growth. Feeling that he can earn his salvation by obedience to the law, man may come to look upon himself as the author of his own salvation. Secondly, the law imposed as the condition of salvation leads man away from knowing himself and understanding other people. For if holiness can be equated with observance, then the law can become a

5. Cf. G. Baum, *The Jews and the Gospel,* Westminster, Md., 1961, pp. 186–207; S. Lionnet, "St. Paul: Liberty and Law," *The Bridge,* J. Oesterreicher (ed.), vol. 4, New York, 1962, pp. 229–251.

screen behind which a man may hide his true feelings and attitudes. As long as he conforms to the rules, he need not look at the hatred, the jealousy, and the envy in his heart. The law which, thanks to his will power, he is able to fulfill may become a platform from which he looks down with contempt on other people less observant than he. Thirdly, the law imposed on man from without as a condition for salvation makes people look upon God as a divine legislator in heaven, who imposes the rules at will, watches man from his judgment seat, rewards them when they obey his rules, and punishes them when they violate them. Thus the law makes men fall into a monstrous misunderstanding of the divine.

Jesus Christ came to save men from the law. He delivered men from the misunderstanding of the divine by proclaiming that God is Father, that he is on the side of man, that he loves man, the sinner, and that this love is the creative principle for the renewal of life. The norm of morality is not imposed on man from without; it is intrinsic to human life and is called divine grace. Morality in the New Testament is not the conformity to a set of rules on which man's salvation depends; it is, rather, the growing conformity to the new life that is being created in man. The Christian grows in holiness according to a living principle created in him through faith, baptism, and the life of the Church. Laws may have a useful role in the life of the community if they are understood as educational helps or means for promoting the common good, as long as they are not looked upon as mediating salvation. For according to the Gospel, the God who is for man and on the side of the sinner becomes the principle of new life and holiness in man as man turns away from the compulsive illusion of self-salvation to faith in the divine Word present to him.

The contrast between law and Gospel, which forms a central theme of the New Testament, must not be understood as a negative judgment on the ancient faith of Israel. Even though the language used sometimes suggests such a judgment, neither Jesus nor Paul intended to condemn the religion of Israel as a religion of law, preventing men from entering into salvation. Both Jesus and Paul acknowledged that the conflict between law and grace was already present in the scriptures of the Old Testament. The ancient prophets of Israel already preached that the law, conceived as an external obligation imposed by God, was a death-dealing, not a life-giving power. The faithful Israelite who followed the law put his trust in God and expected the fulfillment of the divine promises in the expansion of his own moral life. The great men in Israel interiorized the law by accepting it as the visible record of God's redemptive design for his people and hence as mediating, with the obligation, the inner freedom to fulfill it.

The contrast between law and Gospel, which holds such a central place in the New Testament, refers to a conflict that takes place in all religions and even beyond them in secular societies. Man is always prone to make the set of rules inherited from his society the norm of his actions, to think that he can justify himself by living up to these rules, and then to seek peace of mind by the compulsive repetition of these acts. Thus even the secular person may create for himself a dreadful judge, watching him constantly, threatening him with punishment, and continually inflicting pain on him.

The New Testament description of the destructive effects of the law comes close to a description of what in Freudian language is called the superego. There is a sense, then, in which we may rightly say that divine revelation saves men from their superego. God, the Gospel proclaims, is on the side of man. God is not a superego figure. God is alive in human history initiating men into growth and transformation towards the perfect manhood revealed in Christ. The moral quest of man, according to the Christian message, is not his effort to conform his life to a set of laws on the strength of his will power; the quest is, rather, the entry into a new life by faith, the openness to the paschal mystery offered to him, and the growing likeness to Jesus Christ through faith, hope, and love. Even in the Christian Church, we must add, the conflict between law and Gospel remains: Christians continue to be in need of deliverance from the misunderstanding of the law and the power of the superego. As Christians we have to learn again and again that faith in God's presence, and not will power, is the basis of salvation and holiness.

The scriptures, then, are wiser than traditional ascetical teaching. The New Testament does not regard man's exaggerated self-love as the only source of sin in the world, and hence does not advocate the curbing of this self-love as the primary exercise of the quest for holiness. The New Testament puts equal emphasis on the sinful trend by which man separates himself from life. The unjustified man is one who refuses to listen and come to self-knowledge, who is afraid of the new, repeats compulsively the patterns of the past, and declines the painful entry into death and resurrection. To wrestle with this powerful source of sin, a man must do more than seek self-effacement; he seeks faith that God summons him, that he is meant to be a listener all his life, that he is to open himself to the newness offered him, and that he will be ready to grow according to the inner working of the self-revealing God in his life. Man's self-realization is a process including many conversions.

It is a curious coincidence that traditional ascetical teaching and Philip Rieff agree, though for very different reasons, that an ethic of self-realization is destructive of the spiritual and moral values of society. According to the ascetical teaching, self-realization is dangerous because it is not committed to fighting man's self-centeredness, which is the source of his destructive trends, and according to Rieff, self-realization is dangerous because it does not favor the supression of man's instincts, which is the source of his true humanity. Contrary to these two positions, I have defended the view in the preceding pages that man's self-realization is a process in which sacrifice and self-abnegation have an essential role. Since man is born into a situation of ambiguity, life is available to him not by letting himself go but by facing the destructiveness in himself and reaffirming the new life that is offered to him. The quest for self-realization includes the way of the cross. To grow, to become more human, to realize oneself more fully is a process which is, properly speaking, redemptive and which incarnates the paschal mystery revealed by Christ.

Because of the self-deception inevitably present in a man's life, the quest for self-realization always passes through self-knowledge. As we have indicated several times, self-knowledge is a redemptive process. It is not available to man by his own powers. While on the one hand he desires self-knowledge and reaches out for it, he is on the other also afraid of it. He defends himself against coming to know who he is and what is going on in himself. How strong and destructive these defenses can be has been revealed by modern psychotherapy. Many of our attitudes and actions are screens, frantically put up, preventing us from knowing what we really feel. To abandon these screens and come to some self-knowledge is a dramatic process that cannot be produced at will. We have too much invested in our defenses. We fear that if these defenses go, our whole house might fall apart. There are moments in life, however, when a word addressed to a man reveals the illness and creates a community of trust. In such a moment a man may abandon some of his defenses and enter into greater self-knowledge. There are special moments when such a call comes to a man, or even to a community; the scripture speaks of them as *kairoi*. When such a moment is missed, then nothing can be done except to wait for another one; for the entry into self-knowledge is never self-initiated. It is always a response to a summons. It is always painful. There is in it an element of letting go, of falling into darkness, of wondering whether destruction awaits us; and yet there is also an element of hope that we are not totally alone, that protection is available, that something new will emerge in us, and as we fall into the darkness there will be a safe place to stand, safer than the one we had before. Entry into self-knowledge changes man's self-consciousness and hence transforms his entire life.

Jesus Christ revealed to men the unconscious motivations present in their actions. He told men of the power games they play without knowing it. He told them how much of their piety is a hidden way of achieving status, or of evading the demands of love, or of seeking revenge on other people, or of hating life itself. Entry into self-knowledge means conversion. Here again Jesus reveals the universal situation. Something must happen to a man before he can discover in himself the hidden power or sex games, before a man can detect how much his life is determined by unavowed hostility or narcissistic fantasies or concealed guilt feelings or even the hidden love of death itself. A man must be open to the word spoken to him and in a gesture of trust, relying on the possibility of new life still hidden from him, accept the painful truth about himself and abandon some of his attachment to destructive trends. A man can only see these trends as he turns away from them. If there is no willingness to let go, he cannot come to see what is going on. Entry into self-knowledge is always conversion.

A man cannot come to know who he is unless he is told by another. Self-reflection does not produce self-knowledge. A man is in need of being called. Since man's destiny is divine, it is ultimately God's Word that initiates man into self-knowledge. Jesus reveals to us who we are. But the Word, who became incarnate in Christ, is in some way present in human conversation everywhere even when no mention is made of the divine. The divine summons, we have seen, is present in the human dialogue that constitutes man's personal history. Thus we may say that man's entry into self-knowledge across the barrier of his fears is a response to divine revelation. And since this response itself is evoked by the power of the divine call and hence belongs to the total reality of revelation, we may even say that entry into self-knowledge *is* divine revelation.

The quest for self-realization, we repeat, is not a naturalistic process. Since man desires not only life but also self-destruction, self-realization demands conversion, discipline, sacrifice—even if the role of these in human life may be different from that recommended by traditional ascetical teaching. Self-knowledge, we have said, is a process of repeated conversions. Since this wrestling with self-deception brings us in touch with our illness, it leads us to discern the unreal in our desires, our actions, and our achievements and to come face to face with the destructiveness in us. Can we distinguish between the real and the imaginary in our lives? Are we in touch with other people and their true needs? Or are we simply projecting our own unresolved problems on the human environment in which we live? Self-knowledge teaches us that we cannot trust all our impulses for happiness, for pleasure, for sexual love; for these may partially disguise the hidden desire to be unhappy, to experience pain, to be subdued by other people. In order to be well, a man must be in touch with his illness, protect himself and others from it is much as possible, and decide again and again—and this may be painful—to enter the new life available to him and grow in the direction of greater humanity. If it makes sense to speak of the triumph of the therapeutic in a culture, this must refer to a common ethos encouraging men to discern the destructiveness present in their desires and to turn away from the deadly repetition of the past to a more creative encounter with reality. Life has to be chosen again and again, and this demands sacrifice and self-denial. Being human does not come naturally to man; he must be transformed many times in order to enter into his destiny.

The quest for self-realization, which—in our view—is the work of grace in the lives of men, does not destroy the traditional Christian values of sacrifice and self-abnegation. We admit, of course, that the word "self-realization" is sometimes used in a superficial sense, suggesting the compulsive search of some people for the immediate satisfaction of all their desires. A man may speak of his desire to realize himself when in fact he is narcissistically clinging to his own pleasures and his own plans without acknowledging the hidden panic that nourishes his make-believe world. Self-realization in our context means man's entry into his destiny, his humanization. Since the life of a man in this world is profoundly threatened from all sides, it is Good News that a transcendent dynamism offers him liberation from his inner obstacles to put him in touch with reality and empower him to respond to it with courage and creativity. To be well, in Scholastic terminology, is not the work of nature but of grace. Since the ambiguity into which man is born affects all aspects of his life, he is out of touch with reality and in need of grace to be well.

It should be obvious that to be well is not equivalent to being happy. To be well also includes the freedom to be unhappy in the face of human misery. A person would be very sick if he were incapable of being unhappy about the awful things that happen in his life and that of the community. We need much inner freedom to be sad without being depressed. To be well means to be in touch with reality and to respond to it in a fully human way, which is to be happy at times and sad at others. Much of the suffering in our lives has to do, alas, with insignificant issues that lose their hold on us after a while. A person must have been deeply transformed by grace if he is free to suffer about the real evil in the world and his own involvement in it. In the scriptures we hear that Jesus remained well during his passion and his entry into death. Ultimately, we learn from him what it means to be human.

In order to realize himself, man must face the inevitable

dimension of evil. We have described what facing this evil means in regard to man's inner life, but the mention of Jesus' name reminds us that in order to become human a man must also face the evil in his social environment. In order to realize himself, man must face the evil on two fronts, in himself and in the society to which he belongs, and unless he wrestles with evil on both these fronts, he cannot move far on the way to growth and reconciliation. If he confines his struggle to the evil within himself, he will not be able to discern how much his own spiritual values and his ideals for the community are hidden ways of protecting his social and political privileges. In order to become himself, a man must be politicized. In order to discern how he profits from the order of society—and here I include the Church—and how this profit creates a bias in his own understanding of life and its meaning, a man must face the destructive and exploitive trends in his own society. He must be willing to submit his life, his ideals, his religion, to what I have called the Marxian critique. Facing the evil in the life of society will enable him more and more to detect how ideology or communal self-interest has affected his own view of reality. Conversely, if a man only wrestles with the evil in society and refuses to look at the destructive trends in his own life, he takes the risk that his social and political effort will be inspired by an unresolved personal conflict. The man involved in political struggle who refuses to seek self-knowledge may end up in total blindness, be out of touch even with the social reality, and undo the work to which he dedicated his life. The Marxian and the Freudian critiques must never be separated. Man can enter into his self-realization only as he is willing to wrestle with the enemy within and without.

The Blondelian shift, we conclude, does not necessarily produce a soft Gospel. It does not necessarily remove sacrifice and self-denial from the Christian life. On the contrary, in the light of the new focus, the paschal mystery reveals the process of man's becoming man not only in the Church but everywhere.

VI. REINTERPRETING THE DOCTRINE OF GOD

WE have established the thesis, first clearly enunciated by Blondel and later partially acknowledged by Vatican II, that God is redemptively present to the whole of human history. This thesis which in some way, at least implicitly, has always been part of the Christian tradition, has moved into the focal point of the Gospel. In the last chapters we have examined the objections raised against the thesis and tried to show that the thesis, even when radically understood, is in harmony with the Church's teaching. In the light of the new perspective, ecclesiastical dogma assumes a new revelance for the present age.

We now wish to examine the doctrine of God in the light of the new focus. Because Christians have begun to ask many questions about the divine and have new, qualitatively new, difficulties in regard to God, Christian theologians are paying special attention to the doctrine of God at this time. Again I wish to stress the experiential basis of doctrinal development in the Church. The new thinking in regard to God, which is not without its startling aspects, is not imposed on the Christian people by theologians with remote intellectual interests. The contrary is true. Because God has become a problem to vast numbers of people who experience life in a new way, theologians have taken up the doctrine of God and seek to interpret it, faithful to scripture and tradition, in the light of the Church's new experience. The God problem, if I may use this term, has not been created by theologians; it has arisen in the Church's life.

We have seen that Christians have begun to experience the call and meaning of Christ in a new way. In Chapter I we have described the new experience of the Gospel as a new sense of universal brotherhood and a new openness to truth. In the following pages I wish to outline four areas where Christians, especially these "new" Christians, have difficulties in regard to God.

The first area is prayer. For many Christians today, prayer does not work any more. While they enjoyed prayer and worship in the past and much happened to them in these exercises, they are troubled by the realization that prayer has come to mean very little to them. Nothing seems to happen to them any more as they pray. The rebuilding of their lives at one time experienced in worship no longer takes place there. At first these Christians felt guilty: they thought that their own sins created the obstacles that prevented prayer and worship from being the center of strength in their lives. But soon they remembered that they had always been sinners and that God had promised to come to sinners. In the past God came to them in prayer because they confessed their need of redemption. If, therefore, God does not come to them anymore in the old way, it must be because a profound change has taken place in their self-understanding. They experience themselves in a new way. The question that arises is how God comes to men in this new situation. Can we discern the new ways in which

163

God addresses and strengthens the Christian community?

Secondly, Christians today refuse to regard man's secular existence as of secondary importance. As long as they imagined God as the supreme being watching over human history, they were able to divide life into two distinct areas, the religious and the secular. The religious was defined by man's worship of God, and the secular by man's relationship to other men and the creation of their common world. God was present to man in the religious dimension of his life. Only as man turned away from his secular preoccupations and the ordinary things of life, would he be able to find God in worship. The religious side of life held a primacy over the secular.

This approach to life has been largely rejected by Christians today. They feel that if God is present to men only in their pious moments, then he has to do with a marginal aspect of human life and hence cannot, by definition, be God at all. If it makes sense to speak of God, Christians feel, then he must be present at the center of their lives, in that area where they invest most of their intellectual and emotional energies, in other words, in the secular. It is here, in the creation of the human world, that God manifests himself. For this reason Christians have difficulties with the spiritual tradition that exhorts men to turn away from ordinary life to find God in withdrawal and to concentrate on him as if he were a supreme being apart from, and above, human life. To turn away from the secular seems irresponsible to Christians today. If contemplation has a role in their lives, then it is not a time of looking away from, but rather of looking very deeply at, what happens in ordinary life in order to discern in secular experience the redemptive reality of God.

A third source of embarrassment for contemporary

Christians is their inability to look upon the moral life as obedience to a divine lawgiver. When Christians thought of God as the supreme being who first created the world and man and then watched over them, they took for granted that from the beginning God had created the laws according to which his creatures were to move and develop, and inscribed these laws in their very being. Thus man's moral life was simply the obedience to abiding divine laws imprinted in his nature. Today Christians find it difficult to accept this. Man's moral life depends in part at least on the culture which he has created and which creates him. In particular, it depends on the degree of personal responsibility to which man is summoned. Thanks to political and technological developments, the radius of personal responsibility today is greater than it has ever been in human history. Many aspects of life, personal and social, which in the past men were morally justified in accepting passively, have become matters of responsible choice and hence morally significant. Since today men can modify the forms of personal and social life, and even destroy human life on this earth, they have become responsible for their future as never before in history. For this reason, new moral demands are made on man. He has become morally responsible for issues about which his ancestors were still able to shrug their shoulders. Facing these new challenges, Christians find it impossible to understand morality as obedience to laws created by God at the beginning. The demands of morality evolve with the human world which man creates for himself. Is this conviction reconcilable with belief in God?

Finally, the God problem is experienced by Christians in connection with the traditional doctrine of divine providence. If God is the supreme being, all-knowing and all-powerful, watching his creation from above, then he must be thought of as having planned the whole of history to the last day. The entire future of man already exists in the divine mind. Even evil, somehow, has a place in divine providence. While theologians always insisted that God is not responsible for evil, their view of divine omniscience and omnipotence necessarily implied that human sins and crimes are in keeping with God's permissive will. Like some kind of heavenly dictator, God was thought of as permitting evil in the present, for the sake of a greater good to be achieved in the future. Even Auschwitz, according to this theology, had a place in divine providence. Today many Christians find this view of divine providence incredible. They wonder if such a view is not making a monster out of God. They are deeply convinced, moreover, that the future is not fully planned: it is open-ended, to be created by a process in which man's freedom is involved. Man is summoned to create his own future. Is this conviction still reconcilable with a God proclaimed as the Lord of history?

The God problem today, I conclude, is raised by the experience of ordinary Christians. Is it still possible to believe in God, the supreme being and king of the universe? Does this outsider God exist at all? The new focus of the Gospel, based in part on the Spirit-created experience of the Church, will enable us to deal with this problem in a positive and constructive way.

What I have called the focus of the Gospel is the central thrust and message of the Church's proclamation, towards which all her doctrines are orientated. The focus is not simply an important doctrine; it is, rather, the central view in the light of which the entire mystery of salvation is proclaimed and acknowledged. The Church's teaching is not a summary of doctrines or a collection of true propositions about the divine; it is, rather, a single witness, through the interrelation of many doctrines, to God's self-communication in Jesus Christ. All the doctrines of the Church are therefore interconnected and qualify one another. They do not have a meaning as such, looked upon in isolation from the whole; they derive their meaning from their coherence with the whole and their manner of serving God's self-communication to his people. The doctrines of the Church must always be understood in the light of their focus.

This focus, we have shown in another study,[1] can change. When the Church enters a new environment and men ask new salvational questions, the focus of the Gospel may change without, however, affecting the self-identity of the Gospel. This shift of focus is not a worldly process: it is based neither on a new philosophy nor on the demands made by contemporary culture. The shift does not betray the message once and for all delivered to the apostles nor conform evangelical truth to the wisdom of this world. The refocusing of the Gospel is the work of the Spirit. It is brought about by the Church's fidelity to God's Word addressed to her in the present. Through the memory of Jesus Christ, the Christian community is able to discern God's Word addressing it in history now, and through a process of dialogue and some conflict, involving the whole community and eventually even the hierarchy, the entire Church enters into obedience to the divine Word. This is how the focus of the Gospel is shifted. It is based on the Church's Spirit-created experience of what the Gospel means in her own age.

The refocusing of the Gospel demands the reinter-

1. *The Credibility of the Church Today,* pp. 157–173.

pretation of Christian teaching in the light of the new focus. The new central thrust does not break the coherence and interconnectedness of the Church's doctrines, but it reorganizes them, it interrelates them in a new way, and hence it qualifies the meaning of all of them. All the doctrines of the Church serve God's self-communication along the lines of the new focus. In the preceding chapters we have tried to understand the Christian doctrines of Church, eschatology, and the holy life in the new perspective, and we have seen that this method of reinterpretation brings out the relevance and power of traditional teaching in the Church of today. In the following chapters, I wish to apply this method of reinterpretation to the traditional doctrine of God.

This is not the only way of approaching the problem of reinterpretation. Usually theologians adopt an approach based on a particular philosophy. Leslie Dewart, for instance, reconceptualizes the God concept by developing a meta-metaphysics.[2] He rejects a metaphysical understanding of God. He regards God as a reality beyond being and hence beyond metaphysics, and elaborates a language for speaking about God derived from an analysis of human knowing and the formation of consciousness. Other theologians try to use a form of process philosophy to reinterpret the concept of God.[3] Others again, in line with transcendental philosophy, wish to think and speak about God as present in the presuppositions of man's knowledge of the world.[4] I do not deny that these may be valid ap-

2. *The Future of Belief*, New York, 1966; *The Foundations of Belief*, New York, 1969.

3. Cf. S. M. Ogden, *The Reality of God*, New York, 1966.

4. Cf. K. Rahner, *Hearers of the Word*, New York, 1969; E. Coreth, *Metaphysics*, New York, 1968; M. Novak, *Belief and Unbelief*, New York, 1965.

proaches. But I wish to bypass the philosophical issue. I want to bracket the question of being. Instead of seeking a philosophical approach to God, finding arguments in support of it, and eventually deriving from this philosophy a language for talking about the divine, I choose a more strictly theological approach. I raise the issue of God as a Christian, as a member of the Church, acknowledging the mystery of salvation revealed in Christ. In the contemporary perspective, this means that I begin with the faith that God is redemptively present in human life. Is it possible, in terms of this focal point, to gain an understanding of the divine in human life and to develop a language for speaking about the divinity? Since the new focus has enabled us to speak about the Good News in a language drawn from contemporary experience, we anticipate that the reinterpretation of the doctrine of God in the light of this focus will also enable us to speak about the divine in ordinary secular language.

This approach, we immediately add, need not be fideistic. There is no denial here that men outside the Church have some knowledge of God. Since the divine self-communication, fully revealed in Christ, takes place in some way in the lives of all men, it is possible that reflecting on their experience and the meaning of their history men come to acknowledge the God who addresses himself to them. Man's intellectual life is neither as impartial nor as self-made as it may appear. While at one time people were inclined to think that a philosophical inquiry was a purely rational process excluding all options in regard to values, today it is usually recognized that implicit in rational reflection are many presuppositions, some of which are options about values and the meaning of life. Man's basic attitude towards reality or his faith inevitably enters his philosophical quest for truth. The intellectual life is not a purely natural process: God is redemptively involved in man's discovery of the significant truth about life. For this reason, then, we hold that the approach to the knowledge of God through Jesus Christ, adopted in this study, has no fideistic overtones. It does not exclude the philosophical approach. On the contrary, by acknowledging divine revelation as in some sense present in the whole of man's history, this approach provides an explanation as to why and how people in all cultures, simple people as well as the educated, have come to some acknowledgment of the divinity. Since philosophical reflection is always dependent on man's crucial options in regard to the meaning of life, we may confidently affirm that God comes to man even in his rational investigations. Philosophical reflection, though rational in method, may be an attempt to discern the message inscribed in man's experience of reality and hence presupposes a special kind of sensitivity. Because human history is redemptive, because God's Word addresses men wherever they are, it is possible to assert, with Vatican I, that the philosopher reflecting on the reality available to him may come to the acknowledgment of the true God.

FIRST PRINCIPLE OF REINTERPRETATION

Let us now formulate the first principle for reinterpreting the doctrine of God. The focus of the Gospel, we have said, proclaims that God is redemptively present in human life. From this it follows that there is no human standpoint from which God is simply man's over-against. God is involved in man's coming-to-be. It is impossible to think of myself and other men over here, and then of God, the supreme being, as over against us. This is impossible because I and these others have come to be who we are through a process of dialogue and sharing in which God is redemptively involved. Since God's Word is constitutive of who we are as men, it is impossible to conceptualize God as a being, even as a supreme being, facing us. In other words, since God has entered into the definition of man, it would be an error to think of God as a being apart from man and superior to him. We formulate, therefore, as the first principle of reinterpretation that there is no human standpoint from which God is simply man's over-against.

This principle is obviously influenced by a particular view of man. But so is the new focus of the Gospel. What has taken place in the present culture is the transition from a static to a more dynamic understanding of man. If man is a finished substance, if his nature is fully determined at birth, then it does not make sense to speak of God's redemptive presence in man's becoming man. If man is such a substance, then God must be conceived of as extrinsic to him, then there *is* a human standpoint from which God is simply man's over-against. But if man is not a finished substance, if man comes to be in a complex process of dialogue and sharing in which the whole human community is involved, then it is not necessary to think of God as extrinsic to man. Again, if man is a finished reality, it is vague and indeterminate to speak of God's presence to him. Once man is defined simply in terms of his own powers and resources, God becomes an outsider and it is impossible ever to get him back in again. But if man comes to be in a process of dialogue and sharing, then he is an historical, open-ended being in which, by definition, more than he himself is involved. If man comes to be in a process of listening and responding, in which his own freedom is creatively engaged, then it is possible to see how God, summoning and freeing man, enters into the very constitution of who man is and will be. We have analyzed this dialogical structure of man in Chapter II. This dynamic understanding of human life is implicit in the new Spirit-created experience of the Gospel and hence in the doctrinal development of refocusing the Gospel. It is equally implicit in the first principle of reinterpreting the doctrine of God.

There is no hint of pantheism in this first principle. To say that God has entered the definition of man is not to deny the human reality and to suggest that God is everything and man and his world are nothing. Again, if man were conceived statically as a substance whose growth is an unfolding according to laws implicit in his nature, then to deny that God is man's over-against would imply that the substance of man itself is divine. In this context the denial that God may be conceived of as a being extrinsic to man would have pantheistic overtones. In this context, the assertion that God is constitutive of human life would be a denial of the human reality altog.'' ... But if man is not a closed substance but comes to be in a process of dialogue and sharing, then it is possible to affirm at one and the same time that man is truly man and that God is constitutive of his personal being.

This first principle, we note, is not altogether untraditional. Theologians have always insisted that God is both transcendent and immanent to his creatures. They have always realized that any statement made about God as perfect being different from man or as supreme being superior to man has to be qualified by a corresponding statement indicating that in some way this God also engulfs or includes man. After affirming the being of God over against man, theologians always admitted that this being of God in some way pervades man and his world. By insisting that God is infinite, theologians suggested that in a certain sense there can be no being over against him. God is all in all. To say that I am here and that over against me there is the supreme being called God implies a contradiction. Why? Because if I am here and God is conceived of simply as facing me, then he is limited by me, then he is finite and by definition not God at all. There is no limit to God's presence. For this reason any statement affirming God as man's spiritual over-against must be corrected by a statement indicating that in some sense this God is *not* man's over-against but is present in man and includes him in his own mystery. While theologians have always taught God's immanence and even admitted the special way in which man is "a part of God," they have usually done so in peripheral observations without permitting this teaching to modify their entire doctrine of God. Only too often were theologians willing to speak of God as a reality extrinsic to man and his world. Our first principle, then, gives central importance to a traditional insight that has played only a marginal role in theological reflection.

Popular preaching and teaching about God were even more guilty of presenting God as a being extrinsic to man and his world. Preachers preferred the biblical references to God that speak of him as man's over-against, such as Creator, Lord, Almighty, Father, and made little effort to correct this one-sided terminology by the biblical names that speak of God as present in man and his history. When the scriptures call God Truth, Wisdom, Love, or Life, they proclaim the too often forgotten truth that he is operative from within human history in making man grow and in building the human community. Who would deny that vast numbers of Christians, despite this scriptural witness, think of God as a being elevated above men, a supreme person facing them, and hence a special object of human knowledge. This God, however, does not exist.

Traditional philosophy with its static view of reality did not provide theologians with concepts that made it easy for them to speak about God's immanence to human life, except in the vaguest way. Modern philosophy, on the other hand, has found categories that enable theologians to speak about the divine reality without objectifying God as a being over against man. For instance, the distinction between object and subject as worked out by the personalist philosophers of this century has been used by theologians, especially by Karl Barth, in speaking about the divine. According to Karl Barth, man may not objectify the divine reality. God is always and exclusively subject.[5]

Let me explain this terminology. First, what are objects? Objects are the things man looks at, comes to know, and tries to control. Man is superior to objects. It is because of this superior position that he can come to a knowledge of them. He can study them, look at them from all sides, submit them to experiments, and penetrate them with methods devised by him for this purpose. Are people objects? Yes and No. In part people are objects. For it is possible to look at them as objects, to weigh them, to classify them, to regard them as things over which we have control. An engineer making an elevator regards

5. In the following pages I follow James Richmond's interpretation of Karl Barth. Cf J. Richmond, *Faith and Philosophy,* London, 1966, pp. 138–142.

people as objects: "Only six of them," he says, "have room in the cabin; if seven are admitted the elevator might break down." But when we treat other people as objects, we do not learn much about them. In many situations we would even do them a grave injustice. People are never simply objects; they are primarily subjects. They are not open to our view, they are not under our control, they cannot be possessed. They can be known only if they reveal themselves. Only if they speak and if we listen can we come to a knowledge of who they are. Our knowledge of them passes through their freedom. They must want to be known. A subject is, therefore, defined in opposition to an object. An object is inferior to us and knowable by us if we use the correct techniques; a subject is not inferior to us, is not knowable to us unless he decides to be, and hence is misunderstood and even slighted if regarded by us as an object. While we may be tempted to look on other people as objects, to manipulate them and to pretend to know them through external observation, we are always reminded in our relationship with them that they are subjects, that we can know them only if they wish to speak, and that we must treat them as free agents responsible for their life. Only an aspect of other people is object; this aspect may be studied by the sociologist or the engineer. But to reduce people to objects is to violate their nature. Man is primarily subject.

We may distinguish object and subject also by considering the kind of knowledge we may have of them. An object may be studied scientifically. Our knowledge of it is verifiable. We learn to speak about objects in a language that is universally accepted. The more we perfect the techniques of investigation, the greater will be our knowledge of objects. Subjects, however, are not known through scientific reason. Since, by definition, subjects can only be known if they reveal themselves, what is needed is a special sensitivity to the language of the subject. Only if we trust a subject and have some sympathy for him will we be able to listen to him and come to some knowledge of him. Yet this is never verifiable knowledge. It can be tested only by persons to whom the subject is willing to reveal himself. Given certain techniques, an object produces knowledge is me with a certain inevitability, whether I am well disposed or not; a subject, on the other hand, does not automatically produce knowledge in me. In order to know a subject, I am in need of a special openness to him, an openness that passes through my freedom. While a man, once he has undertaken certain steps, is unfree in regard to the knowledge of an object, he is always free and undetermined in regard to the knowledge of a subject. He can only know the subject if he decides to listen.

In terms of this distinction between object and subject characteristic of personalist philosophy, Karl Barth presented his doctrine of God: God is ever and indissolubly subjectivity. God is exclusively subject, and in no way may he be thought of as object. To objectify God or think of him as object would be blasphemous, for to do so would make God in some sense inferior to man, would suggest that he can be looked at from various angles, controlled, classified, and possessed. People are, in part, objects; God is in no way object. God is always and irreducibly subject. There is nothing we can know about him or say about him unless he reveals himself, unless he chooses to speak. There is nothing we can know about God or say about him, based on objective, verifiable, scientific knowledge; what is required for the knowledge of God is a special openness to his voice called faith.

For this reason, we may not even say that God exists. To consider him as existing would be to make him an object of man's knowledge. The objectification of God implied in the statement that God exists makes man a spectator in regard to God. God would no longer be subjectivity. But since God is radical subjectivity, there is nothing about him, not even his existence, that can be known apart from his self-manifestation and apart from man's openness to his voice. For Karl Barth, then, God is always and essentially the coming one. He comes, he manifests himself, he speaks, he affects the lives of men—that is what we know about God from the scriptural witness. Behind this subject-God, there is no object-God. All we know about God is his Word. All we can know about him is his entry into human life, his transforming power, his merciful action, his summons, and his grace. What we know about God is Jesus Christ. In this perspective it is not licit to think of God as a metaphysical being existing behind this self-manifestation. God is total subjectivity. He escapes all objectification. He may not be thought of as a supreme being unless we understand this in a non-metaphysical, religious sense as affirming his power and grace present to man in his history of salvation.

Our first principle of reinterpreting the doctrine of God is very close to the Barthian formula that God is total subjectivity. Where we differ from Karl Barth is in the answer to the question as to how God is coming. For Barth this happens only in Jesus Christ. According to the doctrinal reflections proposed in this study, in keeping with the development of Catholic teaching, God is always and everywhere the coming one. The mystery of God's gracious entry into man's making of man takes place in a hidden and conditional way in the whole of human history. Where

we differ from Karl Barth, secondly, is in the interpretation of God's subjectivity. For Barth, God as subject remains always and everywhere man's over-against: God is
judgment and forgiveness. In keeping with the Protestant
tradition, Barth finds it difficult to acknowledge God's
presence in the important, formative experiences of man,
such as in truth and friendship, that carry him forward
towards growth and communion. For Barth, the never-to-
be objectified God, the gracious God coming into human
life, never really enters the process of man's making of
man. While one may differ from Karl Barth, one must
admire his brilliant attempt to overcome the metaphysical
approach to God. In agreement with conventional athe-
ists, Barth holds that there is no objective being called
God. God is subjectivity. We can only conceptualize him
by expressing the changes he summons forth in human
life.

God is never, we repeat, simply an object of a man's
knowledge. God is not an object of which man may have
an observer knowledge. Why? Because God is present in
the very man who knows God and in the very process of
knowing God. There is no island on which a man can stand,
from which God is simply his heavenly vis-à-vis.

That God is present *in* history and hence not a being
ruling history from above is at the heart of the Christian
revelation. God's revelation in Israel recorded in the Old
Testament encouraged the trend to speak of the true God
as the Lord of history, ruling his people from above. We
acknowledge, of course, that many Old Testament passages reveal God's action within history, but this perspective became decisive only in the New Testament. God's
revelation in Jesus Christ made it impossible to conceptualize God as the supreme outsider and to use a simple

unitary language in reference to him. While the New Testament speaks of God as the author of salvation history, this same God is present as Logos in Jesus Christ and present as Spirit in the hearts of men. God can no longer be conceptualized as the supreme being facing man. While we must speak of God as the destiny of man, summoning him forth towards friendship and truth, we must also think of God as incarnate in Christ acting in history and as Holy Spirit alive in Christ and in all men joined to him in faith. The unitary language about God here gives way to a trinitarian one. In order to proclaim the unity of God, we can no longer speak of him as if he were one supreme being facing man. The divine reality is more complex. Since God is present in man's coming-to-be, we must speak about the one God by referring not only to his transcendence over history but also and at the same time to his presence in the history of men. The New Testament does not first speak of God, and then only turn to God as Father, Son, and Spirit; from the beginning God is spoken of in the trinitarian way.[6] The scriptures tell the story of how Jesus obeyed the Father, how he embodied the divine Word, and how he shared the divine Spirit with those who believe. Jesus reveals the presence of God in history. Since in Christ God reveals his gracious entry into man's coming-to-be, there is no longer a human standpoint from which God is simply man's over-against. The unitary language of God which was still acceptable in the Old Testament can no longer be used in the New. The Christian Church must speak of the one God who is alive in history and transcends it, in trinitarian terms.

In our second chapter we have used the trinitarian

6. Cf. K. Rahner, "Theos in the New Testament," *Theol. Invest.,* vol. 1, Baltimore, 1961, pp. 79–148.

doctine of God to clarify what is meant by God's presence to human life. Man comes to be, we have said, through a process of dialogue and sharing in which the entire community is involved. Man comes to be by listening to others and responding to them; he creates his history by receiving care from others and by extending his love in return. In this process, which is many times interrupted by fear, resistance, and malice, God is present as Word and Spirit, orientating man towards ever greater humanization or, in more traditional terms, making him a son of the Father. God's Word present in the dialogue by which man comes to be becomes manifest in the unconditional character of the summons occasionally addressed to man. And the Spirit present in the gifts which free men to respond to this summons and become more truly human becomes manifest in the radical gratuity implicit in these gifts. God is present in man's making of man as summons and as gift, as Word and as Spirit, leading him and the whole community towards growth and reconciliation as a single people. Word and Spirit constitute humanity as the people of God. Their common destiny is the Father.

Our first principle of reinterpretation raises many problems with which we will have to deal. We are so used to speaking of God as if he were a being superior to man. We often ask questions about him as if he existed independently of man. Thus we entertain questions about the creator prior to the creation of the world and about the redeemer prior to the genesis of human life. If our first principle is correct, these questions with their implicit conceptualization of God have no meaning at all. They are in need of reinterpretation. What do we mean when we call God creator and redeemer?

THE SECOND PRINCIPLE OF REINTERPRETATION

The preceding remarks lead us to the second principle of reinterpretation. We propose that every sentence about God can be translated into a declaration about human life.

This principle sounds startling at first. To some readers it may seem that we seek to reduce the divine to the human. They may be reminded of Feuerbach and the philosophers after him who regarded religion as the projection of man's highest ideals and loftiest sentiments into religious symbolism. According to these philosophers, religion is the symbolic celebration of what is marvelous, healing, and elevating in human life. But religion is not divine. Religion may be useful and even important, for man is in need of projecting his deepest aspirations into symbols and of being transformed by celebrating these symbols in community, but—according to these philosophers—religion is not the living contact with a reality transcending man: there is no reality transcending man. This, obviously, is not our position.

We propose nonetheless that every sentence about God can be translated into a declaration about human life. Since God is present in human life not through a message sent across a distance nor by gifts offered from afar but by his own Word and his own Spirit, his presence to human life is he as he is in himself. The Word of God to man is God himself. The gift of God to man is God himself. This is the Good News proclaimed by Jesus Christ. For this reason we may not suppose that behind God's presence in

181

history there is a God existing in himself. No, the Good News tells us that God's presence to human life *is* God as he is in himself. From this it follows that as we speak about human life in all its dimensions, we are in fact also speaking about God. Since present in human history are not simply some effects of God but God as he is in himself, it should be possible to speak about this God by clarifying certain dimensions of human history. We insist, therefore, that every sentence about God as he is in himself is equivalent to a declaration about human life.

It is Karl Rahner who had made this point very strongly, even though he has perhaps not always applied it consistently.[7] What is revealed to us in Jesus Christ is,

7. According to Karl Rahner, the notional and the economic Trinity are, strictly speaking, identical. Cf. "Remarks on the Dogmatic Treatise 'De Trinitate'," *Theol. Invest.,* vol. 4, Baltimore, 1966, pp. 77–101, especially p. 94; and *The Trinity,* New York, 1970, chapter I. In several articles, especially in "Current Problems in Christology," *Theol. Invest.,* vol. 1, pp. 149–200; and "On the Theology of the Incarnation," *Theol. Invest.,* vol. 4, pp. 105–120, Rahner shows that the divine incarnation in Jesus Christ reveals that God's gift to man is he himself and that it is through this gift that man becomes fully human. God's self-communication is universal and constitutive of man's becoming man. This corresponds to Rahner's attempt, in his earliest writings, to define man in terms of openness to the divine. While he weakened his conclusion at first by introducing the obscure notion of the supernatural existential, he soon taught more consistently that Jesus Christ reveals the universal mystery of man's humanization. Rahner defined man as that which God becomes when he wants to manifest himself to the world, and God as that to which man must open himself in becoming truly human. Because God has thus entered the definition of man, Rahner thought that it was possible, even if not always desirable, to translate God-language into language about man: thus in his article "Anthropologie," *Lex. Theol. Kirch.,* vol. 1, col. 625. It is hard to understand why, in reply to some unkind critics, Rahner wrote a few years ago that the doctrine of God's self-communication as constitutive of human life (or the doctrine of "the anonymous Christian") is a peripheral, not a central theological position, and hence may not become a principle of dogmatic interpretation. Cf. "Die Anonymen Christen," *Schriften,* vol. 6, Einsiedeln, 1965, pp. 545–554. Rahner regards as theological reductions the attempts of such men as R. Bultmann and

according to Rahner, that the God-for-us is in fact the God-in-himself. In Jesus God has revealed himself totally. He has uttered his Word in an unconditional and definitive manner. Nothing remains to be said. We may not think, therefore, of a God behind Jesus, of a God who exists somewhere and reveals something about himself in Jesus; according to the doctrine of the Church, there is no God behind Jesus. Jesus is God's Word. He is consubstantial with the Father. In Jesus we see, therefore, that the God-made-visible-for-us is identical with the God-as-he-is-in-himself. Similarly God's self-communication through Jesus in the community is not a partial spiritual giving, allowing us to think of a God behind this Spirit, who makes himself known in it and at the same time hides himself. According to the doctrine of the Church, the Spirit is consubstantial with the Father and the Word. The Spirit is God. Again, there is no God-in-himself hidden behind the God-for-us. To suppose this would be to deny the divinity of Christ and the divinity of the bond that unites us with him. According to the orthodox teaching, Jesus Christ, as well as our union with him, is in fact the God-in-himself, and for this reason it should be possible to translate every sentence about God-in-himself into a declaration about human life as the locus of the divine.

This teaching of Rahner's is a development of the traditional doctrine of uncreated grace.[8] While theologians

---

Bishop John Robinson to translate God-talk into talk about man. Despite his protest, however, the teaching that God's presence to man is God-as-he-is-in-himself is central to Rahner's theology and offers a new principle of dogmatic interpretation. Cf. also his important essay, first published in English, "Theology and Anthropology," *The Word in History*, T. P. Burke (ed.), New York, 1966, pp. 1–23.

8. Cf. "Some Implications of the Scholastic Concept of Uncreated Grace," *Theol. Invest.*, vol. 1, pp. 319–346.

have usually developed the divine presence to man's life in terms of faith, hope, and love or, more fundamentally, in terms of created grace, they also mentioned at least in passing that the first meaning of grace is God himself. God is grace, uncreated grace. What we call created grace is the modification induced in man by God's self-communication to him. Created grace is the radically new which the encounter with uncreated grace produces in man and which becomes the source of a new mode of human life. But since God is present in human life not simply through some created effect but through his self-communication, it should be possible to translate every sentence about this God into a declaration about human life. To deny this would suggest that God does not communicate himself to man, but only offers him a pledge of his good will. But this does not present the relationship between God and man as preached by the Church. Grace is ultimately uncreated.

God has entered the definition of man. If we think of reality in a static way, then to say this would seem to destroy both the reality of man and the gratuity of God's gift of himself. But since, as we have shown, man comes to be through a process in which the human community is involved and yet which is not wholly reducible to human resources, human life is always and everywhere the realization of a salvational dialogue with God. To say that God has entered the definition of man is another way of saying that history is supernatural. God's gratuitous self-communication is co-constitutive of human history, and since man is who he has come to be and who he will be, God-as-he-is-in-himself enters the historical definition of man. It should be possible, therefore, to translate every sentence about God into a sentence about human life.

Let me apply this principle immediately to the statement

that God exists. This sentence is about God as he is in himself. According to the first principle of reinterpretation, we may not understand this sentence as referring to a being different from man and superior to him. In the light of the new focus of the Gospel, the question "Does God exist?" or the statement "There is a God" does not deal with a being having a supposed existence independently of man. Man may question the being of a planet or make a statement that a star exists. But since God had entered the definition of man, man cannot entertain a question or utter a statement that makes him a spectator in regard to God. According to our second principle, the statement "God exists" must be translated into a declaration about human life. "God exists" means that man is always more than man. It means that wherever people are, something new happens. *It means that man is alive by a principle that transcends him, over which he has no power, which summons him to surpass himself and frees him to be creative.* The sentence "God exists" is here translated into a declaration about human life. Man's tomorrow will be a new day. "God exists" means that man's future will not simply be determined by causes in the present, nor is his future wholly vulnerable to the malice and the blindness that mark his actions today: the new will be created. "God exists" means that tomorrow will be different from today.

This example illustrates why we have said that every sentence about God can be translated into a *declaration* about human life. The doctrine of God proclaims a mystery at work in human history, and hence acknowledging it implies an option and occurs in faith. The doctrine of God is not a description of a supreme being called God. Man can have no observer knowledge of God. The doctrine of God is Good News. It illuminates the human situation. It

185

declares unto man the meaning and the destiny of his life.

Saying that statements about God may be translated into *declarations* about human life indicates that man's knowledge of God is always salvational. The knowledge of God transforms man; it initiates man into a new self-understanding. Our above example, the reinterpretation of the sentence "God exists," shows that the acknowledgment of the true God makes man see himself in a new light: he begins to regard himself as a being summoned to create his own future. Faith in the Good News creates a new consciousness in man. It is the beginning of the new creation in him.

While we do not equate faith with the knowledge of God, we suggest that the knowledge of God is related to faith and based on it. Faith is man's total response to God's Word addressed to him. Faith is man's openness to God's gift of himself as preached by the Church or, at least, as implicit in human conversation. Faith is salvational; it renews; it creates a new consciousness in man. Yet it may happen that the conceptual content of this faith is minimal. Faith may be so implicit in a man's reaction to life that one cannot really attribute to him a knowledge of God. The knowledge of God, in the sense in which we use it, is the conceptual clarification of faith. In this knowledge man lays hold of his faith, understands its meaning, and comes to know whom he believes. Ultimately, it is through Jesus Christ that man comes to the knowledge of the true God. The faith that is gratuitously offered to men wherever they are is clarified and specified by God's Word incarnate in Christ and preached by the Church.

Linking the knowledge of God to faith, we hasten to add, does not limit this knowledge to the Christian Church. For wherever men open themselves to the mystery at work in their interpersonal relations, summoning and gracing them, and wherever they reflect on the message and meaning of their lives, ever questioned and ever renewed, they may come to acknowledge the presence of God in their never-abandoned striving after community and freedom. Because God's Word is present in human history, man reflecting on his own life and the experience of humanity may come to a knowledge of the true God. As we have suggested above, philosophical reflection is not a purely rational process. It is always influenced by non-rational presuppositions. It always embodies some options about the meaning of life. Rational reflection is affected by man's basic approach to reality, by his openness to what is before him, by his willingness to pass beyond the superficial to the profound, by his sensitivity to the orientation of human life to growth and communion. Rational inquiry, even when carried out in logical steps and verified by critical reasoning, may yet be borne by an openness to the mystery alive at the heart of human life and hence lead to a knowledge of the true God. The radical distinction between reason and faith can no longer be upheld today. It is possible, therefore, to affirm without the slightest hint of fideism that wherever men come to know the true God, whether through the preaching of the Church or, more remotely, through reflection on the call addressed to them in their lives, it is always based on faith and hence leads men into new self-consciousness.

Discussing (and dismissing) the argument for God's existence from the unity of the world, Max Scheler made the profound remark that if a man looking at the universe that surrounds him discerns a single world instead of many unconnected and hostile worlds, something marvelous has already happened to him. The God whom he wants to prove has already touched him. God has entered man's reasoning as presupposition. It is not possible, we say, to argue from the one world to a God who is its author; but there is knowledge of God available in a man's reflection on his own history when, while others despair over the absurdity of the universe, he sees one world.

These remarks on faith and the knowledge of God confirm what we have called the irony of the Gospel. According to the teaching of the New Testament, it may happen that the gifts Christ offers within the Church are more intensely present among men outside the Church. It is possible that faith, hope, and love, which are God's gifts to the Christian community, exist more intensely in men who have no connection with the Church. We may meet agnostics who have more faith in the transcendent mystery at work among men, than Christians do; we may meet men of other religions or of no religion who have more hope in the newness available to them and more love for their fellow man than we do. According to the above considerations, it may be that a man who says that he believes in God in fact believes much less in him than another who denies God's existence. It is always possible that the man who says that God exists thinks of him as a perfect being existing over against human history and does not really trust that a mystery is at work among people, a mystery which, despite men's sins and the games they play, summons them and frees them to move forward to greater truth and friendship. At the same time, a man who calls himself an atheist may in fact be borne by a faith, evoked by the divine Word and yet not explicit and fully conscious, that man is always more than man and that he is on the way to a destiny that transcends him.

Is this view of faith and the knowledge of God anti-intellectual? Does it reject or minimize the cognitive content of man's belief in God? The answer is No. The knowledge of God, we have said, cannot be equated with conceptual knowledge; man cannot have an observer knowledge of God. Even the revelation of Christ received in faith does not communicate such a knowledge. Faith and, based on this faith, the knowledge of God leads to a deeper awareness of the meaning and destiny of human life. In faith man becomes more conscious of who he is as person and as community. This new consciousness, needless to say, is not an emotional state induced by the rhetoric of a good preacher or teacher. It is not a strong feeling which makes man see reality less clearly and therefore stimulates his self-appreciation. The new consciousness takes place in man's mind. It involves his entire life, including his feelings, but as greater awareness it brings man in closer touch with himself and the reality facing him. Because faith has to do with man's self-understanding, it has, at least implicitly, an intellectual content. This content may be clarified in the knowledge of God. The knowledge of God is similar to faith in the sense that it makes man enter into new self-awareness. But the knowledge of God differs from faith, and goes beyond it intellectually, in the sense that it clarifies the new consciousness created by faith and reflects on its implications for man's understanding of the whole of reality.

Thus the empirical approach taken in this study has a number of advantages. God, interpreted according to the two principles, is the uncreated depth dimension of human life; he is the transcendent mystery present in history. Every sentence about God, we have said, can be translated into a declaration about human life. This enables us to speak of God in a language drawn from the ordinary conversation and in concepts taken from the description of human life, its fears and its hopes, its pitfalls and its expansion. This sort of secular language about the divine demands no metaphysical commitment and hence will be understood by the people of the present culture.

The more empirical approach that we have adopted will clearly show, moreover, that God makes a difference. The acknowledgment of God influences the decisions men make and the history they create. The question "What difference does it make?" is significant in theology, for if a concept expressing some aspect of the divine mystery would make no difference at all in people's lives, would stir up no new decisions nor inspire a course of action, then nothing would be changed if this concept did not exist at all and thus it would hardly deserve the name of truth. Truth makes a difference. What the Church believes in is not a heavenly reality that may be described in dogmatic terms but has no effect on the lives of men; what the Church believes in, rather, is crucial for human existence and the becoming of human history. We are in need of an empirically-orientated theology because, from the Christian point of view, truth is salvational. The doctrine of God declares man's salvation and mediates man's entry into a new self-understanding.

GOD IS PERSONAL

Let us now apply our principles of reinterpretation to the doctrine that God is personal. It is obvious, after the preceding pages, that God may not be thought of as a person or even as three persons over against men. We cannot look at the people in the room and say "Here we are" and then add "There is also God," for the true God is so present to the community of men and its coming-to-be that there is no standpoint from which he is simply their over-against. What, then, do we mean when we call God personal or insist against those who wish to make God some kind of life force that he is a person?

Before applying our principles of reinterpretation, we must reflect for a moment on what the word "person" has come to mean today. By person we usually understand an historical being, that is a being that not only comes to be in history but that comes to be through a process in which his own freedom is involved. A person is not a determined being, defined as it were by its nature. A person comes to be, in part at least, through his own responses to reality. If this is the meaning of person today, it is obvious that we cannot predicate it of God. For to suggest that God comes to be or that God is historical in the sense that he creates himself in an historical process, goes counter to the entire biblical witness.

It is important, therefore, that we reinterpret the doctrine of God as person. That God is person means that man's relationship to the deepest dimension of his life is personal. Man is related to God not impersonally as the effect is to the cause or the waves to the stream, but personally as a listener to the one who speaks and as the recipient of gifts to the giver. Man's relationship to God cannot be reified; it cannot be reduced to categories that apply to the relationship of things. We have shown more than once that God is present in human life as summons evoking man's response and as gift freeing man to create his future. The deepest dimension of human life is not a blind

191

life force or a necessary, ever-expanding dynamism but a mystery of freely chosen self-disclosure which can only be spoken of in personal terms.

We sometimes meet people who say that they no longer believe in a personal God. They tell us that they still believe in a God, in a divine principle of life present everywhere yet never identical with history, but they deny that this principle is a person. The words they haltingly use to describe this principle is force or power, "something" rather than "someone." And yet as they speak it often becomes clear that they have no intention of claiming some kind of mechanical, quasi-physical relationship between men and the divine principle of life. They simply wish to deny the existence of God, the heavenly person distinct from history, looking at man from a distance and helping him occasionally. They use impersonal words such as "force" to deny that God is person in this sense, but they do not mean to suggest that man's relationship to God can be reified. I have repeatedly found that the university students who say that they believe in God as life force are not rejecting the God of revelation, but rather seek to purify the language about God which suggests that he is a heavenly super-person.

To say that God is person, we repeat, is not a statement about a being, a supreme being called God, who has certain properties which according to some analogy resemble the personal structure of man. Calling God person does not communicate any kind of observer knowledge of God nor does it enable us to speak about his intellect and will as if these were categories describing a heavenly supernatural being. Even if at one time Christians liked to speak and think of God in this manner, we have seen throughout this study that to a growing number of Christians this conceptualization of the divine is becoming increasingly foreign and unassimilable. That God is person, according to our interpretation, means that man's relationship to the transcendent mystery present in his life is personal and can never be reified. Man's relationship to God is dialogical. Man listens and responds to him. To clarify this personal relationship further, we turn to the Church's traditional doctrine of the Trinity.

That man's relationship to God is personal is revealed in the doctrine, testified in scripture and defined by the Church, that God is Father, Word, and Spirit. Let us interpret the traditional teaching according to the principles we have adopted. It should be possible to translate the doctrine of the Trinity into declarations about human life and show how, by believing the doctrine, man is initiated into a new self-awareness. In my study *Faith and Doctrine,*[9] I have given a detailed description of the new consciousness which the divine self-communication as Father, Word, and Spirit creates in man. I shall summarize this description in the following pages.

Man finds himself facing the world. There are other people with their needs, there are the demands made on him by society, there is his body which sometimes bothers him as a faulty and painful vehicle of communication, there is his past which upsets him and will not let him go, and there is his future, as yet unknown to him, in which his dreams and aspirations may be realized or, more likely, frustrated. In this situation man is called upon to decide his present. Often he is frightened; reality scares him. Can he really face it and deal with it courageously? In this human predicament the Gospel proclaims that the reality which he is and which he faces, is, in its totality, not

9. Paramus, N.J., 1969, pp. 15–29.

against him but for him. The ultimate ground of reality is love. The principle of the total reality man faces in himself and in the world is not hostile to him but on his side. It is Father. Since evil is such a powerful factor in human history and deeply affects our own life, is it very difficult to believe the Christian message that God is good? For many people it is only because Jesus has said so and has gone through so much suffering himself that they are able to trust this message. Despite the awful things that happen, man need not be afraid of life for—according to the Good News—the reality he encounters in himself and in others is, in its totality, grounded in a principle that is personal, that is love, that is Father.

What is this principle of reality? Does it refer to the origin of man or the genesis of the universe? When man had a static view of reality, to speak of its principle made him think of what happened at the beginning. We shall see more clearly in the next chapter that today, when man has adopted a dynamic view of reality and regards the world as still coming to be, the principle of reality makes him think of the end of the world-creating process. Since the world is still being constituted, the principle of reality is its destiny. To declare, therefore, that the principle of reality is for man, is love, is Father refers not so much to the origin of man and his world as it does to his marvelous destiny. We need not be afraid of the human reality because it is involved, gratuitously and beyond historical fulfillment or despair, in the never-ending and ever-to-be-renewed process of divine humanization. To say that God is Father means, therefore, that the destiny of man, which is constitutive of his self-making, is a mystery of love.

"God is Father" declares that man is a being with a destiny, defined in terms of growth and communion. To believe that God is Father is to become aware of oneself not as stranger, not as an outsider or an alienated person, but as a son who belongs or a person appointed to a marvelous destiny, which he shares with the whole community. To believe that God is Father means to be able to say "we" in regard to all men.

According to the Good News, God is not only man's gracious destiny; he is also the call addressing man in his life. Wherever a man is, he is summoned to come to self-knowledge, to recognize the destructiveness in himself and his environment, to leave the paralyzing past behind and enter creatively into his destiny. Man need not fear that he will be surrounded by total silence. God is always Word. There is no trap, no prison, no predicament into which a man might fall where the call to new life would not be available to him. This declaration about human life translates the statement that God is Word. To believe that God is Word is to become aware of oneself or experience oneself, as a listener, as open-ended, as essentially unfinished, as still in the process of coming to be.

This Word, Christians believe, has become flesh in Christ. This Word, in dialogue with which every man comes to be, was wholly present in Christ. The divine summons, which in a provisional and conditional manner addresses all men and in response to which they come to be, was present in a definitive and unconditional manner in Jesus and constituted his being in an altogether unique fashion. While God discloses himself in people in a partial manner, he discloses himself totally and exhaustively in Jesus. Jesus is the Word of God.

According to the Good News, the deepest dimension of

reality not only faces man as his gracious destiny (Father) and addresses man as the call to pass beyond himself (Word) but is also alive in the hearts of men as source of creativity and new life (Holy Spirit). The Gospel assures us that alive in man is a precious gift which is power unto new life, yet over which he has no power, which transcends him, and which gratuitously continues to create life out of death. To believe that God is Holy Spirit is to become aware of oneself, and to look upon others as open to the radically new that emerges out of one's inner life yet forever transcends one's own resources.

We have here restated the doctrine of the Trinity, the Church's summary of the Christian message, as the Good News regarding human life. The doctrine of God is truth about human life. The doctrine that God is person brings out the personal character of man's relationship to him. God is not a super-person, not even three super-persons; he is in no way a being, however supreme, of which man can aspire to have a spectator knowledge. That God is person reveals that man is related to the deepest dimension of his life in a personal and never-to-be reified way, by listening, trusting, hoping, receiving gifts, being grateful, and worshiping. But God is not a person objectified as man's over-against.

Even though throughout this book we refer to God as "he," we acknowledge the ambiguity of this language. To be sure, God is not an "it." God is a "he" only in the sense that man's relationship to him is personal. We even have hesitations in regard to the beautiful expression of Martin Buber and Gabriel Marcel that God is man's eternal Thou present in the human thou's he encounters. While it is true that man often turns to God as a thou, or listens and responds to him as a thou, we hesitate to objectify this relationship by calling God a thou or the eternal thou, unless we are willing to submit this expression to the same reinterpretation as the statement that God is person. The principles adopted in this chapter enable us to proclaim God as the Good News for human life without objectifying him in any way.

VII. DIVINE CREATION

WE have claimed that since God is redemptively involved in human history, there is no way of conceiving him as a being apart from man and superior to him. Every sentence about this God, we have said, can be translated into a declaration about human life. This raises many questions. Is this claim not contrary to the obvious sense of the biblical message that God is man's heavenly Father? Does not the Bible continually refer to God as the supreme person, distinct from man and infinitely superior to him, as creator of the universe, as king over the nations, as judge of the living and the dead? In this chapter we want to study the meaning of these divine titles and examine whether we can apply our principles of reinterpretation to them.

Let us begin with the central doctrine of divine creation. This doctrine is often presented as if God, the supreme being, existing from all eternity, brought the cosmos into being in the first moment of time and since then continues as supreme being, existing apart from his creation, to preserve this cosmos in being. The doctrine of divine creation, understood in this way, implies that God must be conceived of as the supreme being over against man and his world.

In recent years, two important factors have produced a modification and reinterpretation of the doctrine of creation. One of these factors is the new biblical research, and the other, the evolutionary understanding of man, characteristic of the present age.

THE BIBLICAL MESSAGE OF CREATION [1]

Israel first experienced God as her liberator. He, the Lord, was the God of the covenant who delivered them from Egyptian bondage and created them as a people in the desert. Even though the story of creation is recorded on the first pages of the Bible, it does not reflect the earliest religious tradition of Israel. First God was the saviour of Israel, present to his people in the covenant. By observing God's law and celebrating his covenant in worship, the people entered more deeply into the divine will and became more firmly established as his people.

God had created Israel through his word. He had summoned forth the people and given them the word of his promise. Because God was faithful to his word, Israel was firmly established as the redeemed people. This creative word of God manifesting the divine will became the law in Israel. The ten commandments and the rules protecting and promoting the life of the community were words of God revealing his will, and by obeying them Israel was

1. In this section we depend on E. Jacob, *Theology of the Old Testament,* New York, 1958, pp. 121–150; G. von Rad, *Old Testament Theology,* vol. 1, New York, 1962, pp. 136–153; W. Eichrodt, *Theology of the Old Testament,* vol. 2, London, 1964, pp. 46–117.

sanctified and became more truly God's holy people. In his law, God continued the creation of Israel.

God was creator and ruler of Israel. The creative word of God present in the law constituted God's rule over Israel. God ruled when his will was done among the people, and hence it was in Israel's obedience to the life-giving law of the covenant that the rule of God consisted. God was king of Israel in the fidelity to his promises and in the people's faithful response to the covenant. God ruled Israel by his word and his spirit: in his word he addressed the people, revealed to them his will and his power, and opened to them the way of life; with his spirit he breathed new life into them, guided them in the grasp of their situation, and made them move forward into a future of greater promise. "You sent forth your spirit and it formed them, and there is no one that can resist your voice" (Judith 16, 17).

Out of this experience of God as creator and ruler of the people, Israel came to raise the question of God's relationship to the cosmos.[2] Israel's understanding of creation was an extension of its own redemptive experience. From the beginning the Israelites had listened to the creation stories told among the tribes and peoples that surrounded them, but they found it difficult to reconcile these stories with their view of God the redeemer. These stories presented the divinity engaged in conflict with other powers, with monsters inhabiting the ocean or with other chaotic forces, a conflict which gave rise to the creation of the world. The Old Testament bears occasional traces of these ancient stories. But with greater consistency the prophets of Israel tried to relate the creation of the cosmos to their saviour God: they presented creation as God's marvelous work preceding, announcing, and validating his marvelous

2. Jacob, *op. cit.,* p. 136.

200

work of the covenant. "Awake, awake, put on your strength, O arm of the Lord! Awake as in the days of old, as in generations long gone. Was it not thou that didst hew Raheb (the sea monster) in pieces, that didst pierce the dragon? Was it not thou that didst dry up the sea, the waters of the mighty deep, that didst make the depth of the sea a way for the redeemed to pass over?" (Is. 51, 9–10). This passage refers to an ancient creation story, yet offers a soteriological interpretation of it. The God who showed his power in the covenant and the establishment of the people was operative in the creation of the world and is still operative in the present history of Israel.

In dialogue with the Babylonian creation stories, Israel eventually developed its own accounts of God's creation of the cosmos.[3] These accounts are recorded on the opening pages of the Bible. But even these accounts are an extension into the past of Israel's redemptive understanding of its own genesis; they convey a redemptive message. They lead almost directly into the story of Abraham, the ancestor of Israel, and they present the creation of the cosmos according to the seven-day week of Israel's liturgical feasts. "Presumptuous as it may sound, creation is part of the aetiology of Israel." [4] The creation stories recorded in the book of Genesis represent the effort of the Hebrew prophets to relate their faith in the redeemer God of Israel to the origin of the whole world and to proclaim that Jahweh, the true God, who created and still creates the people of Israel, also created the cosmos. The creation of the world at the beginning of time is simply the antecedent to the covenant of grace.

Among the theologians of the twentieth century, it was

3. von Rad, *op. cit.*, p. 136.
4. *Ibid.*, p. 138.

above all Karl Barth who brought this result of biblical scholarship to the awareness of the Christian Church.[5] In his vast theological system, based on the biblical research of his day, he presented the creation of the world as the preparation for, and presupposition of, the bestowal of grace. The goal of creation is the redemptive covenant. Only in Jesus Christ, therefore, is the meaning of creation fully revealed to us. Only in him is the nature of man fully disclosed. This theological approach, a turn-about in the history of Christian thought, enabled Karl Barth to overcome the unhappy tradition of distinguishing between creation and redemption as between two distinct modes or steps of divine activity.

The two-step distinction between creation and redemption prevented Christian theologians from explaining how the redemption brought by Christ was related to man's historical existence. If theologians began with the doctrine of creation and looked upon the world as the work of God, they tended to regard redemption as an extrinsic addition to natural life or an elevation above it. Catholics often followed this line. If theologians, on the other hand, began with the doctrine of redemption, they found it extremely difficult to acknowledge the goodness of creation and often tended to look upon the natural order as hostile to the divine. Protestants often followed this road. Karl Barth overcame this dilemma by adopting from the scriptures, understood in the light of modern historical scholarship, the soteriological understanding or creation. God is first of all redeemer: even his creation initiates redemption.

While, as we have said, it has become customary in traditional theology to make a clear distinction between creation and redemption, the scriptures do not always do

5. Jacob, *op. cit.,* p. 136.

this. Second Isaiah in particular unites the redemptive and creative action of God so intimately that creation often becomes a synonym for redemption.[6] Creation is proclaimed as witness and pledge of God's present salvation. The prophet refers to the creation of the world as the sign that God is the redeemer of Israel in both past and present. "Thus says the Lord, the God who created the heavens, and stretched them out, who made the earth and its products, who gives breath to the people upon it, and the spirit to those who walk in it: I the Lord have called you in righteousness and have grasped you by the hand" (Is. 42, 5–6). "Thus says the Lord your redeemer, who formed you from the womb:·I, the Lord, the maker of all, who stretched out the heavens above . . . (Is. 44, 24). "For your husband is your maker, whose name is the Lord of hosts; and your redeemer is the Holy One of Israel, who is called the God of all the earth" (Is. 54, 5). Redemption and creation become synonymous. "Thus says the Lord, who created you, O Jacob, and formed you, O Israel: Fear not, for I have redeemed you; I have called you by your name: you are mine" (Is. 43, 1).

The last verse brings out a central biblical theme: the word of God that offers redemption is the same divine word that creates the world. God revealed himself in his word in a definitive manner in the convenant; but already prior to this event, he had spoken to the ancient patriarchs and produced the world through his word. After the covenant, too, he continues to speak to his people, creating and redeeming them. While some biblical texts refer to

6. "The soteriological understanding of creation is not confined to Deutero-Isaiah" (von Rad, *op. cit.,* p. 138). Cf. also von Rad, "The Theological Problem of the Old Testament Doctrine of Creation," *The Problem of the Hexateuch,* Edinburgh, 1965, pp. 131–143.

creation as an event in the past, for instance the first chapter of Genesis, other biblical passages present divine creation as an ongoing process. In the history of Israel and the nations, God continues his creative work. Even the passage of the seasons and other natural occurrences are understood as the present work of God. "He sends forth his command to the earth; his word runs with utmost speed. He gives snow like wool, he scatters hoarfrost like ashes. He casts forth his ice like crumbs; who can stand before his cold? He sends forth his word and melts them. He makes his wind blow and the water flows. He declares his word to Jacob . . . his statutes and judgments to Israel" (Ps. 147, 15–19). God's creation of the world continues and includes his redemptive work in Israel.

Since God is creator and redeemer of his people, he is their king. He rules the universe. But the preceding paragraphs suggest that the rule of God over the earth is not necessarily understood in analogy to the kings of the nations who from their throne rule their people with commands and laws and the threat of their armed power. God rules history by creating it. God is the uncontested king of Israel and, more remotely, of the whole world, because through his judging and saving action in the history of men he constitutes them as a people and thus creates them. This view of the divine kingship is clarified in the biblical teaching that the instruments by which God rules over the world are his word and his spirit. God acts in human history through his word and his spirit.[7]

The word of God, as mentioned above, founds the covenant and creates the people of Israel. This word manifesting the divine will becomes law in Israel, and as Israel follows this law the people execute the divine will

7. Eichrodt, *op. cit.*, pp. 46–79.

and thereby come to be more truly God's people. This is the first meaning of God's word as the instrument of his rule and his creation. Beyond the law, the word of God addresses Israel in the message of the prophets. Through the prophets, God summons his people to self-knowledge, to lay hold of their situation, to discern their infidelity and repent of their sins, and finally, to be again converted to him and hope in his mercy. The creative summons present in the prophetic utterances addressed to Israel is the central and most consistent meaning of God's word. This word is spoken in power. The word summons forth strength in the people who listen to it, it judges them and restores them. This word rules Israel. The word of God declares the future because it creates it. This word is present in Israel also in the written record of the prophetic utterances and the written account of the people's redemptive history: in the sacred scriptures, Israel believed, God is present to them, manifesting his will and creating their life anew.

This same word, the Bible tells us, is the divine instrument of creation. God creates the world in his word. "God said, 'Let there be light!' and there was light . . . God said, 'Let there be a firmament in the middle of the waters to divide the waters in two!', and so it was" (Gen. 1, 3. 6). This creative word of God is acknowledged in the psalms. "By the word of the Lord the heavens were made, and by the breath [spirit] of his mouth all their host . . . he spoke and it was, he commanded and it stood fast" (Ps. 33, 6. 9). "The voice of the Lord is above the waters; the glory of God thunders . . . The voice of the Lord is mighty, the voice of the Lord is majestic. The voice of the Lord breaks the cedars . . . " (Ps. 29, 3. 4–5). "Though the nations roar, the kingdoms totter,

God utters his voice, the earth melts. The Lord of Hosts is with us" (Ps. 46, 6–7). "Fire and hail, snow and fog, stormy winds, all fulfilling his word" (Ps. 148, 8). Through his mighty word, God is creator and redeemer of the world. This divine kingship, this redemptive and ever-new creation is expressed in the celebrated passage from Second Isaiah: "As the rain comes down, and the snow from heaven, and returns not thither, without having watered the earth, and made it bring forth and sprout, giving seed to the sower and bread to the eater, so shall my word be that goes out of my mouth . . . it shall not return to me fruitless, without having done the thing that I pleased, and accomplishing the purpose for which I sent it" (Is. 55, 10–11).

Closely linked to the word of God is his spirit. The imagery itself suggests this relationship, for the spirit or breath (wind) is the power in which a word is spoken. But as the word confronts a man, clarifies the situation, and demands understanding, the breath (wind) or spirit is an invisible power and produces a motion which surprises men and escapes their understanding. The scriptures abound in references to the spirit of God. This spirit is, first of all, the principle of life. Man comes to be a living being because God breathes his spirit into him (cf. Gen. 2, 7), and as he dies in his body this spirit returns to God. The spirit of God, moreover, is the invisible actor in the Israel's history of salvation. The judges are led by the spirit, the kings anointed by the spirit, and the prophets seized by the spirit. The promises for the future are announced by God in terms of a powerful advent of the spirit. The coming messiah will not only be led by the spirit, anointed and seized by him, but, we are told, "the spirit of the Lord will rest upon him, the spirit of knowledge and the fear of the Lord" (Is. 11, 2). The spirit is the power by which God transforms life from within, opens the hearts of men to his wisdom, and makes them enter into newness of life. The messianic future is thus often described as an outpouring of the spirit. As the falling rain gives new life to the ground (Is. 32, 15; 44, 3; Ez. 36, 25) and the animating breath puts life into dry bones (Ez. 37), so will God pour out the fullness of his spirit in the hearts of his people, making them sensitive and faithful to his word and creating in them the impulse to worship and praise. The transformation affected by the spirit will be like a new creation (Is. 65, 17; 66, 22). So closely, it is hoped, will God identify himself with his people, so much new life will God create in them, that the prophet proclaims the message: "I will no longer hide my face from the people, for I have poured out my spirit upon the house of Israel" (Ez. 39, 29). Thus as the word of God is the instrument of his ongoing redemptive creation, so too is his spirit. God rules in his spirit, God saves and recreates in his spirit.

The Old Testament does not speculate a great deal on what this word and this spirit are. With the exception of a few passages, neither word nor spirit are hypostasized or regarded in any sense as persons. Usually they are spoken of as effects produced by God in the history of man and the coming-to-be of the world. Sometimes they seem to be used as synonyms for God: they are a way of saying God is present and acts. Even if it is only in the New Testament that God's word and his spirit are fully identified with the divine reality, the teaching of the Old Testament, that we have examined suggests that already Israel declined to conceive of God as the creator king of the world, ruling human history from his throne in heaven, a kind of Hebrew

Zeus, but rather, thought of God as involved, through his word and his spirit, in the genesis of Israel and the creation of the entire universe. The Lord is creator; but this meant to the Hebrews primarily that he is redemptively at work in the history of men and thus is now creating their human world. God is king; but this meant that he manifests his will in his word, his law, and his utterances and that he enables men, by the power of his spirit, to do his will and thus to create their history and become more truly his people.

How does this understanding of God fit into the cosmological views of Israel? It is well-known that Israel shared its cosmological ideas with the ancient cultures of the Near-East.[8] As evidenced by the creation story recorded in Genesis and many earlier biblical passages, the Israelites took for granted that the cosmos was made up of three storeys, the heavens above, the earth, and the underworld below. This cosmological picture fitted well in the Near-Eastern religions, in which the divinity that was worshipped had to fight for his supreme position against the monsters of the sea or other forces of the deep, and had generated the earth in the course of this very struggle. Here the divinity was indeed the god of heaven; yet in the underworld his dominion was still disputed, and even on earth the struggle between this god and the chaotic powers still continued. These primitive creation myths of the Near-East, however, did not fit very well into Israel's religious understanding. While we find occasional references to these creation myths in the Old Testament, the teachers and prophets of Israel were unable to adopt them in their religious teaching. Only much later, only in contact with the Babylonian creation myths, did Israel develop its own

8. Jacob, *op. cit.*, p. 145.

story of a divine creation at the beginning of time. But while there was this hesitation—as we have seen—in regard to the primitive creation myths, the Israelites adopted quite readily the cosmology of the Near-Eastern cultures. They took the cosmological picture for granted, even if they were unable to integrate it with their religious understanding of the universe. "The cosmological conceptions of the Israelites do not seem to have been directly influenced by their religious beliefs." [9] Yahweh was not the god of heaven whose dominion was denied in the underworld and whose reign was still disputed on the earth. The God of Israel was presently involved, as he had been from the beginning, in the redemptive creation of Israel and, with it, of the entire world in an ongoing dominion exercised through his word and his spirit. The cosmological view adopted by the Israelites was "so little influenced by their religion that it was an obstacle rather than an aid to faith."[10] Yahweh, creator of the world and king of Israel, was not a god enthroned in heaven—an outsider-God; according to the religious teaching of the Old Testament, despite its cosmological terminology, Yahweh was, through his word and spirit, the insider-God creating history and establishing the world in its course yesterday, today, and tomorrow.

DIVINE CREATION AS ONGOING

A second factor in modifying and reinterpretating the doctrine of creation is the evolutionary understanding of the universe. Even if it is by no means certain whether the

9. *Ibid.*
10. *Ibid.*, p. 146.

world is an ongoing development towards greater per-
fection—there is some evidence against such a theory—
what is no longer questioned by anyone is that man and
his world are not static realities with fixed natures, but
that they have come to be through a complex evolutionary
process and that they are still in a state of development.
Being is developmental. This does not mean that it will
always evolve; there seems to be no reason why regression
or decomposition should not also be possible. But what is
quite certain for the men of our age is that being is not
static but dynamic.

Because reality is developmental, it is necessarily unfinished. It is still in a process of becoming. In the past,
with a more static view of the world, although we readily
admitted that things develop and change in the course of
time, we thought that essentially a thing is what it is from
the beginning. It has an abiding nature. The whole nature
of man, for instance, is given, at least implicitly, right at
birth or even at conception; what takes place in his history is simply the passage from potency to act. The future
is contained in the past. Today, having adopted a dynamic
view of reality, we have learned to acknowledge the unfinished character of man and his world. A man is not
what he is but what he will be; his future, as yet un-
realized and even unknown, is part of his nature. For, if
being is developmental, then in order to know a man, we
cannot be content with a static definition of what he is
now; we must, rather, describe his development and the
direction in which he is moving.

We note in passing that since man's destiny is known
to him only by divine revelation, we cannot come to knowledge of man apart from God's self-disclosure. Since the
orientation of man is part of who he is, we cannot speak

of man without also speaking of God. From this it follows that every judgment about the meaning and value of human life is in fact a theological decision. Whether people know it or not, whether they call themselves theists or not, every judgment about man implicit in their action and in their understanding of life is, in fact, a theological statement.

This developmental understanding of reality demands a re-reading of the scriptures.[11] Many passages of the scriptures are not only based on a particular oriental cosmology—and for that reason are in need of reinterpretation—but also imply a static concept of reality which until recently was commonly acknowledged in Western culture and now demands critical reconsideration. It was possible at one time to understand literally the biblical passages that speak of divine creation as an event in the past, as something that took place a long time ago and is now completed. Today such a literal interpretation has become impossible. It is no longer possible to think that at the beginning God created the earth with its plants, its animals, and its human population and that, since that time, God keeps his creation in being (divine preservation) and rules over human history on this earth (divine government). If it makes sense to speak of divine creation, then it must refer to an ongoing divine activity through which things and people have come to be and are still being created. If we can speak of the end of creation at all, then it must refer to the last day when humanity, having caught up with its destiny, is finally and definitively completed. To speak of the end of creation is eschatological language. This shift from a static to a dynamic understanding of reality, therefore, demands a re-reading of the scriptures.

11. Cf. A. Hulsbosch, *God's Creation,* London, 1965, chapters 1–3.

It becomes necessary to stress the biblical passages that speak of creation as ongoing and as being fulfilled in the future, and to interpret in the light of these, the passages in which creation is spoken of as past and finished.

It is obvious that we must also reinterpret ecclesiastical teaching. For in the Church's tradition we paid almost exclusive attention to the creation story recorded in Genesis and tended to think of creation simply as an event in the past. When Christians say that God created the world, they spontaneously think of an occurrence that took place a long time ago and gave being to the stage on which history moves forward and to the actors who participate in it. We tend to imagine a supreme being, existing by himself for all eternity, creating the world and the things in it, including man. This moment was the beginning of history. In this way, we come to imagine God as a supreme being apart from the world and superior to it. This picture of God is deeply rooted in the Christian imagination, and even if it no longer makes sense, we still carry it around with us. For many people, this remains the only way to think of God; and hence when they eventually abandon the static view of the world in favor of a more dynamic one, they feel compelled to give up their belief in God altogether. What is required at this time, therefore, is a reinterpretation of the Christian doctrine of creation and, more important still, a correction of the inherited religious imagination.

The developmental understanding of reality demands that we think of creation principally as ongoing.[12] Creation takes place now. God is present as Word and Spirit in the coming to be of man and his history. As man listens

12. Cf. P. Smulders, *The Design of Teilhard de Chardin,* Westminster, Md., 1967, pp. 45–59; E. Baltazar, *Teilhard and the Supernatural,* Baltimore, 1966.

to the summons addressed to him and responds with the freedom granted to him, he enters into God's new creation. In this way, God rules history as king. Creation is now, in the coming to be of the human world.

If we want to give meaning to the scriptural passages dealing with divine creation as closed and completed, we will have to apply them not to some moment of the past, but rather to the last day of the universe. Only at the end will creation be finished. We must give an eschatological interpretation to the biblical story of Adam, telling us about the perfect man, his freedom and his happiness, the garden in which he walked and the communion with God that gave peace to his life. When the scriptures speak of the beginning of man, they reveal the divinely-given orientation of human life and the end towards which man has been appointed. There are scripture scholars who say that this eschatological shift in the understanding of the creation story is demanded by hermeneutical principles drawn from the study of the bible itself.[13] It is **not** merely, they say, an adaptation of the biblical message to an evolutionary understanding of reality. The whole pull of life, according to scripture, is towards the future. The eschatological message stands at the center, and hence there is good evidence for saying that the stories the biblical author records of the beginning of mankind in fact refer to man's promised destiny. Creation is always new creation. But even if the purely biblical arguments for an eschatological interpretation of the creation story are inadequate, what counts for us is that scriptural teaching presents divine creation as ongoing, as taking place now, as leading man into a redemptive future, as being God's rule in history, as establishing mankind as God's people.

13. Cf. Hulsbosch, *op. cit.,* pp. 30–40.

Since, according to the New Testament, the word and the spirit by which God performs his creative work are identical with God, since, in other words, creation takes place through God's presence to human life as Word and Spirit, we can no longer make a neat distinction between the creative and redemptive orders. We can no longer claim that the creative order embraces man and his world, "the natural order," established by God at the beginning, and that the redemptive order is the new life offered to man as forgiveness of sin and elevation to divine friendship. Since creation is ongoing, since creation moves man towards his gracious destiny, the Father, since it takes place through God's gratuitous presence to man as Word and Spirit, it includes forgiveness of sins and the new life. In the strict sense, therefore, creation is always new creation. The order of creation is not the closed reality that traditional theology has imagined: there is no finished natural order. The seven days of creation are still going on. We may not think of God as acting in two distinct gestures, first creating man and his universe and then, reaching over the abyss produced by human sin, initiating him into redemption. God's ongoing creation is the redemption of mankind. Since, according to the divine self-revelation in Jesus, God's Word and God's Spirit are God himself, the creation of man takes place through the self-communication of the divine life. Man's entry into his humanity is a participation in the life of God.

Even though the divine creation, ongoing and ever new, includes the redemptive work of God, present from the beginning in a hidden way and fully revealed and hence available in Jesus, it is still possible and necessary to distinguish between creation and redemption. But this distinction is taken wholly *ex parte hominis,* from the effects in human life. It is possible to say that creation is God's gift of himself, or his self-communication, in a process where man is a passive recipient, while redemption is the same divine self-communication in a process that implies the active participation of man in faith, hope, and love.[14] This is a useful and important distinction, but it is never perfectly clear. Since man's cooperation with the divine summons and the grace of freedom is not always conscious to him, since it may take place on deep levels of his personality which are partially hidden from him, he is unable to distinguish in himself which is of creation and which is of redemption. But it makes sense, and is in keeping with traditional religious language, to speak of *creation* when we think of the world in which we find ourselves as such and such persons, and to speak of *redemption* when we think of the newness that is being offered to us, the freedom to leave the destructive past behind and to move forward into greater truth and love. Our environment, our history, ourselves—this is God's *creation* wounded by sin; and Jesus is God's *redemption* coming upon us. This distinction is useful and necessary, but we must always remember that it is based on a difference in human life and not on a difference in God's self-communication. From the viewpoint of the revealed mystery itself, creation is new creation, and the ongoing self-gift of God is the creation that redeems the world.

GOD THE CREATOR

We now turn to the question posed at the beginning of this chapter. Does calling God the creator of the world and

14. Cf. Dewart, *The Foundation of Belief,* pp. 372–373.

the king of human history necessarily imply the concept of the supreme being over-against man? Or is it possible to interpret the Church's profession of faith that God is creator and ruler as the proclamation of a mystery that takes place within human life? Since divine creation is the ongoing mystery of God's self-communication in the coming to be of man and his world, and since his rule of kingship lies in the manifestation of his will in the Word and in man's response to this Word through the power of the Spirit, we conclude that it should indeed be possible to translate the doctrine of God as creator and king into declarations about human life.

"God is creator" means that man's life is unfinished and still in the process of being created. "God is creator" means that the process of man's coming to be is not the unfolding of a dynamism put into him at the beginning but includes the unaccountable and wholly gratuitous production of the new in his history. The irreducibly new takes place in human life. Man's development as person and as community is not a necessary evolution according to some built-in mechanism or the organic unfolding of a seed; what takes place, rather, is the repeated creation of the new, in no way derived from the elements that preceded it in time. To say that God is creator is thus a declaration about human life, and to believe that God is creator is man's entry into a new self-understanding as an unfinished being open to the new in present and future.

To say that God is king is a declaration about human life. It declares that the summons and the gifts available in the life of man and society build up mankind as a single people. This orientation of man towards universal fellowship is not chosen by him nor is it the product of his own imagination; it is, rather, a gratuitous dimension of history which transcends man's understanding and power and into which he enters through obedience.

Whether we speak of God as existing, as Trinity, as person, creator, king, or redeemer, the reference is always to the same transcendent mystery that takes place in human life, and the acknowledgment of which in faith leads man into a new self-understanding and thus radically transforms him. That God exists, we said, means that man is always more than man. "God is Father" means that human life is orientated towards a gracious future, and "God is Word and Spirit" means that a summons revealing sin and the gift of freedom to move beyond it into newness are offered to man in his life, constituting the orientation towards his gracious future. "God is person" means that man is related to the deepest dimension of his life in a personal way, that he listens to the summons addressed to him and responds to the gifts offered him. "God is creator" means that man is unfinished and open to the irreducibly new. "God is king" means that the mystery at work in human life is stronger than sinful man, overpowers him, and establishes him on the way of reconciliation. "God is redeemer" means that this selfsame mystery which saves man from the ambiguity into which he is born and which he confirms by his life, again and again, beyond expectation and desert, offers him the possibility of escaping the destructive past and entering into new life, into an ever-recreated new way of being, beyond all death.

We note that the divine mystery present in human life, expressed by calling God existing, person, creator, king, and redeemer is always the trinitarian mystery of God's presence as Word and Spirit orientating man and his history, through growth and reconciliation, towards a gracious future, the Father, who as man's absolute future is the source of his life.

The reader may have noticed that we have completely avoided any cosmological reference in interpreting the doctrine of God as creator. We have not said a word about God's relationship to matter, to the physical world, to the cosmos as a whole. This has been consistent with our method. For divine revelation, we have said, is not information about God nor, therefore, an explanation of the universe and its origin, but self-revelation and hence the initiation of man into a new self-consciousness. Divine revelation recreates man. If, therefore, we interpret the doctrine that God is creator, we must understand it as a declaration about human life, the faithful acknowledgment of which saves man and establishes him on the way of redemption, and not as information about a supreme, uncreated being nor an explanation of the genesis of the world. Divine revelation, we wish to insist, is not information about the past. God has summoned forth the prophets and sent Jesus Christ as his special messenger to disclose to us the truth about human life, to announce to men who they are, where they are going, what threatens their life, and where healing, growth, and communion are available to them. Christ came to be the saviour of mankind, not the explainer of world genesis. The revealed doctrine of divine creation, therefore, has to do with the coming-to-be of man.

This man-centered understanding of divine creation is in keeping with the general tenor of the scriptures. It is quite generally acknowledged that the scriptures assign an altogether central place to man in the universe and show an almost exclusive concern for human life and history. The earth is simply the human environment, the garden or the wilderness in which men live. The reason why the personalist philosophers of the twentieth century, with their unwillingness to put persons and things in the same category of being, had such a profound influence on Christian theology is precisely because their view of man came close to that of the scriptures. The Bible does not acknowledge a hierarchy of beings, in which man is assigned a special place; instead, the Bible is almost exclusively concerned with man and his history and considers the material world only inasmuch as it contributes to man's life. The biblical accounts dealing with the cosmic order simply illustrate, announce, or confirm the transformations that take place in people. This becomes apparent, for instance, in the creation story of Genesis. Here man is the very purpose of the cosmos; the natural order exists simply as the human environment. It is to be the garden in which man lives. Even the animals are destined to serve human life. Later, when man sins and is excluded from the friendship of God, the whole order of nature is disturbed. The fall of man is symbolized by the deterioration of the natural universe. In line with this symbolism, the scripture often proclaims the promised redemption in terms of the cosmic transformations that shall accompany it. In the messianic age, the hostility of the animals will be transmuted into peace between lion and lamb; the threatening jungle and the overgrown field, miraculously, will be replaced by the fruitful garden. In line with the same symbolism, the biblical stories often record the manifestations of the divine introducing man into salvation as accompanied by cosmic wonders and miraculous events. All this is too well known to require specific references. In a multitude of stories the cosmic is totally subordinated to the proclamation of human redemption. For this reason, it would seem, the Bible does not encourage us to understand its message of creation as having anything to do with information about the origin of the world or its cosmic future. Divine revelation recorded in scripture is salvational: it initiates man into a new awareness of the mystery at work in him and in others, and hence into a new consciousness of who he is, as person and as community.

It is nonetheless important to speculate about the origin of the world and of matter, and to devise theories about the future development of the cosmos. The biblical doctrine of creation lends itself to such speculation. Since the process of man's coming-to-be is one in which God is creatively present, since, in other words, man develops or evolves in virtue of an orientation which is divine and of an ongoing creation of the new which, again, is divine, it is tempting to extrapolate this view of creation to the whole universe and suppose that the world comes to be through precisely such a process, a process, that is, which in its orientation and hence its origin is divine and which includes special moments, pivotal points when the new is being created. In other words, if the biblical teaching regarding the coming-to-be of man is extended to apply to the entire cosmic order, then we have a theory of evolution—not indeed an evolution that is the unfolding of reality according to a built-in dynamism, but rather an evolution that continues to depend on God's creative presence. This sort of speculation has its own significance and importance, but it has nothing directly to do with divine revelation and the knowledge of God. Theologians and philosophers may work out various theories regarding the evolution of the world and God's relation to this, but these theories belong purely to the intellectual order and cannot be looked upon as salvational truth. They provide interesting explanations and fill out man's intellectual picture, but as theories they may be true or false. They are not revelational truth; they are not constituted by man's response to the divine self-disclosure. They do not belong to the knowledge of God.

We reach here the limit of our principles of reinterpretation. We can translate into a declaration about human life the sentence "God is the creator of the universe" only to the extent that this sentence communicates the knowledge of God and initiates men into salvation. "God is creator," we have said above, reveals how we come to be and hence introduces us into a new self-understanding. To believe that God is creator is to acknowledge oneself and one's community as unfinished, as open to the new, as orientated towards growth and reconciliation.

The doctrine that God is creator of matter may indeed have a salvational meaning. But this has hardly been worked out. We may eventually see that this doctrine discloses unto man his relationship to his own body, to his sexuality, to his voice, to his ear: in brief, it may disclose unto him his mode of communication with the entire universe. It should be possible, therefore, to translate into a salvational message about human life the doctrine that God creates matter.

GOD THE JUDGE

Let us now turn to another title which the scriptures frequently give to God. God is judge. What does this title mean? Does it necessarily imply that God is a super-person facing man? Or is it possible to understand this title also

221

as the proclamation of the redemptive mystery present in human history? But even beyond the issue whether God is outsider or insider, the question in what sense God is judge is of tremendous religious importance. Is God really a judge? May we picture him sitting on a throne, rewarding the good and punishing the wicked? Is a literal interpretation of this picture in harmony with the whole biblical message about God or must we, to be faithful to biblical revelation, interpret the language about the divine judge metaphorically? [15]

It is my intention to show that when the scriptures are understood in the light of the central themes, it is not licit to think of God as punishing in a literal sense. God is not a punisher. God is always saviour. Since the image of God as judge meting out punishment has deeply affected the Christian imagination and finds expression in ecclesiastical art and religious language, it is of utmost importance that we examine the concept at this point. Even the imagination of people no longer connected with the Christian Church still associates the name of God with judgment and punishment. Intellectually, educated people realize that the central message of the Bible is that God is good, that he is Father, that he is redeemer, that he forgives sins and recreates the world of men, yet they often remain, on an emotional level, deeply attached to the image of God as punisher. What are the reasons for this corruption of the biblical message?

I wish to propose two reasons why the Christian world has become so attached to the image of God as punisher. The first has to do with the pathology of the institution. The Gospel as proclaimed by the official Church has often en-

15. T. Sartory, *A New Interpretation of Faith,* Westminster, Md., 1967, pp. 38–54.

couraged people to think of God as heavenly judge. If ecclesiastical superiors understand their own authority in terms of jurisdiction including the power of coercion, they will tend, consciously or unconsciously, to present God as the supreme lawgiver who enforces obedience through divine sanctions. Such a view of the divinity protects the earthly authorities, ecclesiastical and secular. There is an ideological taint in the image of God as supreme authority.

By concentrating on a few biblical passages and understanding them in separation from the central message, the Christian Church even developed a theology of atonement that made God the angry father in heaven who demanded the punishment of sinful mankind and was eventually appeased by the bloody sacrifice of his own son. The passion and death of Jesus, according to this theology, paid for the transgression of mankind, and since justice was thus re-established between heaven and earth, the offended deity was again willing to accept mankind into his friendship. For many, this theory made a monster of the divinity. The reason why this doctrine did not do too much harm in the Christian Church is that it was so far removed from the Good News that no Christian ever quite believed it in a literal sense.

A second reason why the image of God the punisher has flourished in the Christian and even post-Christian imagination is drawn from personal pathology. The idea of God as judge on a throne, meting out punishment, corresponds to a self-destructive trend of the human psyche. On a previous page we have mentioned man's primitive conscience or, as Freud called it, his superego.[16] The person who is dominated by his superego—

16. Cf. p. 143 above.

and no one is able to escape it altogether—has the accuser, judge, and tormentor all wrapt in one, built into his own psychic make-up. When such a person hears the Christian message with the accent on God the judge, he can project his superego on the divinity and then use religion as an instrument to subject himself to this court and, unknown to himself, to promote his own unconscious self-hatred. As we mentioned more than once in these pages, Jesus has come to save men from their superego. God is not punisher; God saves.

Let us now examine the biblical teaching.[17] What did Israel mean when it called God "just" or "the just One"? What is the justice of God? According to the Old Testament, the justice of God is not the quality whereby God rewards the good and punishes the wicked; God is just, rather, when he intervenes in the lives of the unprotected to save them from the injustices of men. "He executes justice for the fatherless and the widow, and loves the sojourner, giving him food and clothing" (Deut. 10, 18). God is just when he defends the cause of the innocent. He is just when he establishes those who have been exploited by wicked men. He is just when he saves the poor.

This original concept of divine justice received a wider meaning in the writings of the later prophets. The justice of God, we hear, is God's intervention in the history of men to save them from the enemies of life. The psalmist repeatedly pleaded, "in your justice, give me life!" (Ps.

17. For the following remarks on the meaning of biblical concepts, cf. these excellent works: *A Companion to the Bible,* J.-J. von Allmen (ed.), New York, 1958; *Dictionary of Biblical Theology,* X. Léon-Dufour (ed.), New York, 1967; *Bibeltheologisches Wörterbuch,* ed. J. B. Bauer, Graz, Austria.

119, 40). In this petition the believer did not ask God to deal justly with him, that is to reward him for his good deeds and punish him for his evil works; on the contrary, he pleaded that God manifest his justice by giving life to those whose life was being threatened. God is just when he grants gifts that exceed the expectation of men and saves them from destruction. "They shall publish the memory of thy great goodness, they shall joyfully proclaim thy justice . . . The Lord is just in all his ways, he is gracious in all his works" (Ps. 145, 7. 17). Ultimately—by a radical transvaluation of language—God is just when he forgives sins. God revealed his justice when he had mercy on Israel and saved it from the Egyptian bondage. Second Isaiah proclaims the justice of God as the act of divine mercy by which he intervenes in the history of Israel and the nations to prepare the salvation of the entire human race. The justice of God equals divine salvation.

In the New Testament this teaching is literally adopted by St. Paul. In his Letter to the Romans he tells us that in the Gospel of Christ "the justice of God is revealed" (Rom. 1, 17). This justice is the power of God unto salvation unto everyone who believes. In the New Testament God is just when he justifies sinners. God is just when he saves.

What do the scriptures mean by God's judgment? In what sense is God the judge of man's life? According to biblical teaching, God is judge in his Word. The Word of God is described as a double-edged sword penetrating deeply into the consciences of men. In his Word God judges man's innermost heart. The divine Word accuses man of sin; it reveals to him his hidden faults and the destructive inclination alive in him. God's Word brings man face to face with what he really is and hence produces in him the acknowledgment of sin and the readiness to be converted again.

According to biblical teaching, this Word of God revealing the sin of man was present to Israel in the law and in the utterances of the prophets. Wherever this Word was celebrated in the community, God again became the judge of the people, disclosed to them their sins, and summoned them to turn away from the past to new life. This Word of God, according to New Testament teaching, is bodily present in Jesus Christ. He, the redeemer of mankind, discloses the sinfulness of the human race. Since Jesus is the true man who, filled with the Spirit, was totally open to the Father, the encounter with Jesus discloses to men their hidden opposition to life and love, their secret hatreds, their closed minds, their arrogant pretensions. In this sense we must say that God is judge of men in Jesus Christ. Wherever Christ is proclaimed and celebrated, in liturgical worship or in any other context, the divine judgment is available to the community.

Judgment is part of the Gospel. God reveals sin before he forgives it. God's Word discloses the illness before he applies the remedy. Judgment and grace belong together. The initiation of man into healing does not close his eyes to the sickness in himself and his environment; on the contrary, according to the biblical teaching, divine grace is discernment and critique before it is salvation. God is judge precisely as he is saviour. It is because God comes to men as saviour that they enter into self-knowledge and come to see what is really going on. Through his critique God saves men from their self-deception.

This Word of God is present not only in the experience of Israel and in the person of Jesus Christ; it is present in a provisional and conditional manner in the entire history of man and qualifies all human experience. God as judgment is operative in the lives of men everywhere. In a strict doctrinal sense, then, we encounter the divine judgment in conversation with other people, in the incidents of our lives, in the happenings of history. It is part of our task as Christians to discern this divine critique in our personal and communal lives, and to be willing to be accused and renewed by it. This is what it means to believe in God as judge. God is judge, we conclude, because he approaches man as saviour.

There are many biblical passages, however, in which God is depicted as passing judgment on people and inflicting punishment on them for their sins. How are we to understand these passages? The sin of man, according to the biblical view of life, causes confusion and disorder in the universe created by God. Sin creates chaos. Sin destroys the human relations that permit men to grow and become more truly themselves. Sin, we note, is much more than a violation of a divine commandment. Sin is the dimension of man's life, both personal and social, by which he resists entering into his divinely appointed destiny. In sin man turns away from the life-giving Word which alone offers him the possibility of finding truth and entering into fellowship. Sin resists the divine Spirit in man. The destruction which sin initiates is like a terrible disease that spreads in the human fabric and affects an ever widening area of man's personal and social life. The sin of man generates a web of evil consequences, a pattern of destruction, that cannot be contained by human power. Man cannot stop this web of destruction from growing. Eventually, the widening circle of destruction will come upon him as his punishment—not, indeed, as a punishment imposed by God, but as a punishment inevitably and ineluctably linked to his sin. Between sin and punishment there is an automatic connection, a necessary chain, which no man is able to interrupt. Man, the sinner, is caught. He may escape the chaos initiated by his sin for a time, but eventually it will catch up with him, and be his punishment.

The above paragraph should not be understood in the individualistic and moralistic sense sometimes encouraged by the ecclesiastical teaching on sin. If we think of sin simply as a conscious transgression of a divine commandment, as some Catholic catechisms did, we gravely underestimate the depth to which evil has affected human existence. If we define sin simply as a violation of a divine commandment, the preceding remarks on the relation of sin and punishment could foster the superstitious fear that every unhappy and painful incident in our lives is a retribution for a particular sin that we have committed. According to the scriptures, sin is a much more pervasive reality. It is a dimension of man's life which goes deeper than a conscious opposition to a divine commandment. It is man's pathological resistance to growing up. This sin finds expression in man's social life: it is never simply his own. Sin is man's conscious and unconscious unwillingness to enter into new life, expressed and disguised in a multitude of ways, both personal and social; it opposes God's gracious gift of himself and thus prevents man from entering into his destiny. It is this sin that inevitably causes the havoc of which we have spoken. This sin produces its own punishment.

According to the Gospel, God comes into the lives of men as saviour. God offers to break the automatic connection between sin and its punishment. He is ready to deliver man from the impending destruction that his sinful life has created. God is never punisher; on the contrary, God saves from punishment. The God who has revealed himself in Israel and in Christ is always mercifully and gratuitously saving men from their self-generated destruction.

It is, therefore, necessary to interpret as metaphor the biblical passages that depict God as the judge, sitting on a throne, rewarding the good and punishing the wicked. It is true that God, whose judgment is in his Word, reveals the sinful dimension of human life. God's life-giving, accusing, and yet redeeming Word leads those who are open to it to new life and establishes them on the way towards a gracious destiny. However, the same redemptive Word remains without effect among those who refuse to listen and thus leaves them in their self-isolation. This interpretation, we add, is in harmony with Catholic teaching on the judgment after death. Here, too, God is always saviour. As we mentioned in a previous chapter Christ's teaching on eternal life is not information about another world but a witness to God's self-communication as saviour, as life-giver, as one who creates life out of death. In this perspective it is reasonable to hold that in a man who believes the Word and is alive in the Spirit, new life is being created as he dies; and that in a man who makes himself hard of hearing and eventually totally deaf, nothing happens as he dies. Since such a man cannot hear the call of salvation, he remains in the death he has chosen. The doctrine of hell, seen in this perspective, is not information about another world. It reveals, rather, an existential possibility of man. It is possible for a man, the doctrine of hell says, to destroy his ears and close the doors and windows of his soul, to let himself be overpowered by his self-deception, and thus lose all contact with reality, to orientate his life away from hearing in such a radical way that the God who is Word can no longer reach him in his self-chosen prison. There is no limit to human sickness. We may conclude, therefore, that the doctrine that God is saviour and never punisher is in harmony with traditional ecclesiastical teaching on life after death.

Some biblical passages rejoice in the wrath God has appointed for the wicked. The apocalyptic literature glories in the punishment, the plagues, the destruction that God will send upon the world on the day of judgment. God will judge history. While in the present the powerful, the rich and successful, all the mighty institutions exploit the ordinary people in a hidden way and slowly squeeze the life out of them, though no one dares to raise an accusing finger at them, on the day of days God will reveal their wickedness. The powerful shall come under God's judgment. Their sins shall be proclaimed and terrible will be their punishment.

The meaning of these apocalyptical passages is clear and their message comforting. They replied to the anguished question, posed by the simple people who accepted the Gospel, as to why God permitted wickedness in high places. What is God's attitude towards the empires that multiply evil and inflict unspeakable suffering on innocent men? The slaves wanted to know if God is on the side of the masters. The exploited asked themselves why the exploiters seem to flourish in the world. Does God approve of what is going on in history? The apocalyptic literature replies to this question. God is radically against evil.

He has nothing whatever to do with the kings and mighty institutions that exploit and devour human life. God is no accomplice of evil. The awful things that take place in history are completely against his will. Yet his Word is judgment, and the revelation of this wickedness has already begun in history. One day it shall all be made manifest. The apocalyptic images depicting God as the destroyer of nations do not reveal that God is, in a literal sense, a punisher; rather, they reveal the Good News that God is radically and totally against evil. We shall see the implications of this message further on in connection with the problem of evil.

Before we leave the subject of God as punisher, we must recall that there are doctrines of the atonement, faithful to scripture and tradition, that do not depict God as an offended deity demanding satisfaction and obtaining it in the bloody sacrifice of Christ. We have shown in a previous chapter that it is possible to understand the redemption wrought by Christ, including his sacrifice, as a way of divine self-revelation.[18] God makes himself known in, and communicates himself through the life of Jesus Christ, including his death and resurrection. Christians may participate in Christ's perfect self-surrender to the Father, present in his whole life, but especially in his passion, as they approach him in faith and celebrate his paschal mystery in the Church's liturgy. Christ's surrender to the Father's will was painful not because obstacles existed within him but, rather, because he was sent to reveal sin as well as grace and hence had to denounce the evil present in his society. Because he put into accusing words the hidden evil at work in the established powers, he was

18. Cf. chapter II, "Redemptive Immanence."

hated by them and eventually killed. Christ's fidelity to God led him into persecution and death. It is possible, we repeat, to present a theology of redemption and sacrifice that does not presuppose that God is a punisher. The biblical teaching of God, creator, redeemer, and judge, proclaims the mystery of new life present in human history and hence may be translated into declarations about human life.

VIII. DIVINE TRANSCENDENCE

WE now come to the most difficult question. Does the passage from the outsider- to the insider-God weaken or invalidate God's transcendence? Or is it possible to apply our principles of reinterpretation to the doctrine of divine transcendence?

Catholic theologians supported by the ecclesiastical magisterium have always acknowledged God's immanence as well as his transcendence, but there is some evidence for saying that the stress on divine transcendence was usually greater, so great in fact that the divine immanence, acknowledged in a special chapter, did not affect and qualify the elaboration of the doctrine of God in its details. In speaking of God as a transcendent being, theologians usually created the impression that God was a super-person facing man and his history. They were thus quite ready to make statements about his personality, his intellect, and his will and claim that the future of every man and human history as a whole were already foreknown and predestined in the divine mind. Divine providence, it would seem, is the crucial teaching which inevitably reveals whether a Christian regards God as an insider to human history or whether he does acknowledge a human standpoint from which God may simply be regarded as a being over-against man. In discussing divine providence, a theologian must put his cards on the table.

The task of the theologian today is to give an account of divine transcendence that does not make God an outsider to human life. He must show that divine transcendence is Good News for human life. If God were not transcendent, man would be caught in the mess he has made of history and that would be bad news. If God were not transcendent, the mystery at work in human history, of which we have spoken in these pages, would simply be a dynamic principle built into life itself. This would give rise to the naïve belief in an inevitable progress or to the depressing view that man is caught in a mechanical or organic process which will eventually devour him. Without divine transcendence human life canot be free.

Reinterpreting the doctrine of divine transcendence with the help of the principles we have established will in a sense repeat what we have already said in regard to God, Father, Word, and Spirit, present in human history. Everything that is said about God—whether we speak of him as creator, redeemer, king, judge—is just a restatement of the Gospel that a (trinitarian) mystery is at work in human life or, more specifically, that a summons not of man's making and a gift that he has not solicited are available in his life, orientating him towards growth and reconciliation. Interpreting divine transcendence as a declaration about human life will be essentially a restatement of this trinitarian mystery.

DIVINE TRANSCENDENCE

God's Word transcends human life as critique. Because man is sinner, he is tempted to elevate a finite element of his experience to the ultimate norm, in the light of which he evaluates the whole of reality. Idolatry is a constant temptation for him. Even if the modern age no longer encourages the primitive forms of idol worship, men remain tempted by a strong absolutizing trend operative in their lives to single out a finite element of the world, to attach themselves whole-heartedly to this element, to draw it into the center of their lives, to defend it compulsively as the most precious thing, and to measure the whole of reality in its light. Preachers are quite ready to denounce the possibility of money, power, sex, or success becoming an absolute value for people. But, alas, no one is safe from idolatry. It also touches the spiritual man. Even the Church can become an idol. Even the doctrine through which we come to know the living God can be elevated as the supreme value and crimes can be committed in its name. Christians are always tempted to worship the dogma rather than the true God to whom dogma gives witness.

We can never be totally free from idolatry. Many cultural and religious values, though conditional, enter our hearts in such a subtle way that we actually identify them with God and defend them as if they were divine. While God is indeed present in many of our experiences—especially in the conversation we have with others and the friendship that unites us to them—he can never be identified with any of them. After we have acknowledged the divine Word in a conversation, we must immediately pro-

235

ceed to discern how this conversation differs from God's Word. And after we recognize God's presence in human fellowship, we must discover why this fellowship is not divine, where it is threatened, and how it is still in need of being redeemed. God is present in human life, but never identical with it. God is always different. God's presence remains critique. The divine Word present in human history (and present in a privileged way in Israel and in the definitive and unconditional way in Christ) always reveals the sickness and the sin of man. In God people everywhere are summoned to abandon their self-deception and enter into self-knowledge. In particular, the divine Word reveals to men their unconditional attachment to things that are conditional. There is nothing in life and history (apart from the person of Christ) that may be identified with the absolute. The ultimate transcends any and every human reality. History is not its own measure. Thanks to this divine Word, we are repeatedly confronted with our idolatry, we are enabled painfully to detach ourselves from the values we have loved as absolutes, we remain forever open-ended in regard to the ongoing divine self-communication. We may translate God's transcendence into a declaration about human life—the declaration that human life is in need of an ongoing critique.

We note that the acknowledgment of divine transcendence is salvational knowledge. By accepting God's transcendence in faith, a man acknowledges that his life is in need of critique and thus enters more deeply into salvation. If God were a being or an entity, he could become the object of man's understanding: and man could aspire to a purely intellectual knowledge of God's properties. Thus, in traditional theology, we tried to construct a concept of divine transcendence that the human intellect by itself could accept. In these terms, even the devil (if he existed) could have known divine transcendence. In our theological approach, we reject the idea that God is an object of the intellect and that his properties can be known in a conceptual manner. The knowledge of God is always salvational. The devil, by definition, could never acknowledge divine transcendence. To acknowledge divine transcendence, we repeat, is not the assimilation of a special concept about a supreme being called God; to acknowledge divine transcendence is a salvational process by which a man is ready again and again to detect the absolutizing trend in himself and in his culture and is willing, by a painful step, to abandon his idolatry. Divine transcendence cannot be accepted by a man once and for all; it is not an idea which he acquires and then carries around with him. Divine transcendence must be acknowledged again and again, for every new insight becomes the occasion of a new temptation. It is only because God is Word, offering himself to us as critique, that we have the hope of not losing ourselves in the cultural and religious idolatry that pervades our lives. To the extent that we are idolators, we do not know divine transcendence.

It belongs to the irony of the Gospel that the people who loudly affirm divine transcendence need not be the ones who eagerly submit their idols to critique; conversely, people who deny divine transcendence in their words may in fact be open to the ongoing critique addressed to them and willing to discern the self-aggrandizement in their greatest loves and the self-deception in their highest truths. We sometimes hear of ecclesiastical princes who loudly defend divine transcendence and suspect modern theologians of having neglected or abandoned it, while they surround themselves with symbols of divinity, regard incidental developments in the Church as absolutes, and reveal an eager attachment to the historical forms of their own authority. The princes of the Church hesitate to declare openly that all human life, including the ecclesiastical institution, is in need of an ongoing critique.

Who, then, acknowledges divine transcendence? Only Jesus does so perfectly. Only he was totally free of idols: he saw through everything, even through the institution founded and operated in the name of God. Because in him the divine critique became fully revealed, they crucified him.

This leads us to the otherness of God. Even the otherness of God, we want to stress, does not demand an objectification of the divine. God, communicating himself as Word, as summons, revealing human sin and manifesting the radical difference between man and the divine, produces in people the experience of his otherness, which is universal in the history of religions. God faces man, confronts him, makes him tremble, impresses upon him his otherness, destroys his easy self-confidence. These universal experiences, confirmed by the biblical witness that God is the holy one, may very well be acknowledged without making God a metaphysical entity over-against the human world. The otherness of God is in harmony with our concept of the insider-God. For God's self-communication as Word, which at times confronts man with his own nothingness, is not apart from history but graciously and gratuitously constitutive of it. The otherness of God is a declaration about human life: it means that human history, personal and social, is always sinful, and that this is brought again and again to man's consciousness through the summons present in his life, in a painful, humiliating, annihilating, and yet hope-filled and redeeming way.

We have tried, so far, to formulate God's transcendence in terms of his Word. We can also formulate it in terms of his Spirit. The life of man, we believe, is not fully determined by his own resources and possibilities; it is open to the new. The Spirit is present to history, freeing man to respond creatively to the challenges he encounters. The human future is not wholly determined by man's limited powers nor wholly vulnerable by the stupid and sinful things he does. God's presence in history means precisely that the new, the irreducibly new, does take place in human life. The process by which man comes to be is not a passage from potency to act, as if the beginning in some sense already contained the future; rather, the process is one of dialogue and participation which includes the new, the unaccountably new, transcending man's power, expectation, and desert. The Spirit, in other words, transcends human life.

Here again we are able to express God's transcendence without making him into a supreme being. Divine transcendence is not a metaphysical concept in the ordinary sense of that word; divine transcendence proclaims salvation. It can be translated into a declaration about human life—the declaration that human life is open to the new. Man is not defined by his nature. Because of God's presence to life, man is again and again graced to transcend what he is at any time. Tomorrow will be different from today. This is another way of putting it. While the future of the physical world is wholly determined by causes in the present and hence moves according to a principle that is wholly immanent (or so it would seem), according to the Gospel this is not true for man. Man's tomorrow is not wholly determined by causes present to him today. His life is not simply the unfolding of his nature. To believe in divine transcendence is to acknowledge that man ever has a new future.

Again, the knowledge of divine transcendence is not the assimilation of a concept. It is salvational: it implies a change in man's consciousness, an inner resituating of himself in regard to the future. Hence it is possible—we have called this the irony of the Gospel—that some who profess divine transcendence do not believe that tomorrow can be different, while some who deny transcendence in their speech in fact believe in it.

We should also be able to express God's transcendence in terms of the Father. God's presence to history in Word and Spirit orientates man, as person and as community, towards the Father. This gracious destiny is the source of all life. Thus the Father transcends human history. While man's destiny, revealed in Christ, moves him to growth and reconciliation, we are radically unable to define what precisely and concretely this growth and reconciliation will mean. There is no ceiling to this movement. It never stops. Man grows when he becomes more conscious of who he is, when he is able to determine by his own choice ever more factors making up his life and his environment, when he becomes more responsible for his own future. Men are reconciled when communication among them leads all of them towards growth, when they find a language by which they are able to communicate across diversity while remaining themselves in their own way, when their increasing participation in a common life is accompanied by a greater sense of their self-identity as individual persons. We experience this orientation operative in our lives at certain times.

The Church is the privileged area where growth and reconciliation take place; at least, we celebrate this blessed community symbolically in the sacraments. But while we may be able to describe this orientation towards the Father in terms of process, we are radically unable to describe what this process will ultimately lead to: the process has no ceiling. God remains man's future, his absolute future. He remains ahead of man as his orientation. He can never be caught up with. He is *uneinholbar, unüberbietbar* as the Germans say. Again, then, we are able to translate divine transcendence into a declaration about human life: there is no ceiling to the process of humanization.

The transcendence of God as Father, Son, and Spirit, we note, cannot simply be equated with the self-transcendence of man. While it is true that man is not caught in any of the stages of his development and hence may be called self-transcendent, what must be specified immediately is that this self-transcendence is not due to a principle which belongs to man, which he can take for granted, and over which he has power. Man's self-transcendence is due to a gratuitous and ever surprising mystery present in him, over which he has no authority, a mystery which is God's gift to him.

PROVIDENCE AND EVIL

Let us now turn to the doctrine of divine providence. I have called this the test issue, where a theologian must reveal how he understands the relation between divine immanence and transcendence. Here it becomes evident whether he understands God's transcendence without qualifying it by his immanence and thus thinks of him as super-person above history, or whether he acknowledges a transcendent mystery immanent in the process of man's becoming and hence refuses to think of God as a supreme being over against man. In line with our theological approach, we are unable to accept the existence of a supreme being, called God, with an omniscient mind and an omnipotent will, who has planned the world of men in all its detail and who rules over history with a power no one can resist. God is not provident, we say, in the sense that as ruler of the world he has a master plan for human history by which he provides help for the people in need, especially those who ask him for it, and by which he guides the lives of men, even while acknowledging their freedom, towards the necessary fulfillment of his will. God is not provident in the sense that he has impressed finalities on all things from the beginning so that through their interaction the world moves inevitably, even if freely, towards its destiny. We cannot accept a divine master plan in which God has permitted evil and, from the beginning, calculated its damaging effects and compensated for them in the final outcome. History is not finished in God's mind from the very beginning. This view of God, we have shown, is not compatible with man's present self-understanding and his Christian experience. We must reinterpret the doctrine of divine providence according to the principles outlined above.

We must translate divine providence into a declaration about human life. God is provident in the sense that in whatever trap a man falls, a summons continues to address him and offer him new life that makes him more truly human. This is Good News. Misery invades us from all sides. Yet the Gospel proclaims that man is never totally determined by his limitations. When he is locked in a prison, when no door seems to open for him, when his life seems to move on a dead-end street, there is still available to him, gratuitously and beyond expectation, the summons and the freedom either to change his external situation or, at least, to be internally resituated and thus to become more truly human. God's providence is a message of hope in regard to human life.

What does this understanding of providence do to God's omniscience and his omnipotence? They, too, have to be reinterpreted according to the same principles. It is no longer possible for us to think of God as a super-person with an intellect and a will and then specify what this intellect is like—omniscient—and what this will is like—omnipotent. The image of God as heavenly person no longer corresponds to the Church's experience of the divine. The wisdom and the power of God remain a central aspect of the Gospel, but their meaning has to be understood in the light of the new perspective. Divine omniscience and omnipotence are not characteristic of a supreme being, of whom man is the observer. They are Good News, and hence they can be translated into declarations about human life.

The wisdom of God refers to the Good News that man is always summoned to greater insight, that despite the blindness and stupidity produced by sin, a mystery is at work among men as they enter into conversation and reflect on their experience, a mystery that leads them into greater truth. God is omniscient in the sense that there exists no human situation, however difficult, however obscure, however frightening, in which God remains silent or, avoiding the word "God," in which a summons to greater insight is not available. Similarly, we may say that the power of God refers to the Good News that men are always graced to become more creative, that despite the sinful resistance to growing up, a mystery is at work among them, strengthening them to see, to respond, to do, and to be in a new way. God is omnipotent in the sense that there is no earthly power oppressing man that is stronger than the divine grace that frees him to wrestle with it in some way and to become more human in the process. Or, if we want to avoid the word "God," divine omnipotence means that there is no situation, however destructive, in which an inner strength is not offered to man, allowing him to assume greater possession of his humanity.

As the terms are ordinarily used, God is neither omniscient nor omnipotent. The questions "What does God know?" and "What can God do?" are based on the presupposition that God is a super-person, of whom man can have some kind of spectator knowledge, however analogical. But if God is in no way a super-person, then these questions have no meaning whatever. Yet when reinterpreted, we may continue to speak of God's wisdom and power, recite the poetry of the scriptures praising God's omniscience and omnipotence, and marvel at the transcendent mystery, immanent in man's making of man, by whose wisdom he enters into truth and by whose will he recreates his life.

This interpretation of divine providence enables us to deal with the problem of evil in a new way. We may now say that evil is purely and simply against the divine will. There is a radical opposition between God and evil. When we conceptualized God as a supreme being ruling the world from above, it was difficult to absolve God altogether from complicity in the awful things that happen in human history. While we insisted on the biblical doctrine that there is no shadow of darkness in God, that God is love, source of life, and saviour of men, we had to admit,

244

nonetheless, that since nothing takes place against God's will, he must at least give permission for evil. Evil, we said, is in accord with God's permissive will. Theologians tried to find reasons why God would give permission to evil, usually proposing that God permits evil things to happen in the present for the sake of a greater good to be achieved in the future.

If one applies this sort of reasoning to concrete situations, it becomes quite terrible. Thinking of the torments people go through, especially innocent children, thinking of the sickness, the accidents, the wars, the exploitations, the cruelty afflicted on helpless men and women, it makes a monster out of God to suggest that he permits these dreadful things to happen for a greater manifestation of his mercy in the future. For some people God has become this heavenly monster. They think that even Auschwitz has a place in God's providence. If we conceptualize God as an omniscient and omnipotent king governing the world from above, then there seems to be no other way of relating God to evil. To deny that God gives permission to evil would, in such a theology, imply that God is not king and ruler at all.

Yet once we reinterpret the doctrine of God and understand his kingship in a new way, we are able to affirm the radical opposition between God and evil. In no sense of the word is evil permitted by him. God overcomes evil. God is constantly at work among men, summoning them and gracing them to discern the evil in human life, to wrestle against it, to be converted away from it, to correct their environment, to redirect history, to transform the human community. The death that destroys is never the will of God. On the contrary, God is the never-ending summons to life. The transcendent mystery present in man's becoming always creates life out of death. This is fully revealed in Christ's resurrection.

We may not think of God as giving permission for sickness, accidents, wars, exploitations; God is against all evil. The question "Why doesn't he stop all this at once?" is based on the presupposition that God is the heavenly outsider, the supreme ruler, all-knowing and all-powerful. But this God, we have seen, does not exist. The true God opposes evil. His self-revelation in Jesus Christ manifests this. God opposes evil by summoning and gracing men to deal with their lives, to understand what is going on, to face up to the destructive powers, to gain increasing mastery over evil, and to assume more and more responsibility for their human future. God has triumphed over evil in the orientation of mankind towards growth and reconciliation. Our reinterpretation of the doctrine of God enables us to affirm in a more uncompromising fashion than previous theologies that God is the author of good and of good alone and that there is no shadow of darkness in him.

Where, then, does evil come from? The scriptures do not offer an explanation for the origin of evil. We here recall the general principle: divine revelation is not information about God nor an explanation of the genesis of the world; rather, it is self-revelation and hence man's initiation into a new consciousness and thus a new way of being.

To look for a definitive theory explaining the origin of evil in the scriptures is futile. What the scriptures reveal is that evil is a never-to-be-overlooked dimension of human life and that God is not its remote author but its radical foe. Divine revelation discloses the hidden presence of evil and clarifies, with its talk about the demonic, that while man is associated with the production of evil, its destructive power greatly transcends human malice. The Christian Church has tried to express the biblical teaching on evil in the doctrine of original sin: every man, we are told, is born into an inevitably sinful situation, where he cannot grow up without becoming a sinner himself. The self-destructive drive is a dimension of human life that a man must face lest he become more vulnerable to it—and that a man is able to face in the knowledge that God is good and stronger than evil. Where sin abounded, grace abounds even more. But the scriptures do not offer a definitive explanation of where evil comes from. Evil is with us, and divine revelation enables us to discern it, face it, denounce it, abhor it, and sometimes overcome it.

We repeat in this context what we have said in connection with the origin of the cosmos. It is interesting and important to speculate about the origin of evil. Theologians and philosophers have engaged in inquiries of this kind throughout the ages. Their achievements are significant theories. But these speculations do not belong to the salvational knowledge which divine revelation communicates. The question as to where evil comes from torments us, but apart from the fact that God is not its author and that man is connected with it, the scriptures give us no definite reply. Evil is here, even though its depth and extension are often disguised. What the scriptures do communicate is the vision and strength to face this evil.

When a man of great faith is overwhelmed by bad news about people he loves or is struck down by sickness, an accident or a terrible crime, he may possibly say, "This is God's will." Such a statement would be a magnificent expression of his faith. The statement does not mean, of course, that God has wanted this terrible thing to happen or even that he has given permission for it. What the man of faith means is that he continues to trust in God: he believes that despite the calamity God continues to be wise and powerful in his life, summoning forth new insights and creating life out of death in unexpected ways. A man of faith who suffers great loss may indeed say "This is God's will." But no one else may say this for him! No one may call the evil that befalls another the will of God.

Jesus saw in the cross the will of the Father. Jesus realized that his mission as prophet and revealer would provoke the enmity of the established class and eventually lead to his violent death. His fidelity to this mission and his entry into suffering and death was for him the will of God. But no one else could say this for him. The men of the institution who persecuted him certainly could not say, except as a terrible lie, that it was God's will that Jesus die. Suffering, injustice, and death are always against the divine will. In our generation, Jewish men and women on the way to the extermination chambers may have said to themselves that this incomprehensible and groundless evil was in some mysterious way God's will—in the sense that they continued to trust in God. But on the lips of an observer such a statement would be a dreadful blasphemy.

God's power over the world is dialogical. God is not the first cause who produces at will the effects he desires; he is not the heavenly king who predestines and foresees every detail of the historical process. The transcendent God, we have tried to show, is related to the world of man through dialogue. It is through the summons addressed to man and the grace to respond that God exercises his power in the world. God is opposed to evil; his power in overcoming it is present among the people who, enlightened by his Word and strengthened by his Spirit, resist evil and find ways of conquering it. God is opposed to cancer; he is at work in the urgency with which men, doctors and researchers, dedicate themselves to finding a cure for the terrible disease. God's power over the world is not the miraculous action by which he makes things happen as he pleases, but the redemptive action by which he enables men to deal with their own problems. When we repeat with the scriptures that God is omnipotent, we interpret this to mean that God is related to the world, as insider, through his word, his creative Word uttered in the power of his Spirit.

PRAYER

Is it possible to pray to the insider-God? Since prayer is an acknowledgment of divine transcendence, we must examine the question in this chapter.

We have already referred to the difficulties present-day Christians experience in regard to prayer. Many Christians who enjoyed prayer at one time have found, to their surprise, that the customary prayer does not work for them any more. The theologian is bound to acknowledge this witness and to try to interpret its meaning. Theology is an empirical study in the sense that it takes seriously what Christians in fact think, do, and feel, and uses the Church's Spirit-created experience as a key for the understanding of the Gospel. The widespread difficulties with prayer manifest a change in man's self-understanding and hence, inevitably, a change in his encounter with the divine.

Let us briefly analyze the inner obstacles many Christians experience in regard to prayer. First, we note that the customary teaching on prayer tended to visualize man as facing two worlds, the world of ordinary life and the world of God. On the one hand, there is man's secular existence, his friendship, his love, his building of the human world, his political action; on the other, there is the supernatural world where God is ready to encounter him. The inner gesture of prayer, understood in this perspective, is a turning away from history and ordinary life to the supernatural world of God and his grace. The gesture of prayer is withdrawal from life.

This withdrawal has become problematic to modern man. He feels that it would be irresponsible to look away from his secular existence; he will not let out of sight what he regards as his essential task in the hope of finding God away from it. Since in this self-critical age man has become aware of his own fear of life and his resistance to assuming responsibility for himself, he regards the flight from reality as his constant temptation. The Christian asks himself whether there is not an element of flight in the prayer he enjoyed for so long. He is ready to admit that there is a kind of prayerful turning to God which is an escape from the pressure of history and a shrugging of the shoulders at issues that demand action. Fearing this tendency in himself, the Christian finds it difficult to perform the inner withdrawal that meant so much to him at one time.

Prayer seems to increase men's dependence on God. The customary teaching on prayer often presented God as the good father, and man as his trusting child: in prayer we lean on God and ask him to take our hand and lead us. Today, in a more self-critical mood, men have become aware of the deadly passivity in them that often prevents them from growing up and assuming responsibility for their lives; they wonder whether the prayer they have learned does not in part encourage this unhappy trend in them. Christians today reach out for the God who summons them to assume greater responsibility for themselves, who will make them less dependent on himself, and who helps them to overcome their sinful inclination to desire others to make decisions for them.

Since prayer was presented as a strict obligation in the traditional teaching, Christians tried to engage in it whether they felt like it or not, even if it meant very little to them. In a more critical age they have begun to wonder whether such prayer may not be a technique of self-persuasion, of talking oneself into something. Is there an element of brainwashing in the prayers made obligatory by ecclesiastical authorities? The Christian who has learned to acknowledge the ambiguity of life will readily admit that prayer is not necessarily an exercise that delivers man from his self-deception but that it may also be, in varying degrees, a self-induced confirmation of his favorite illusions. Today many Christians find it almost impossible to pray when they do not feel inclined to do so.

These, then, are three reasons why prayer has become problematic for present-day Christians. Since they realize that prayer is not exempt from the ambiguity of life, they fear that the surrender to God which was easy and enjoyable at one time may in part have been a flight from reality, an endorsement of their passivity, and a defense of their self-deceptions. Is there a God who calls men into reality?

Our reinterpretation of the doctrine of God will shed some light on the difficult and important subject of prayer. Let us begin with public worship. We have said that God is present to human life as Word and Spirit. This divine presence gives rise to four distinct actions on the part of man, namely listening, responding, receiving gifts, and expressing gratitude for them. These four actions enter into the definition of public worship. The divine presence, which offers man salvation everywhere and which is fully revealed in Jesus Christ, is proclaimed and celebrated in the Church's liturgy. Here the proclamation of the revealed message and the celebration of the sacraments render God present to his people. Together the Christian community listens to the divine Word, responds to it in song, receives the sacramental gifts, and expresses gratitude for the forgiveness and newness available in them. The presence of Word and Spirit, revealed in Jesus Christ, creates the community of believers and orientates them towards the Father. The Church acknowledges this orientation by praise. The believing community at worship celebrates the mystery of redemption present in Christ and praises God as the author of life and the term of man's destiny.

At worship the Church celebrates the redemptive mystery that takes place everywhere. For this reason the sacred does not sever men from the ordinary things of life happening every day; on the contrary, the sacred as the celebration of the depth dimension of human life enables men to lay hold of the ordinary daily reality in a new way. Worship, understood in this way, unites a man more closely to his entire life. Word and sacrament enable him to interpret the meaning of secular life and discern the divine presence in his relationship with people and the building of the human world. The proclamation of the Gospel at worship enables the Christian to hear the summons addressing him in his life situation, and the celebration of the sacramental gestures enables him to open himself to divine grace offered in the gestures that create the human community, such as eating together, conversing, forgiving one another, and bearing the burden together.

In the above paragraph we have rejected a monopolistic understanding of the Church's sacramental liturgy. The first means of grace is life itself. It is here that God is redemptively present to man. This divine presence, fully disclosed in Jesus Christ, is celebrated at worship. Liturgy understood in this way should teach Christians to discern God's redemptive call and gifts in the ordinary situations of life and hence, in a sense, make them more independent of the liturgy.

It follows from these remarks that it is possible to elaborate a theology of worship based on the concept of God the insider. It is possible to worship and to speak about worship in a meaningful way, even if we refuse to think of God as a super-person facing man and his history. The shift from the outsider- to the insider-God is symbolically expressed by the recent change in the liturgical structure of the worshiping community. When the priest celebrated Mass with his back to the people, the position of priest and people together looking forward symbolized that the divine mystery they worshiped exists in some sense beyond them. Together they turned in the same direction. Now that the priest has changed his position and faces the congregation, the symbolism of the Mass is significantly altered. The new liturgical structure signifies that the divine mystery who is being worshiped is present within the community. God is present in the people. In worship the believing community acknowledges the deepest dimension of its life, opens itself to the redemptive summons, and praises the mystery that is the source of its ever-renewed vitality.

The Christians who find it almost impossible to pray usually have no special difficulties with public worship. When the liturgy is celebrated well, they find it joyful, challenging, and transforming to take an active part in it. In public worship it is not necessary to project a divine thou beyond oneself and imagine God as a super-person above the community. In the liturgy the spiritual attention of the worshipers constantly shifts. They listen to the scriptural text, they let themselves be impressed by its deep meaning, they respond to the gospel with greater trust, and they express their common fidelity in song and recitation. The emphasis is on the whole community. The worshipers stand up and kneel down together. They eat the same redemptive food in a common meal. Liturgy is action. Together they join Christ in his self-surrender to the Father. Some Christians, accustomed to an older type of piety, find participational worship distracting. Paying attention to other people and relating themselves to a common action prevent them from concentrating on the invisible God they want to worship. But the Christians formed by the Church's renewal do not experience the attention given to others and the effort to cooperate in gesture and song as something distracting. The divinity they worship is not an entity existing apart from the community; God, for them, is present in the community as a constitutive element —as its source and deepest dimension. Liturgy occasionally leads the worshiper to acknowledge God as a thou addressing him and awaiting his response, but this is simply one among many aspects that make up the entire worship. In liturgy the Christian celebrates the divine mystery, present in the community, to whom he relates himself through a multitude of inner acts and outer words and gestures.

Private prayer has become more of a problem. In private prayer as it is customarily conceived (not, of course, by the great mystics!), it seems to be necessary to concentrate on a heavenly thou before and above us. The definition of prayer as an elevation of the mind and heart to God suggests that God is the supreme being over against man and that prayer demands a turning away from the earthly to the heavenly realities. With such an image of the divinity, the Christian regards it as his duty to project God as his invisible thou and to address himself to this thou in much speaking. This effort of the will to imagine God as the invisible partner in a conversation has become highly problematic for Christians of the present age.

A brief reflection on the definition of prayer as the elevation of the mind and heart to God shows that this definition is inadequate and misleading. Prayer, as any salvational relation between God and man, always begins with God. This has been the constant teaching of the Church.[1] We may not define prayer, therefore, as if it were a conversation that begins with man! Prayer is always and every time initiated by God. God speaks first; man then listens and responds. Listening always precedes the response. Prayer must, therefore, be defined as man's listening and responding to the divine Word.

The character of private prayer depends largely on where one expects the divine Word to be sounded. If we suppose that the divine Word is present almost exclusively in Jesus Christ, the scriptural witness to him and the ecclesiastical celebration of him, then prayer will always be a specifically religious act connected with ecclesiastical life. We let ourselves be addressed by Jesus Christ, either through the Bible or through his manifold presence in the Church, and we respond to the divine Word in meditation, in inner commitment, in words and invocations. But if the divine Word is not only present in Israel and Jesus Christ, but also, conditionally and provisionally, in the

---

1. Cf. the forceful rejection of the so-called semi-Pelagian positions at the Second Council of Orange, *Denz.*, 370–395, especially 373: "If anyone says that divine grace is bestowed because of man's invocation rather than that this divine grace brings about that it be invoked by man, he contradicts [divine revelation] . . ."

entire community of men, that is in man's personal and social history, then the listening and responding to this Word, which we have called prayer, will not necessarily have anything to do with conventional religion and the ecclesiastical setting. The Christian who reflects on his own experience and on that of the community, who seeks to discern in these the divine voice, and who wants to respond to it by redirecting his life, is—theologically speaking—engaged in prayer.

Discerning reflection on human history is prayer. Reading the newspaper, for instance, and seeking to hear in it the Word of God is prayer. For through the reports of the press we may come to greater self-knowledge, see more clearly our sin, detect how far we are involved in exploitation, and prejudice; we may also discern some marvelous signs of God's presence to life, the healing produced by dialogue and cooperation, the bridges overcoming old divisions. As we read the paper, trying to detect the divine voice and respond to it by adjusting our political judgments and, possibly, preparing ourselves for action, we are in a strict theological sense engaged in prayer. (We recall at this point that the Christian is able to detect the Word addressed to him in history because he is familiar with Jesus Christ from the scriptures and the Church's life.[2])

Discerning reflection on personal life, too, may be prayer. For instance, I may reflect on the friendship I have with another person and wonder if in it there is a message addressed to me. I may discover the destructive things I do to the other and possibly the harmful influence he has on me. There may be a message here, revealing to me the true nature of friendship, telling me whether to find a better way of being close to him or rather seek a

2. *The Credibility of the Church Today,* pp. 162–164.

greater distance from him. Or the message I hear by reflecting on the friendship may be the call to be interested in aspects of life I neglected before and to become morally sensitive to areas of life where before I simply shrugged my shoulders. This sort of discerning reflection accompanied by the readiness to respond is, in the strict theological sense, prayer.

We may add that without this sort of contemplative dimension no man can grow to maturity. Prayer is nothing specifically Christian. Even the person who does not acknowledge God's existence in a conceptual way must again and again open himself to the summons available in his life, interpret its meaning, and seek to respond to it with courage and generosity. Prayer may be secular; the contemplation produced by God's Word and man's listening may be expressed in secular terms. The prayer Jesus taught the Church simply clarifies and intensifies the prayer God produces in people wherever they try to become more truly themselves.

Since, as we explained many times, listening and responding to the divine Word take place in conversation among people, especially in the Church, conversation, too, is an occasion of prayer. This theoretical conclusion is strongly supported by contemporary Christian experience. Many Christians for whom customary private prayer has become almost impossible have discovered in dialogue carried on in the community one of the principal means by which God comes to them. There, in conversation, they hear the Word addressed to them; there they are unsettled, initiated into self-knowledge, brought to conversion, confirmed and rebuilt by God's Spirit. This contemporary Christian experience gives special meaning to the biblical teaching that the temple of the new covenant, the temple in whom God is present to his people and is worshiped by them, is the body of Jesus, that is the Christian community.[3] The temple is the people. This is true not only in an abstract ecclesiological sense but also in a concrete, experiential, spiritual sense referring to the prayer that occurs in communication.

Christians for whom traditional private prayer has become almost impossible are not by this fact alone cut off from the divine Word. We have seen that it is possible to understand public worship as the celebration of the insider-God and that even private prayer is available to them in discerning reflection on life and conversation in the community. But what about the prayer that is directly addressed to God as the gracious thou? Is this sort of prayer still possible?

To imagine God as an abiding partner, an eternal thou, an invisible companion, or a heavenly father has become increasingly difficult. God is present to human life. According to the principle of reinterpretation that we have established, there is no human standpoint from which God is simply man's over-against. The divine mystery offers itself to man again and again as summons, as challenge, as gift, and hence it often becomes a thou addressing man and awaiting his response; but this does not mean that one may conceptualize the divine mystery as a super-person in conversation with man. While we admit that God addresses us as Word and in this sense is a thou, we must add that conceiving of God as a thou must be corrected immediately by the acknowledgment that God is also present in

3. The new temple, not made by human hands, which is the place of God's presence in the new covenant, is the body of Jesus Christ. "Destroy this temple, Jesus said, and in three days I will raise it up . . . He spoke of the temple of his body" (Jn. 2, 19–21). Cf. Mt. 24, 2; 26, 61; 27, 40; 1 Cor. 3, 9. 16–17; 2 Cor. 6, 16; Eph. 2, 19–22.

us as we listen to him, that he is present in our response to him, in our gratitude, in our praise. The brilliant use made of the "I-thou" relationship by Martin Buber and Gabriel Marcel has its limitations. What is characteristic of the divine thou, according to Buber and Marcel, is that it is ever and unchangeably a thou. God is never an object *about whom* we speak; he is always and only someone *to whom* we speak. This position has the advantage of making the knowledge of God a salvational, not a rational, truth. It has the advantage of preventing the conceptualization of God as object. But one wonders whether the definition of God as the eternal thou in the I-thou relationship does not make the I, the ego, the standpoint from which God is simply man's over-against. In this study we have defined divine transcendence differently. To call God a person or a thou, we have said, does not mean that we may imagine him as a super-person facing man; it means, rather, that man's relationship to the divine mystery, the deepest dimension of his life, is personal, that is to say it is constituted by listening and responding, by receiving gifts and by being grateful for them. God is never simply a thou over against man because he is present in the very coming to be of man.

Why is this a point of practical importance? If God were the supreme thou that man encounters in and through other people, then the believer would regard it as his duty to concentrate on this divine thou, to make a special act by which he acknowledges and addresses himself to this divine over-against. He would regard himself as lacking in faith, as unreligious, as having no contact with the divine if he did not consciously focus on the divine thou. No one would be open to the divine unless he conceived the divine mystery as a thou over against himself, to whom he listened and spoke. This, however, does not correspond to our analysis of God's presence in human life as Word and Spirit. Faith, or man's faithful openness to God's coming, does not demand that he mentally create for himself a God who is facing him and to whom he speaks. The entire ascetical effort by which a man forces himself to imagine such a divinity, by which he interrupts the meaning of life itself to turn away from what happens now to a being who is conceived of as separate, has become highly problematic to the modern Christian. To some it seems like mental gymnastics, which they can no longer perform with a good conscience. According to our reinterpretation of doctrine, there is no need for this kind of ascetical effort. God offers himself as Word and Spirit in the ordinary, secular, day-to-day life of man, enabling him to become more human, to grow, and to enter into reconciliation with others. A man is in touch with God not necessarily when he focuses on him as a supreme thou, but when he is open to the summons that leads to self-knowledge and the discernment of life, and when he creatively responds, with the freedom offered by the Spirit, to the word that has been spoken to him.

There are many ways in which men are related to God in a personal way. One of these is the experience in which they encounter God as another thou. If this is what takes place in the lives of Christians, then their prayer will unfold according to an I-thou pattern, and the traditional form of private prayer will be meaningful to them. But if this is not the way in which a man is personally related to God, then—and this is my point in this section—there is no need for him to force himself into this piety, to project the divinity before himself, and to feel obliged to keep talking to this divinity as if he were an invisible companion.

For many Christians this is precisely the kind of prayer that has become next to impossible.

What about prayers of petition? Do they necessarily imply an outsider-God? There can be no doubt that the Old and the New Testament strongly recommend petitionary prayers. Such prayers were regarded as special signs of faith and hence deserving of special blessing. It would seem that implicit in these prayers of petition, more than in any other form of prayer, is the concept of God as supreme ruler of the universe, able to determine events in time and space as he pleases, who may be moved by the humble intercession of his children to intervene in the course of history. This conceptualization, we have said, is no longer acceptable. What happens to petitionary prayer when we reinterpret the doctrine of God? I hold that prayers of petition remain spiritually meaningful. For as we pray to God, asking him to protect us and his people, and plead with him to save us from the calamities of life and lead us to greater happiness, we give a concrete manifestation of our faith that human history (and hence our future) is not a necessary sequence of events related to one another as cause and effect, nor the slow unfolding of a dynamic built in from the beginning, but that history is open-ended, that God is alive in it, or, in secular words, that the new, the irreducibly new, takes place in it again and again. By praying to God for his blessing and his help, we show our faith that creation continues and that tomorrow may be different from today. Petitionary prayer gives concrete expression to the faith that the deepest dimension of human life is not a blind force, not a necessary metaphysical principle, not a neutral ground of some kind, but is personal and gracious wholly in favor of man.

The petitionary prayer most in keeping with the understanding of God proposed in these pages is the call for mercy, for help, for a new message, for more light, for greater freedom, for a deeper entry into man's humanity. The "Lord's Prayer" remains the classical interpretation of what petition means in the Church's life. What has become more difficult, if not impossible, for Christians is to make detailed petitions to God, asking him for this or that precise favor, as if he were the supreme ruler of the universe in total control of historical events. Even a petition, we insist, is man's response to a call that comes from God; a prayer of petition is not man-initiated. According to the experience of many Christians, the inner call to address themselves to God with petitions comes to them much less frequently than it did in the past, when they thought of God as the gracious Lord of heaven. The intercession which they are called to offer has to do, almost exclusively, with the more general plea that God be God, that his kingdom come, that he be present to the recreation of human life. Petitionary prayer, then, at least when understood in a more general sense, is in harmony with the concept of God as the transcendent mystery present in man's making of man.

We now return to the question as to whether private prayer, addressed to God as the invisible, eternal thou, is still possible. We have seen that the concept of God as trancendent insider provides us with a deep appreciation of public worship, with its multi-faceted attention on God's presence in the community, and stimulates the special forms of private prayer that we have called discerning reflection on life and conversation in fellowship. But is it possible to understand God as insider and still address him as an eternal thou in private prayer?

I venture to give the following positive reply. There is

some evidence that Christians who have enjoyed prayer in the past and then abandoned it for a few years as no longer making sense to them, are discovering a new kind of prayer corresponding to the new way in which they discern God's presence in their lives. The inner gesture of this new form of prayer is different. The best way to illustrate the shift that has taken place in man's inner life is to refer again to the recent change in the liturgical structure of the Mass. When the priest at worship had his back to the people, he and the congregation together faced the divine mystery before them and symbolized the community's reaching out to the God alive beyond it as its divine thou. The new liturgy in which the priest faces the congregation at worship symbolizes that the divine mystery that is being celebrated is present in the community. Similarly, the customary forms of private prayer (I exclude those of the great mystics) had the inner gesture of reaching out. Prayer was an inner turning away from oneself and ordinary life and a stretching out towards an invisible other, the divine thou. The analogy by which prayer was understood was the turning of a man to his friend or the bowing down of a servant before his gracious king. The new form of prayer has a different inner structure. Instead of reaching out beyond himself, the Christian in his inner concentration remains close to the ordinary things of life, tries to be in touch with himself, with all of himself, with his mind and his body, and to open himself to the deepest dimension of his being, the inexhaustible source of life that remains forever hidden. To pray to God means to remain where we are, to lay hold of what is there, to pass through the superficial layers to the profound meaning, to integrate our mind by self-knowledge and to possess our body, including our sexuality, in reconciliation. This sort

263

of prayer acknowledges a divine transcendence that is not in contradiction to divine immanence but, rather, clarifies it. To pray is to be in touch with oneself in a new way: to listen to the melody, not made by ourselves, that sounds at the core of our being and, from beyond the sickness that deafens us, summons us to be alive. Since God is redemptively present in man's coming to be, prayer is a way of holding or possessing oneself. This kind of prayer is not a moving away from oneself and reaching out for another, but rather a being in communion with oneself across many obstacles, and a laying hold of oneself in and through the gift dimension that is constitutive of one's being. This prayer is supremely possible only in Christ because only in him is revealed to us who we are and who God is.

Prayer as the turning in on the mystery of one's history is not a move towards individualism and isolation. On the contrary, the mystery that takes place in my own life and that has entered into my personal being is God's gift of himself that is present also in the lives of other men and that constitutes the history of mankind. The prayer by which I assimilate myself according to the gift dimension of my being unites me, therefore, with other people, with the community and the entire world of men. This form of prayer has its own pain, for while it is open to God's presence in man's becoming, it also registers the sin, the self-destruction, the unwillingness to grow, by which men oppose the coming of the kingdom.

This form of private prayer acknowledges that God is personal, in the sense explained above, but it does not demand the mental concentration on a God conceived as an invisible thou to whom we address ourselves in word and feeling.

It may well be that the change in man's self-understanding and his openness to the divine explains the great interest many people in the West have shown in the Eastern forms of prayer. According to the great Hindu tradition, God is alive in the self or even identical with it, and prayer consists, therefore, not in a reaching away from oneself into the distance but, rather, in the peaceful acknowledgment, across many hurdles of self-elevation, that the self is God. The Hindu formulation that *brahman* is *atman* and *atman brahman* may sound pantheistic to Western ears, but there is no need to interpret it as such. There is no way of speaking of God that does not sound pantheistic. It may well be that the present Western trend of looking at the world as historical and developmental and of understanding God as the transcendent mystery creatively present in man's coming to be make the spirituality of the East appear as an appealing and realistic way of dealing with life and, furthermore, brings the Christian experience of prayer into greater proximity to the Eastern tradition.

MIRACLES

The reinterpretation of divine transcendence leads us inevitably to examine the place of miracles in the Christian message. In the history of Christian theology, miracles were usually regarded as witnesses and even guarantees of God's transcendence and the whole supernatural order. In the nineteenth century in particular, the Catholic Church's official teaching defended miracles as the visible and hence historically verifiable proofs that God is not caught in the causality of the cosmos and that, transcending the order of nature, he intervenes in the lives of men for their salvation. Miracles were looked upon as the founda-

265

tion of the Church's apologetical stance, and hence as an essential part of the Christian Gospel.

We observe immediately, however, that miracles are signs of God's transcendence only if we have adopted an extrinsicist concept of God. If it is possible to separate the world from its creator, if it is possible to regard the world as a closed system created by God at the beginning, which is now moving according to laws implicit in this first act of creation, then these startling violations of the laws of nature, that is the miracles, are indeed signs that God transcends the created order and is graciously at work in it. In the disruption of the causality proper to the created order, God manifests his authority over the natural universe and his mercy towards men.

Maurice Blondel, at the turn of the century, was the first Catholic thinker to reject such a view of miracles. In Chapter I, we dealt with Blondel's critique of the extrinsicist concept of God implicit in much of the Church's official theology on divine revelation, the relation of nature and grace, and the apologetical system. Blondel said that since God is redemptively involved in man's becoming man, it is not possible to separate the world of man from its creator and redeemer, and hence it is not legitimate to think of God as the supreme outsider who occasionally puts his finger into the clockwork to alleviate suffering or offer salvation. Blondel repudiated such an extrinsicist view of miracles. Since God is graciously present to human history, the new, the unexpected, the gratuitous, the marvelous is part of history itself, and the startling manifestations of God's mercy in miracles simply reveals a hidden dimension of the whole of human life.

In his early work, *The Letter on Apologetics*, Blondel

composed a passage on miracles [4] which, I think, is the best that has ever been written on the subject, a passage that challenged him all his life and to which he could never totally live up, a passage that revealed the radical consequences of his thought, of which, at a later time and under some pressure from the authorities, he may even have been a little afraid.

In the first place, Blondel emphasized that nature is not a closed system. "Let us use the strictest language about this: since for philosophy no contingent fact is impossible, since the idea of fixed general laws of nature or of nature itself is an idol, since every phenomenon is a special case and a unique solution, there is nothing more in a miracle, if one thinks it out fully, than in the most ordinary events: equally there is nothing less in the most ordinary events that there is in a miracle." [5] Because of God's presence to human life as ongoing creation, nature or the created order is not a closed definable system. The new takes place again and again in the becoming of the human

4. *The Letter on Apologetics, and History of Dogma,* London, 1964, pp. 134–135. This single paragraph on miracles is more profound, more honest, and more realistic than anything written by Catholic theologians since then. (For literature see L. Monden, *Signs and Wonders,* New York, 1966.) None of the authors fully deals with the issues raised by Blondel. They suppose that the ecclesiastical magisterium has committed itself on a particular view of miracles, to which they must conform. Even Blondel seems to have softened his view of miracles later in life. Great theologians like K. Rahner and J.-B. Metz propose principles for the rethinking of miracles, but instead of applying them they tend to lose themselves in obscure remarks. (Cf. the articles "Wunder" in *Kleines Theologisches Wörterbuch* and *Lex. Theol. Kirch.*) The patristic tradition on miracles, however, is very wide and leaves much freedom to the Catholic theologian: see, for example, P. de Voogt's studies on the concept of miracle in St. Augustine, *Recherches de théologie ancienne et médievale,* 1938, pp. 317–343, and 1939, pp. 1–16, 197–222.

5. *Ibid,* p. 135.

world. For this reason, the ordinary events of life are not simply due to the unfolding of fixed laws; ordinary events are, in part at least, the result of God's redemptive presence in human life and hence as much surprising and gratuitous as are miracles.

Miracles, Blondel said, are signs. They speak a sign language. They are meant to signify God's redemptive action in human history. "The purpose of these interventions, which provoke reflection into making conclusions of a more general character, into breaking through the deadening effect of routine, is to show that the divine is to be found not only in what seems to surpass the familiar powers of men and of nature but everywhere, even when we are tempted to think that man and nature are sufficient: so miracles are truly miraculous only for those who are already ready to recognize the divine action in the most usual events." [6] The sign language of miracles can only be understood by a person already familiar with it, to whom it recalls what he has known many times before, even if, under the pressure of life, he has not always paid sufficient attention to it. Miracles are startling events that go against men's immediate expectations, but they are signs to men only if they call to mind the ever startling grace of God operative in their lives. This is the reason why miracles that enlighten some blind others. What counts is the faith of the beholder; what is decisive is whether the beholder is open to God's gracious presence to man and is able to decipher the sign language of the miracle, or whether he is insensitive to the newness of life offered to him and hence remains unaware of what the miracle means. To people who do not believe, miracles mean nothing.

With these reflections Blondel destroyed the use of

6. *Ibid.*

miracles in ecclesiastical apologetics. Miracles are not violations of the natural order, helping us to prove the existence of a transcendent God and the loving concern he has for human life. Miracles are not even divine signs revealing the power of God and confirming the message preached in his name. Miracles, for Blondel, are simply startling events that bring out the startling character implicit in all of human life and hence have meaning only for men who already acknowledge the marvelous as a dimension of human history. The representatives of the official theology attacked Blondel bitterly. Some of his opponents even felt that he reduced the nature of miracles to such an extent that it no longer made a difference whether miracles ever took place or not, or worse, that miracles are not what people had thought they are, namely violations of the natural order, and hence that there really are no such things as miracles at all. Blondel, who was quite traditional in the interpretation of scripture, accepted the biblical miracles as actual occurrences, but by constructing an apologetical theology which was quite independent of miracles, he assigned to them an altogether subordinate place in the genesis of faith and the understanding of the Gospel.

Several years after Blondel had written *The Letter on Apologetics,* he discovered, in his efforts to defend himself against accusations, that already in the nineteenth century Cardinal Dechamps had devised an apologetical approach similar to his own in that it was independent of miracles.[7] Allusions to Dechamps' approach are actually to be found in the conciliar documents of Vatican Council I. Anticipating Blondel's method of immanence, Dechamps had

7. F. Rodé, *Le miracle dans la controverse moderniste,* Paris, 1965, pp. 166–172.

taught that God is redemptively involved in the lives of all men. The redemptive immanence of God produces what Dechamps called "the inner fact." Life itself brings people to ask urgent questions about its meaning. The inner fact is the Spirit-created search for the ultimate answers to the questions that inevitably arise in people's lives. These answers, Dechamps believed, are available in the Church: this is "the outer fact" produced by God. When these two facts are brought together in man's conscience, he becomes a believer. Dechamps held that the answers to life's urgent questions are present in the Church not simply as abstract doctrines: they are lived, they permit people to participate in them in a vital way, they are celebrated, they constitute the community. The Church as the community of truth and love, Dechamps held, gives witness to its own authenticity. The Church is the great marvel that guarantees the divine presence to those who are interiorly prepared for it. According to Dechamps' apologetics, it is not so much the miracles of the past that establish the rational foundation of faith, as the marvels of the present, the living fellowship of the Church.[8]

While the constitution *Dei Filius* of Vatican Council I insisted in one paragraph[9] on the role of miracles in the genesis of the Christian faith, it admitted in another that the Church by its life, by its present life, is a powerful motive of credibility (*magnum quoddam et perpetuum motivum credibilitatis*),[10] and hence acknowledged, at least implicitly, that there is an alternative approach to apologetics, based not on past miracles but on present marvels.

8. Cf. R. Aubert, *Le problème de l'acte de foi*, Louvain, 3rd ed., 1958, pp. 142–145, 341–342.
9. *Denz.*, 3009.
10. *Denz.*, 3013.

Miracles are still an intellectual problem in the Church today. While the scriptures recorded miracles to inspire people to believe in God and to praise his mercy and power, and while the Church throughout the centuries felt that miracles make the proclamation of the Gospel more powerful and persuade people to put their trust in the divine message, in modern times miracles have turned out to be an obstacle rather than a help to faith. Miracles often create special problems for believers. Ordinary Christians find it difficult to reconcile the world of the Bible, in which miracles are a common occurrence, with the world of their own experience, and even when they are willing to accept miracles as the work of God, they must make a special effort to do so. Miracles are no longer a bridge to faith. What happens, rather, is that Christians of strong faith make the special effort to acknowledge miracles. Today many Catholics question whether miracles belong to the core of the Gospel and hence play an essential role in the life of faith, or whether their existence is a marginal issue on which Catholics may have different views. For instance, could a person become a Catholic when he comes to believe that God has revealed himself in Christ and that the new life of resurrection is available, through the Spirit, in the sacramental fellowship of the Catholic Church, even if miracles are so far removed from his world view that it does not occur to him to accept them as historical occurrences? Or would he have to be told that in addition to God's self-revelation in Christ and its availability in the Catholic Church, he would also have to accept this or that miraculous event? In the following pages, I wish to expand the Blondelian view of miracles in the terms adopted in this study to show that miracles are marginal to the Gospel of Christ. From the viewpoint of faith, of saving faith, it does not make any difference whether or not miracles are accepted as actual occurrences.

I wish to introduce a distinction that will enable us to explain the biblical view of miracles and deal in a new way with the Church's official teaching on the subject. I wish to distinguish between *miracles* and *marvels*. Miracles are inexplicable events in the order of nature; marvels are inexplicable events in the order of persons. Miracles have to do with the physical world; marvels have to do with personal and social history. Miracles are surprising and unaccountable cosmic or molecular transformations, such as fire falling from the sky or water turning into wine; marvels are surprising and unaccountable transformations of personal or social life, such as the conversion from sin, entry into new life, or the creation of fellowship. In the scriptures, I propose, the miracles are signs of marvels: they signify and proclaim the marvelous works of God.

It is generally acknowledged that the people of Israel did not regard miracles as occurrences that violate the fixed order of the universe and hence as proofs of God's transcendence and the sovereignty of his mercy. The people of the Bible did not regard the world as a closed system with fixed laws of nature. The modern problem of miracles was unknown to them. In the Old Testament all events, whether they take place in the cosmic order or in personal life, are presented as effects of God's marvelous power.[11] Creation is called a miracle. The preservation of the universe and the history of men on earth are also miraculous: they are extraordinary events produced by divine power, inspiring men with awe and wonder. They

11. Cf. W. Vollborn, "Wunder" (OT), *Rel. Gesch. Gegen.*, vol. 6, cols. 1833–1834.

are no less marvelous than the extraordinary occurrences, such as the plagues of Egypt or the feeding in the desert, associated with the redemption of Israel. These very special miraculous events signify and proclaim the marvelous works of God in saving Israel from destruction and establishing it on the way of salvation. These miracles point to the time of fulfillment, promised for the future, when miracles will be multiplied and God's mercy be revealed in the transformation of his people beyond all imagination.

The Israelites accepted the miracles as historical events. While some Old Testament passages suggest that the writer uses miracle stories as a special literary form, other present convincing evidence that the writer looked upon miracles as actual occurrences. Since the Israelites did not look upon the universe as determined by fixed laws of nature, they did not find it difficult to accept miracles as historical events. They lived in a world where prodigies were taken for granted. Miracles were performed not only by holy men; false prophets and priests of pagan cults were also able to work miracles. To acknowledge miracles, therefore, was in no way a special sign of faith and did not as such signify a holy trust in God. In Israel, by contrast, faith in God, the redeemer, is to accept the miracles of Israel's history as the sign of God's marvelous works in creating his people. Faith is the trusting acknowledgment of the marvels the miracles signified.

The cultural setting of the New Testament is the same as that of the Old Testament. In the New Testament the miraculous was taken for granted: God rules the entire universe, and all events, whether cosmic or historical, are the effects of the divine will. This is as true for the extraordinary occurrences as for the ordinary course of history. Central in the New Testament is Jesus Christ as healer of the sick and exorcist with power over demons. We read that Christ's preaching was accompanied by many miracles. When he sent his apostles on their mission, their preaching, too, was to be accompanied by miracles; they were to do even greater works than he did (cf. Jn. 14, 12). In this context these miracles are the sign that the messianic age has come. They are signs vouching for Christ's mission not because they disturb a supposedly fixed order of nature and hence demonstrate God's transcendent power, but because they are the fulfillment of the promises made for the messianic age.[12]

When the disciples of John the Baptist came to Jesus to inquire whether he was the one who was to come, he replied: "Go and tell John what you have seen and heard: the blind receive their sight, the lame walk, lepers are cleansed, and the deaf hear, the dead are raised up, the poor have the good news preached to them. And blessed is he who takes no offense at me" (Lk. 7, 22–23). Jesus foretold that these same signs would accompany the preaching of the Church and vouch for the advent of the messianic age: "These signs will accompany those who believe: in my name they will cast out devils, they will speak in new tongues, they will pick up serpents, and if they drink any deadly thing, it will not hurt them, they will lay their hands on the sick and they will recover" (Mk. 16, 17–18). These passages refer to the miracles foretold for the days of the fulfillment: "Then shall the eyes of the blind be opened, and the ears of the deaf shall be unstopped, then shall the lame leap like a hart, and the tongue of the dumb shall sing" (Is. 35, 5–6).

How are we to look upon the miracles of Christ? There

12. Cf. A. Vögtle, "Wunder" (NT), *Lex. Theol. Kirch.*, vol. 10, cols. 1255–1261.

can be little doubt that the New Testament presents Christ as prophet and miracle worker. His miracles profoundly impressed the early Christian community, for they gave ample witness to the marvelous works performed by the Lord. While the relating of the miracles often reflects a highly schematic pattern, almost a set literary form, and while these reports often depend on Old Testament passages, it seems impossible to explain the miracles of Christ simply as symbolic representations of the Good News. The evangelists wanted to present an historical picture of Christ as the man who walked about doing good, who had power over demons, and who showed his mercy by saving people from suffering and even death.[13]

At the same time, we must acknowledge that the New Testament still regards miracles as common occurrences. Devils and angels had the power to work them. Human beings, some connected with Jesus and some not, are reported to have performed them. The scribes and Pharisees hostile to Jesus had no difficulty in acknowledging the miracles worked by him, but they interpreted them as works of the devil (cf. Mt. 12, 22–28). Hence while we admit that Christ's miracles are recorded in the New Testament for the greater part as historical events, we deny that it is salvational to accept them as facts: even Christ's enemies did that. According to the New Testament, what counts for salvation is to acknowledge the miracles as signs of redemption, as proclamation of the Good News, as witnesses to grace: what counts is their meaning.

The New Testament does not know the modern problem of miracles. Miracles belonged to the world view of the people among whom Christ lived. Christ's opponents

13. Cf. E. Käsemann, "Wunder" (NT), *Rel. Gesch. Gegen.*, vol. 6, cols. 1835–1837.

had no intellectual difficulties with miracles; they had a spiritual difficulty with Christ and his message. *To make the issue of whether miracles are historical events or not of crucial significance is to introduce a new and extraneous element into the scriptural faith.* It is true, of course, that miracles are often recorded as signs in support of Christs message, but this is done not because the miracles violate the order of nature and hence demonstrate the supernatural origin of Christ, but rather because they manifest Christ's mercy, clarify the nature of his mission, confirm the Old Testament prophecies, and as such symbolize the redemption offered to mankind. The factual problem does not exist in the New Testament. What is decisive for faith is to acknowledge the marvels signified by the miracles. While the evangelists present many of the miracles as historical facts, their facticity is in no way an issue of faith. The modern problem, created by a new understanding of the cosmos, is peripheral to the biblical faith.

Even though the issue may not be central to the Gospel, what are we to think of Christ's miracles? The Christian Church has usually accepted them as descriptions of what actually happened and hence as manifestations of God's power and mercy. In terms of the common philosophy, they were regarded as violations of the natural order. This view was congenial to Christians when they regarded God as the supreme ruler of the universe, responsible for all the events taking place in history. In the perspective adopted in this study, the traditional view of miracles has become problematic. But besides the common view that miracles are events *contra naturam,* there is another view, also traditional, that miracles are simply events *praeter naturam:* they are exceptional events at the very limit of what is still possible in a graced nature. According to this view, miracles are homogeneous with nature and life, even though they occur at the edge of the possible.[14] According to this view, Jesus Christ, anointed by the Spirit, had such deep insight into the process of man's becoming and the possibilities of healing through touch and conversation, that he performed cures and liberated people in ways that were unexpected and beyond the grasp of his followers, even if they were not essentially different from the ways in which God is present to all of human life.

Christians have divergent views in regard to miracles, usually depending on their view of the physical universe and their conception of the divine. But whatever their view, miracles are not central. The marvel belongs to the core of the Gospel, but the question about the miraculous is peripheral.

The resurrection of Jesus Christ, we hasten to add, was first of all and essentially a marvel. God raised his son from the dead. Christ became the living Lord. The inexplicable that took place belonged to the order of persons, that is to say it affected Christ's personal being, his history, his future existence and hence the existence of the Church and all those men who were to encounter him in faith. The resurrection is the marvel at the heart of the Gospel.

14. This is the view of miracles adopted in the new Dutch catechism. "The one thing we can say with certainty [about miracles] is that—always linked with salvation and judgement, and above all always linked with Christ—mighty forces are released for man's benefit. There is no reason to regard this as an arbitrary and extrinsic intervention on the part of God, as though God were thwarting his own work of creation. On the contrary, the miracles do not resist the forces of nature. They leave them to act with marvellous success and effectiveness, in keeping with 'the longing' and 'groaning' which live deeply within nature itself (Rom. 8:22) . . . After all, what do we know of the relationship between the new creation, which is here breaking through, and the laws of nature?" *A New Catechism*, New York, 1967, p. 107.

It sums up the preaching of the early Church. The marvel that Christ is alive totally discloses God's redemptive presence to man.

But, we may ask, is the resurrection also a miracle? Does it imply the inexplicable in the cosmic or molecular order? In other words, does it tell us anything about the cells of Christ's body? Usually, it is true, Christians have accepted the resurrection as miraculous: the same body that was laid in the tomb came to life again. On the other hand, Christians have never regarded the resurrection simply as the resuscitation of a dead body—as described, for instance, in the raisings from the dead performed by Christ —but always as an elevation or glorification, as an entry of Christ into a new way of being, enabling him to be present to the whole community. Christ's bodily existence, or his "spiritual body," was not imagined as something in direct physical continuity with his earthly body: the bodily continuity lay, rather, in the personal self-identity of the risen Lord. We may propose, therefore, that the question as to whether the great marvel of the resurrection is also a miracle remains open.[15] The apostle Paul, for one, proclaimed the risen Lord and his presence in the Church without any reference to the empty tomb. What counts for Christian faith is the resurrection as marvel, revealing God's victory and making visible the future of mankind.

The distinction between marvel and miracle also enables us to deal in a new way with the defined teaching of the Catholic Church. In the nineteenth century, the Catholic Church defended the existence of miracles against various rationalistic and positivistic trends of thought and taught that miracles are visible signs and empirical facts,

15. For literature see Max Brändle, *Orientierung,* 31 (1967), pp. 65–71, 108–112.

guaranteeing and manifesting the supernaturaal order. To deny the miracles of the scriptures or to question the existence of miracles in the Church's life was regarded by the ecclesiastical magisterium as the denial of the entire Christian dispensation. In their attitude towards miracles, men reveal whether they are believers or unbelievers.

This attitude found expression in the documents of Vatican Council I: "If anyone say that miracles could not happen and that therefore all the accounts of them, even those contained in the scriptures, should be counted among fables and myths, or that miracles could never be known with certainty and used to prove the divine origin of the Christian religion, let him be anathema." [16] This position was reaffirmed in the Anti-Modernist Oath of Pius X [17] and the encyclical *Humani Generis* of Pius XII.[18] The acknowledgment of miracles had become the touchstone of Christian faith and the principal argument vouching for the rationality of the Gospel.

In the intellectual culture created by the enlightenment and the positivistic outlook of the nineteenth cenury, man and his world were looked upon as a closed, autonomous system, determined by fixed laws and principles that can be studied, known, and ultimately fully understood. Man's rationality is up to reality. The thinkers of the enlightenment thought that man is a nature, that he can be defined and hence fully understood, and that his life is due to the unfolding of the laws proper to this nature. The positivists, a few generations later, rejected this philosophical rationalism, but they trusted that the more empirical scientific approach is able to come to a reliable picture of the world

16. *Denz.*, 3034.
17. *Ibid.*, 3539.
18. *Ibid.*, 3876.

including man and that the whole of reality corresponds to this picture. Rationalists and positivists, though working with different presuppositions and different methods, looked upon the world and man as a closed system, the future of which is wholly determined by causes within the system. There is no room for a creative mystery. To proclaim the transcendent God in this intellectual environment meant to affirm the existence of a supreme being beyond the system who has power over the system and reveals himself by miraculous events violating its fixed laws.

The intellectual climate of the enlightenment influenced Catholic thought. Even Catholic theologians tended to understand nature, including human nature, in highly rationalistic terms and to look upon the universe, no longer —as the Bible did—as the manifestation of God's power and mercy and hence always open to the unexpected, but as a closed system defined by principles wholly intrinsic to it, over which God, the creator, retains sovereign power. In this theological climate, miracles are the guarantee that the system is open-ended despite its fixed laws. Miracles give witness to the transcendent God and to the mercy by which he intervenes in the lives of men. No wonder, then, that in the nineteenth century the Catholic Church defined miracles as belonging to the very substance of the Gospel. Given these presuppositions, this is the only way to proclaim the Christian message.

Maurice Blondel was the first to criticize the strain of rationalism implicit in the Scholasticism of his century. He saw that this theological approach inevitably leads to an extrinsicist understanding of God. For him the world is not a closed system, for God is creatively and redemptively present to it. In other words, marvels belong to the essence of history. Wherever people are, the inexplicable happens. The witness to God's power and mercy is not a group of isolated events that startle because they are physically unlikely; the witness is the whole of human life when looked upon in a discerning way and acknowledged as the locus of death and resurrection. History testifies to the transcendent God and his grace. The question as to whether or not there are miracles is of little consequence.

The nineteenth century could not make the distinction between marvels and miracles, based as it is on the personalist philosophy of the twentieth. Neither the scientifically oriented people who denied miracles nor the Catholic theologians and teachers who affirmed them were able to express themselves in terms of this distinction. As it stands, the Church's official position has become incomprehensible to us. Since the days when it was defined, our understanding of reality has changed considerably. But if we reinterpret the official nineteenth century teaching on miracles in the light of the new distinction, then this teaching is as valid now as it was then. What the Church affirms, against the rationalists of any age, is that marvels occur and that they belong to the core of the Gospel. To reject the possibility of marvels is to deny the Christian faith. For marvels are the visible sign of God's transcendence and the manifestation of his redemptive presence in human life.

CONCLUSION

THE God immanent in human history radically transcends it. We have shown in the last chapter that the reinterpretation of the doctrine of God does not involve us in a theological reductionism. We have not reduced the divine to a factor immanent in history and determined by it. God is not caught in the human dynamics. God is the more than human in human life. This "more than human" is his transcendence situated at the heart of his immanence. While God is wholly immanent to history—and there is no standpoint from which he is simply man's over-against—he can never be identified with any aspect of history. God is always different. God's presence in history is not dominated or exhausted by it. God rules history from within. God is always transcendent to human life as critique, as newness, as orientation.

The reinterpretation of the doctrine of God has enabled us to speak about the divine mystery in words drawn from ordinary day-to-day speech and in concepts taken from man's experience of his own history. The Blondelian shift, by rejecting extrinsicism, conceives of God as the transcendent mystery present in history. Without in any way abandoning or weakening divine transcendence, we have avoided any objectification of God. God is not a supreme being or a supreme person. The divine mystery revealed in the New Testament is a dimension of human life: God is present to human life as its orientation and its source of newness and expansion. The traditional doctrine of the Trinity has enabled us to discern an empirical basis for speaking of God's presence to man: God is present, as summons and gift, in the conversation and communion by which men enter into their humanity.

The principles of reinterpretation that we have adopted enable us to translate the Christian creed into ordinary secular language without mentioning the word God. As Karl Rahner has reminded us more than once,[1] it was possible at one time to compose a Christian creed by beginning with God. At one time everyone knew what this word refers to. Christians could express their faith to others by speaking about the divinity. But today, Rahner says, to begin the creed with a reference to God makes it impossible to communicate the Church's faith to men of the present culture. People do not know any more what the word "God" refers to. Should it not be possible for the Church to compose a creed which proclaims the Gospel of Christ and declares the divine redemption present in human life in ordinary secular language—and only then, on the basis of the preceding, explain what Christians mean by the word God? Since our principles of reinterpretation have enabled us to translate the traditional titles of God into declarations about human life, they could become the basis for writing a creed in modern language expressing the traditional Gospel once for all delivered to the apostles.

1. Cf. "In Search of a Short Formula of the Christian Faith," *Concilium,* vol. 23 (K. Rahner, ed.), New York, 1967, pp. 70–82.

It is possible to proclaim the Gospel without mentioning God by name. The Church's silence about God would enable Christians to overcome the objectification of God to which they have become accustomed and thus to remove the great obstacle for the Christian faith in the modern world. At the same time, the silence about God must be broken occasionally. Truth is always threatened in this life. It is possible for people to forget that the mystery at work in their history radically transcends it. It is possible for them to identify the success of their culture with the promised kingdom or to assume that certain cultural values are the unqualified embodiment of the divine. Then the need arises to utter the divine name. Even though the divine reality revealed in Christ can be expressed in an-anthropological terms, this translation must never be exclusive. There will always be times when we can only speak about God by mentioning his name.

Divine revelation can be translated into anthropological terms. Karl Rahner, as we mentioned above, has brilliantly demonstrated that this assertion is not a theological reductionism but, rather, the clarification of the heart of the Gospel.[2] God has revealed in Jesus Christ—the doctrine of the incarnation—that his gift to man is himself. The triune God has revealed himself in Jesus as present, as he is in himself, in the humanization of man. Human destiny is truly filled with the divine. God's presence of man is God himself. To call this a theological reductionism would be to deny the divinity of the man Jesus and the divinity of man's link with him. God has revealed himself as the destiny and the source of human life.

In our study we have limited the translation of doctrine

2. Cf. "Theology and Anthropology," *The Word in History,* T. P. Burke (ed.), New York, 1966, pp. 1–23.

to human terms to what we have called salvational knowledge. The doctrine of God, we have said, is Good News. It creates faith in man and thus transforms his consciousness. The anthropological interpretation of the doctrine of God are, therefore, not factual statements about human life; they are, rather, declarations about the marvelous things that happen wherever people are. The doctrine of God can be translated into anthropological terms only to the extent that it is Good News.

We do not claim that this is the only approach to the problem of God. For beyond the salvational knowledge of faith there is the more exclusively intellectual knowledge of theology. It should be possible to approach the insider-God with the methods and tools of philosophical reasoning. The more restrictive approach that we have adopted, however, has many advantages. It has enabled us to speak about God and his revelation in ordinary, largely non-technical terms, to bypass many philosophical issues which, in our age, seem to divide rather than unite people, and to create a language about the divine that can be used in preaching and teaching to men with no special academic background. In our approach the doctrine of God remains, strictly speaking, Good News. In Schillebeeck's happy phrase, God is the Good News that humanity is possible.